▍▍ spring into ▍▍▍

Linux®

■■spring into■■■ series

Spring Into... a series of short, concise, fast-paced tutorials for professionals transitioning to new technologies.

Find us online at **www.awprofessional.com/springinto/**

Spring Into Windows XP Service Pack 2
Brian Culp
ISBN 0-13-167983-X

Spring Into PHP 5
Steven Holzner
ISBN 0-13-149862-2

Spring Into HTML and CSS
Molly E. Holzschlag
ISBN 0-13-185586-7

Spring Into Technical Writing for Engineers and Scientists
Barry J. Rosenberg
ISBN 0-13-149863-0

Spring Into Linux®
Janet Valade
ISBN 0-13-185354-6

YOUR OPINION IS IMPORTANT TO US!

We would like to hear from you regarding the Spring Into... Series. Please visit **www.awprofessional.com/springintosurvey/** to complete our survey. Survey participants will receive a special offer for sharing their opinions.

From the Series Editor

Barry J. Rosenberg

A few years ago, I found myself in a new job in which I had to master many new skills in a very short time. I didn't have to become an instant expert, but I did have to become instantly competent.

I went to the bookstore but was shocked by how much the publishing world had changed. At a place where wit and intelligence had once been celebrated, dummies were now venerated. What happened?

Photograph courtesy of Ed Raduns

Well, I made a few phone calls, got Aunt Barbara to sew up a few costumes, and convinced Uncle Ed to let us use the barn as a stage. Oh wait… that was a different problem. Actually, I made a few phone calls and got some really talented friends to write books that clever people wouldn't be ashamed to read. We called the series "Spring Into…" because all the good names were already taken.

With Spring Into…, we feel that we've created the perfect series for busy professionals. However, there's the rub—we can't be sure unless you tell us. Maybe we're hitting the ball out of the park and straight through the uprights, bending it like Beckham, and finding nothing but net. On the other hand, maybe we've simply spun a twisted ball of clichés. Only you can tell us. Therefore, if anything—positive or negative—is on your mind about these books, please email me at

barry.rosenberg@awl.com

I promise not to add you to any email lists, spam you, or perform immoral acts with your address.

Sincerely,
Barry

▮▮ spring into ▮▮

Linux®

Janet Valade

✦ Addison-Wesley

Upper Saddle River, NJ • Boston• Indianapolis • San Francisco
New York • Toronto • Montreal • London • Munich • Paris • Madrid
Capetown • Sydney • Tokyo • Singapore • Mexico City

The publisher offers excellent discounts on this book when ordered in quantity for bulk purchases or special sales, which may include electronic versions and/or custom covers and content particular to your business, training goals, marketing focus, and branding interests. For more information, please contact:

U. S. Corporate and Government Sales
(800) 382-3419
corpsales@pearsontechgroup.com

For sales outside the U. S., please contact:

International Sales
international@pearsoned.com

Visit us on the Web: www.awprofessional.com/springinto/

Library of Congress Catalog Control Number: 2005920919

ISBN 0-13-185354-6
Text printed in the United States on recycled paper at R.R. Donnelley in Crawfordsville, Indiana.
First printing, April, 2005

*To my mother, with thanks for passing on a writing gene,
along with many other things.*

Contents

Preface

I am not only a writer of technical books, I am also a consumer of technical books. I like learning from books. All the information is pulled together for me, arranged in a logical learning sequence by someone who understands the subject. I learn much faster when a good book on the subject is available. This applies to all areas of my life, not just computing. I have a library that includes how-to books for everything I have ever tried to do—from meditating to playing the guitar to fixing my dryer to growing herbs.

This book is the book I needed when I was learning Linux. The essential information is inside, organized into compact chunks—a lot of information in a small space. This book is too small to be a good doorstop or stepping stool to the top shelf, but just right for getting up and productive with Linux in no time at all.

Who Should Read This Book?

The book is meant for computer users who are new to Linux. Your understanding of computer concepts and experience with another operating system allows you to grasp the Linux information quickly. You do not need to be told how to press the power switch. You are way beyond this. You can get your work done on Windows (or Mac or UNIX); you just need a quick start guide for working on Linux.

It is not impossible to learn Linux from this book without a background in computers—just difficult. The book assumes an understanding of concepts and computer use that you may not possess. However, if you appreciate a book that assumes you can understand quickly and delivers information in a compact form, without distractions and repetitive explanations, give this one a try. It might work for you.

How Is This Book Organized?

This book is organized in 19 chapters. Each chapter focuses on a topic, providing an overview and how-to information. The chapters are as follows:

- **Chapter 1, Understanding Open Source Software:** Describes open source beliefs and practices. See how they differ from the beliefs and practices prevalent with proprietary software.

- **Chapter 2, Choosing a Linux Distribution:** Provides the information needed to choose among the many Linux flavors.

- **Chapter 3, Getting Ready to Install Linux:** Instructions for preparing your computer for a Linux install.

- **Chapter 4, Installation:** Installation steps.

- **Chapter 5, Interacting with Linux:** How to get work done using Linux.

- **Chapter 6, Using Your Desktop:** How to use the two major Linux desktops—KDE and GNOME.

- **Chapter 7, Using the Command Line:** How to enter commands directly into Linux, without using the desktop.

- **Chapter 8, Linux Accounts:** No work can be done on a Linux system without using a Linux account. This chapter describes how to create accounts and associated information, such as passwords, owners, groups, and so forth.

- **Chapter 9, File Management:** How to create, copy, rename, delete, and otherwise manage Linux files.

- **Chapter 10, Applications and Programs:** How to download, install, and run Linux applications and programs.

- **Chapter 11, Word Processing:** How to use the OpenOffice word processing application.

- **Chapter 12, Spreadsheets:** How to use the OpenOffice spreadsheet application.

- **Chapter 13, Graphics:** How to create, edit, and manipulate different types of graphics files.

- **Chapter 14, Printing:** How to set up and use a printer on Linux.

- **Chapter 15, The Internet:** How to access and browse the Internet.

- **Chapter 16, Multimedia:** How to play sound and video files on Linux.

- **Chapter 17, Email, Messaging, and News:** How to communicate with other people over the Internet.

- **Chapter 18, Editing Text Files:** How to create and edit text files, such as HTML files, program source code, and Linux configuration files.

- **Chapter 19, Shell Scripts:** How to write and use shell scripts.

Two appendixes are also included:

- **Appendix A, Regular Expressions:** How to build regular expressions, patterns used by many different Linux applications.

- **Appendix B, Command Reference:** Description and information about the commands available for use with the CLI.

What's Unusual About This Book?

This book—like the other books in the Spring Into … Series—provides the following eccentricities:

- Each topic is explained in a discrete one- or two-page unit called a "chunk."

- Each chunk builds on the previous chunks in that chapter.

- Most chunks contain one or more examples. I learn best from examples. I don't think my learning style is unique. I believe I have company in my appreciation for examples.

- The heading for each chunk appears in the table of contents. The small chunk size means the chunk heading pinpoints small amounts of information. Finding information is *so* easy.

Information is packed densely in each chunk. I have toiled to make each word contribute to your understanding of Linux. The result is focussed information—information you can find when you need it.

Who Helped Me Write This Book?

Linux is the motivation for this book. I am a huge Linux fan. So, I would have to say that all the Linux developers in the world helped me write this book. What would I have to say if Linux were not the great operating system that it is?

Of course, having something to say is not sufficient. You must say it clearly and accurately. Editors have the difficult job of keeping an author on track toward clear and accurate. My editors are extraordinarily good at this part of their job. Without my editors, this book would veer much further toward what-in-the-world-does-that-mean and that-can't-be-right.

About the Author

Janet Valade has 20 years experience in the computing field. Her background includes experience as a technical writer for several companies, as a Web designer/programmer for an engineering firm, and as a systems analyst in a university environment where, for over 10 years, she supervised the installation and operation of computing resources, designed and developed a state-wide data archive, provided technical support to faculty and staff, wrote numerous technical papers and documentation, and designed and presented seminars and workshops on a variety of technology topics.

Janet currently has two published books—*PHP & MySQL for Dummies, Second Edition*, and *PHP 5 for Dummies*. In addition, she has authored chapters for several Linux and Web development books.

About the Series Editor

Barry Rosenberg wrote the cult classic, *KornShell Programming Tutorial* (Addison-Wesley, 1991), which pioneered many of the chunk-oriented techniques found in the Spring Into… Series. He is the author of more than sixty corporate technical manuals, primarily on programming. An experienced instructor, Barry has taught everything from high-school physics to weeklong corporate seminars on data structures.

Most recently, Barry spent four semesters at MIT where he taught advanced technical writing. Barry is also a professional juggler who has performed more than 1,200 shows, including a three-week run in Japan. Juggling serves as the backdrop for his novel, *Cascade* (not yet published). Barry currently works as the documentation manager at 170 Systems.

CHAPTER 1

Understanding Open Source Software

If this is your first venture into open source software, you need to understand open source beliefs and practices. If you come from a background in Windows and/or other commercial, proprietary software, you'll find that the open source viewpoint is quite different from the viewpoint of proprietary software vendors. Open source software is developed and distributed differently. Your procedures for obtaining the software and its updates are very different. Your methods of obtaining support for your use of the software are different, as well. This chapter explains the philosophy and practices of the open source community of software developers and users.

Open Source Software

Open source means exactly what it says—the source of the software must be open, available to everyone, not secret. The source is the program code that produces the functionality of the software (that is, the underlying program code that makes a spell checker check spelling and an address book store addresses). The source code is written in a known programming language, such as C or Java. Many people know this language. Therefore, anyone who sees the source knows how the program does its job.

Open source software provides the source with the software. The source is considered to be free, as in free speech. Anyone is free to use the program for any purpose, to modify the program, or to redistribute the program. No permission required.

The alternative to open source software is proprietary software—software that is exclusively owned by one or more individuals or by a company. The owner's permission is required for any use of the software. Many commercial software companies make a profit by owning the software and charging customers to use it. For these companies, the software is the company's product. The source code is the company's trade secret, the basis for its hopes of profit, an asset to be guarded. Much of the commercial software you are familiar with, such as Windows, MS Office, and Photoshop, is proprietary software. The company provides the software to those who pay for it in a format (binary code) that hides the source code. The software users can see what the software does (e.g., finds incorrect spelling) but don't know how the software accomplishes the task.

Most open source software development is organized as a project. Volunteer developers, often located throughout the world, coordinate their work via the Internet. Open source projects communicate with their users, and the world, via a project Web site where the software is available for download. The Web site also often provides information about the software and its developers, documentation for the software, a bug database and procedures for entering bug reports into the database, mailing lists or forums where users can discuss the software, and other related information.

Open source software development is open. That is, the software source is posted on the Web as it is being developed, available for any interested person to use or to work on. The users are a diverse group, with varying uses for the software and levels of skill in using the software, who have direct access to the developers through the Web site. The result is quick identification of bugs and problems, feedback on useful and not-so-useful features, bug fixes provided by users, and suggestions for new features and/or feature implementation.

Open source proponents believe that software produced by this process—openly, publicly, with a great deal of testing, input, review, criticism, and discussion—is higher-quality software. The fact that developers are motivated by interest, rather than by employment considerations, is believed to increase quality as well. Some open source software has certainly succeeded well. Apache is probably the best known success story, a classic open source project that has succeeded quite well. Currently, Apache has approximately 67% of the Web server market. Linux as open source software is discussed later in this chapter.

Commercial software companies in the open source world don't depend on proprietary software for profit. Customers are charged for enhancements to the software or for services related to the software, as shown in the following examples:

- Developing and providing bundles of software combined to work well together
- Developing versions of the software with simple installation procedures
- Providing technical support for users of the software
- Providing consulting and programming expertise for the software
- Providing modified versions of the software for special purposes

The only restriction is that the open source software may not be converted into proprietary software for any purpose. The source must remain open.

Users of commercial proprietary software expect a phone number they can call when they have problems. Users of commercial open source software can expect the same. This doesn't mean there is no help for users who download and install open source software themselves. Quite the contrary. Open source users support each other. Information is available from many sources, not just one. Mailing lists and forums for open source software abound on the Web where hundreds of knowledgeable users, often including the developers, voluntarily help newbies. When you ask a question on a mailing list, the answer often shows up in your mailbox within seconds.

Open source software releases are irregular and arbitrary. A new software version is released when the developers believe it's ready, often with little prior notice. A new version can be released in response to a bug or a security problem within a day. Users of open source software must keep themselves informed. Otherwise, a new version that solves an annoying problem or the identification of a security problem may go unnoticed.

Open Source License

Software falls under copyright law. Written program code is copyrighted, by default, automatically. If anyone uses the code without permission from the owner of the copyright, it's theft. Piracy. The copyright owner can, of course, allow anyone to use the software, setting any conditions the owner chooses. Software licenses provide the conditions under which the copyright owner allows you to use the software.

If you have ever purchased or installed software, you have probably encountered a license. Commercial software usually includes a written license. If you download software, there's usually a screen that requires you to click your agreement to the license before you can actually install/use the software. Such a license is called the end user license agreement, also not so affectionately known as the EULA.

When you read a EULA, you discover that you haven't actually purchased the software. You have, instead, purchased a license to use the software. The EULA specifies the conditions, or terms, under which you can use the software. The EULA may include some restrictive conditions, such as limiting the software to installation on one computer. It's wise to read the EULA so you know your legal rights and responsibilities. The EULA is generally not open for negotiation.

Open source software also comes with a license. The most common open source license is the General Public License (GPL). The GPL is quite unrestricted. It states that you can use the software for any purpose. You can change it if you want. You can redistribute it if you want. However, you cannot redistribute it as proprietary software. It must remain open source. Anyone receiving the software from you has the right to the source and has the right to change it or redistribute it.

The GPL was developed by GNU (discussed later in this chapter). It's often referred to as copyleft, defined by GNU as a general method for making a program free software and requiring all modified and extended versions of the program to be free software as well. You can see the entire text of the GPL, as well as other information regarding its use, at www.gnu.org/licenses/licenses.html#TOCGPL.

Other open source software licenses are available, such as a license for documentation. You can see information about open source licenses at www.gnu.org/licenses/licenses.html.

Linux Is Open Source Software

Linux is an operating system. It makes your computer hardware into a usable machine. It interacts with the hardware to perform the tasks you need done, such as store information in files, display information on the screen, send data to the printer, add two numbers together. Anything you do on your computer is mediated by the operating system.

Linux is not one big, monolithic program. It is a collection of many programs that together make your computer into a useful tool. The heart of Linux is the kernel where the low-level operations take place. Without the kernel, there's nothing. However, the kernel by itself is not enough. Many other programs combine to make up the Linux operating system that sits on your computer. More details regarding the programs required are provided in Chapter 2.

Linux is based on the UNIX operating system, which was developed in the 1970s to run on mainframe and minicomputers. In 1991, a student at the University of Helsinki in Finland, named Linus Torvalds, wanted an operating system like UNIX to run on his PC. Because nothing meeting his requirements existed, he set out to write one. The current Linux kernel is the result—produced by the work of developers all over the world, coordinated by Torvalds. When he posted his project to the Web early in its development, he found a great deal of interest. It seemed many people wanted an operating system like this and jumped in to help. Linux was released almost every week and immediate feedback from hundred of users was incorporated into its development, facilitated by the rapid growth of the World Wide Web.

From the beginning, Linux was open source. It was distributed freely to anyone who wanted it. The official Web site for Linux, where the latest news is available and the current source can be downloaded, is www.linuxhq.org (Linux Headquarters).

Other programs that make Linux useful on your computer can be downloaded from various Web sites. A central source for Linux utilities, compilers, applications, and other software is GNU (discussed later in this chapter). Many other individual project and company Web sites exist for software that is part of a complete, installed Linux system.

Although any user can download the Linux kernel and download all the components of a complete Linux system, it's not simple. Very few users install Linux in this manner. Rather, most Linux systems are installed from a distribution—a collection of programs put together by a group or a company, often with a simplified installation procedure. Linux distributions are discussed in Chapter 2.

What Is GNU?

GNU stands for GNU's Not UNIX, a project started by Richard M. Stallman in 1984. The goal was to develop an open source operating system that would be freely distributed to anyone who wanted it. At that time, there were no viable operating systems that were not proprietary. GNU was intended to remedy the situation.

GNU intended to develop all the programs needed to produce a complete operating system, including a kernel, a shell (the program that interfaces between the user and the kernel), utilities, compilers, text editors, mail software, etc. GNU intended to provide all the programs necessary so that users would not need to use any proprietary software. GNU is philosophically opposed to proprietary software.

GNU coordinated the development of many programs simultaneously, guided by a to-do list of programs needed/wanted. Programs were released as soon as they were developed, not waiting for the complete system to be ready. Many users downloaded the programs and used them on UNIX systems. Among the first programs to be released were a GNU c compiler (gcc) and a text editor (EMACS). GNU continues developing software into the present and the foreseeable future, as well as maintaining and updating its existing programs.

By 1992, GNU had all the necessary programs, except that their kernel wasn't ready. However, Linus Torvald's Linux kernel was available, so GNU combined their software with the Linux kernel to make a complete operating system. The Linux kernel plus GNU programs plus additional programs and applications comprise the Linux system that sits on most computers today. The combination of programs is put together by individuals or companies into distributions, the software package that is installed on most computers. Linux distributions are discussed in Chapter 2.

Summary

The open source viewpoint is quite different from the viewpoint of proprietary software vendors. The source of the software must be open, available to everyone, not secret. Anyone is free to use the program for any purpose, to modify the program, or to redistribute the program. No permission required.

Most open source software development is organized as a project with volunteer developers, often located throughout the world, coordinating their work via the Internet. Open source software is posted on the Web as it is being developed, available for any interested person to use or to work on. Commercial companies in the open source world charge for enhancements to the software or for services related to the software, not for the software itself, as proprietary software companies do.

Like any other software, open source software comes with a license. The most common open source license is the General Public License (GPL). The GPL is quite unrestricted. It states that you can use the software for any purpose. You can change it if you want. You can redistribute it if you want. However, you cannot redistribute it as proprietary software. It must remain open source. Anyone receiving the software from you has the right to the source and has the right to change it or redistribute it.

Linux is an open source operating system. The heart of Linux is the kernel, but many additional programs are required to make your computer into a useful tool. Many of the additional programs are developed by the GNU (GNU's Not UNIX) project. The Linux kernel plus GNU programs plus additional programs and applications comprise the Linux system that sits on most computers today.

Although any user can download the Linux kernel and download all the components of a complete Linux system, it's not simple. Very few users install Linux in this manner. Rather, most Linux systems are installed from a distribution—a collection of programs put together by a group or a company, often with a simplified installation procedure.

The characteristics of Linux distributions are discussed in Chapter 2. The range of distributions available and the focus of each are explained.

▌▌ CHAPTER 2 ▐▐▐

Choosing a Linux Distribution

The Linux operating system that's installed on your computer is not a single, huge program. It's a collection of many programs. You can get each component of the Linux system yourself, downloading and installing them separately to create exactly the system that fits your needs. However, it's not simple; you must know Linux well to do this. Most users don't install the pieces themselves. Rather, they install a Linux distribution.

A distribution (often called a distro) is a collection of programs put together by a group or a company. It includes all the components needed to provide a complete Linux system when it's installed on your computer. However, distributions can differ in the components included, focusing on different aspects. For instance, one distribution may emphasize easy use and installation whereas another emphasizes providing a large set of applications.

Fedora Core, the successor to the very popular Red Hat Linux, is the main distribution discussed in this book. In addition, the Mandrake and SuSE distributions are described. These three distributions are oriented toward desktop computer users and provide installation procedures similar to Windows installation procedures. Many, many other distributions are available. This chapter describes the major distributions. More complete coverage of distributions is available at www.distrowatch.org, which maintains a database of 320 distributions.

Distribution Contents

Linux distributions can include the following components:

- **Linux kernel:** The core of Linux. The kernel interacts with the hardware to perform the tasks you require of your computer, such as save text in a file, display text or graphics on the screen, or send text or graphics to the printer. There is no operating system without the kernel.

- **Shell:** A program that interfaces between the computer user and the kernel. The most common shell used on Linux is the Bash (Born again shell) shell, so named because it is derived from an earlier shell called the Bourne shell. The interfaces for Linux are described further in Chapter 5.

- **Linux commands, utilities, and applications:** Programs that perform tasks. The task may be simple, such as displaying the contents of a file on the screen. Or the task may be quite complex, such as word processing with its complex functionality. Whenever you type a Linux command or start an application, you run a program that provides the functionality you need.

- **Compilers:** Compilers translate the language that humans understand into language that the computer understands. That is, humans write programs in languages, such as C or Java, similar to human languages. Compilers convert the C or Java code into machine language so that the computer can run the program.

- **Desktops:** Applications that provide a graphical interface to Linux. Several desktops are available, allowing you to select the one that best fits your needs. Some desktops provide an interface that is similar to the Windows interface. The interfaces for Linux are described further in Chapter 5.

Some components are required to provide a usable Linux system, such as the kernel, a shell, and many Linux commands and utilities. All distributions provide the minimum requirements. However, most distributions provide more than the bare minimum. Distributions differ on the following characteristics:

- **More or fewer applications:** Distributions provide different applications. For instance, almost all distributions provide word processing applications. In fact, most distributions include OpenOffice, an office application similar to Microsoft Office. However, not all distributions include it. Other word processing applications are available, such as KOffice, an office suite developed for use with the KDE desktop. Some distributions offer more than one office application.

  A distribution can include hundreds or thousands of applications. You can see which applications are included at the distribution Web site. In addition, DistroWatch reports on a list of applications, showing whether a distribution includes the applications. For instance, the list of applications for Fedora is provided at www.distrowatch.org/table.php?distribution=fedora.

The presence or absence of any single application is not a sufficient reason for choosing a distribution. Any application can be added after Linux is installed. However, if a distribution includes all the applications you need and installs them during the installation procedure, it's easier than downloading and adding applications separately later.

- **More or less up-to-date versions of their components:** Linux software is updated frequently. Some distributions include the newest releases, striving to be the most cutting-edge. Other distributions emphasize stability, not including new software releases until the version has proven stable. Some distributions provide procedures to keep your Linux current after it's installed. For instance, Fedora includes a utility called up2date that keeps track of your current versions and automatically gets and installs updates for you when they become available. Installing and updating software is discussed in Chapter 10.

- **Different desktops:** Most distributions provide a desktop. The two main desktops are KDE and GNOME, but more are available. Most distributions provide KDE, GNOME, or both.

- **Utilities developed specifically for the distribution:** Some companies develop utilities specifically for their distributions, making maintenance and administration easier for users. For instance, SuSE has developed YaST (Yet Another Setup Tool) to simplify installing and configuring their distribution.

- **Different installation procedures:** In the past, Linux had a reputation for difficult installation. In response, several distributions developed procedures to make installation simpler. Mandrake, for instance, has focused on developing an installation procedure that detects hardware efficiently and is easy to use. Mandrake's popularity has increased since its reputation for easy installation and use has spread.

- **Varying levels of support:** Some Linux distributions provide official support, equivalent to proprietary software support. For instance, Mandrake provides 30 days of telephone support, with more available for purchase, and SuSE provides free installation support, with other support provided for a fee. Other distributions expect users to solve their own problems.

Each distribution has a Web site providing information about the distribution. You can generally download the distribution at the Web site. The files you download are usually CD images (ISO images) that you write to CD; then you install from the CDs. Some distributions are also sold in a boxed set, with CDs and perhaps a manual.

l Hat/Fedora

Even if you have no experience with Linux, you've probably heard of Red Hat—the most well-known commercial version of Linux. Red Hat has recently undergone some organizational changes. Free Red Hat Linux has been replaced by Fedora Core, released by the Fedora project, which is initiated, supported, and contributed to by Red Hat. Fedora is an open source developer project with public testing, participation, and feedback. Fedora includes only open source software. Information on Fedora is available at fedora.redhat.com. Red Hat now only sells Red Hat Enterprise Linux—commercial software appropriate for organization-wide use, emphasizing stability, reliability, and commercial support.

You can't buy Fedora from Red Hat. Red Hat only sells Red Hat Enterprise, a commercial version of Linux. To obtain Fedora, you download files from the Fedora Project Web site: fedora.redhat.com/download/. The files are images of installation CDs, which you can write to CD or install from disk. Installation is discussed in Chapter 4. However, the files are huge and downloading them over a dial-up connection is painful. You can purchase installation CDs through various vendors. The vendors don't provide a nice boxed set of software and manuals, such as you receive when you purchase Windows or a commercial distribution of Linux; they just provide CDs. A list of vendors is available at fedora.red-hat.com/download/vendors.html.

Fedora features include the following:

- **Multiple desktops:** Provides both GNOME and KDE. GNOME is the default.

- **Software updates:** Red Hat provides a utility called up2date that keeps track of your current versions and automatically gets and installs updates for you when they become available.

- **System utilities:** Provides system tools developed by the Fedora project. Tools have an easy-to-use graphical interface, as well as a text-based interface. The names begin with redhat-config, such as redhat-config-network.

- **Installation procedure:** Provides either graphical or text interface for the installation procedure, using its own installer called Anaconda. The installation procedure detects and configures the system hardware. Provides Kickstart, a utility that allows scripted, unattended installation useful for system administrators.

- **Well supported:** One of the best supported distributions. Red Had maintains a mailing list at www.redhat.com/mailman/listinfo/fedora-list. Also try the Fedora Forum at fedoraforum.org and the Fedora forum on Linux Questions at www.linuxquestions.org/questions/forumdisplay.php?forumid=35.

Mandrake

Mandrake Linux is particularly oriented toward Linux novices and home users. Mandrake focuses on user-friendly graphical installation and utilities. It's the easiest distribution to install, allowing successful installation by users without any Linux experience. It's very competent at recognizing hardware during the installation process.

Mandrake Linux has two major versions:

- **Mandrake Distribution:** The stable, official Mandrake Distribution is available for download from the Web site (mandrakelinux.com) in files that are CD images (ISO files). It's also available in three boxed sets:

  - **Discovery:** A simplified package that provides the essentials for a desktop user, with an automated installation procedure and a handpicked selection of applications. It includes 2 CDs and a manual.

  - **Power Pack:** An advanced desktop package that provides thousands of open source and commercial applications. It includes 6 CDs and 2 manuals.

  - **Power Pack Plus**: An advanced package that provides a powerful desktop plus the server tools necessary to create and manage a small to medium size network. It includes 8 CDs, 1 DVD, and 2 manuals.

- **Cooker:** The developmental version of Mandrake Linux, Cooker is constantly evolving. New packages can appear daily. It's released frequently for testing, bug reporting, and feedback. When a cooker version is deemed ready, it's frozen, meaning no new features are added, only bug fixes, and it becomes the beta for the official Mandrake Distribution.

If you want the cutting-edge software, install Cooker. If you like your software a little more stable, install the official Distribution.

Mandrake features include the following:

- **Multiple desktops:** Provides both GNOME and KDE. KDE is the default.

- **Mandrake Club:** Provides help forums and other extras. Provides early software downloads. Provides extra software. Requires a small fee to join.

- **Mandrake Experts:** A Web site (www.mandrakeexpert.com) where volunteer experts answer questions. A list of experts is available. Or post your question publicly for any expert to choose. Phone consultation with experts is possible.

SuSE

SuSE (pronounced sue suh) has a desktop focus. The SuSE developers have developed an easy-to-use installer and simple configuration tools. SuSE has the best documentation of any distribution, thorough and understandable.

SuSE is developed privately, not publicly. The software is not available during the development process. It's developed by the SuSE developers, depending on sales of boxed sets for much of its revenue. SuSE includes some commercial software, in addition to the free open source software. Two boxed sets are available:

- **Personal:** A version that provides the essentials for a desktop user, including office applications, email software, Internet applications, and others. The documentation includes only an installation guide. The user's guide is only available online.

- **Professional:** A version that includes more software. It provides server and network utilities and development tools, in addition to personal desktop applications. It includes a printed user's guide and an administrator's guide.

SuSE also provides business software such as an enterprise server.

SuSE provides the opportunity to install its software free of charge directly from FTP. The FTP version is mainly the same, except that some of the commercial software included on the CDs is removed. This is not something you want to do via a dial-up connection.

SuSE features include the following:

- **Multiple desktops:** Provides both GNOME and KDE. KDE is the default.

- **Linux with Windows:** SuSE Linux installs easily alongside a Windows system. The installation procedure will make room for the Linux system on the hard disk in the space (partition) where Windows is already installed by resizing the Windows space.

- **Well supported:** SuSE supports a very active mailing list at www.suse.co.uk/uk/ private/support/online_help/mailinglists/index.html. Several forums are available at forums.suselinuxsupport.de/, such as general questions, install problems, and network problems. Or try the SuSE forum at Linux Forums at www.linuxforums.org/forum/viewforum.php?f=36.

Other Distributions

Fedora, Mandrake, and SuSE are the distributions discussed in this book. Other popular major distributions include the following:

- **Slackware:** The oldest surviving Linux distribution. It's most suitable for users who want to learn Linux thoroughly. Slackware has not focused on ease of use. It has no distribution specific utilities or tools. Its strength is consistency, stability, and security, making it very useful for servers. www.slackware.org

- **Debian:** A pure open source project. Three versions of Debian are available at all times: stable release (the current stable release); testing (contains packages that haven't been accepted into the stable release yet—more cutting-edge, but not as stable); and unstable (the distribution where active development is taking place). Debian has a reputation for being difficult to install unless you know your hardware very well, but it's working to improve the installation procedure. Once it's installed, it's easy to keep up-to-date. www.debian.org

- **MEPIS:** The newest arrival. MEPIS is based on the Debian distribution. It comes with nonfree applications, such as Java and Macromedia Flash. If you need some of the extra applications it includes, it's much easier to install MEPIS than to install the applications individually on another distribution. www.mepis.org

- **Xandros:** The easiest Linux of all. It's meant for beginners. Fewer applications are included, but the included applications work well. It's based on Debian, but designed to look as much like Windows as possible. It includes graphical tools designed for Xandros to make tasks, such as file management, easier for the user. www.xandros.org

- **Linspire** (formerly named Lindows): Another easy Linux, meant for beginners. It features quick and easy installation. It offers a one-click software installation feature that installs software from their own software pool. www.linspire.com

- **Gentoo:** A source-based Linux. Gentoo emphasizes installing most of your Linux system from source, compiling it on your computer. The installation procedure is more difficult and longer, but the result is a system that's tailored to your hardware and your needs. Gentoo has excellent documentation. www.gentoo.org

The database at DistroWatch currently includes over 300 active distributions. Most distributions are modifications of Red Hat/Fedora or Debian. If you have a specific purpose for your Linux, you can probably find a distribution that provides what you need.

Live CDs

A Live CD is Linux on a CD that can run a computer. You boot from the CD and have a working Linux computer, running from the CD. You can use the Linux tools and applications without installing anything on the hard disk. The Live CD can contain many applications by using on-the-fly decompression techniques. Linux on the Live CDs can access floppy disk and CD drives, printers, and other hardware. Live CDs are useful for the following:

- **Evaluation:** You can try out Linux. You can see how it works and/or learn to use it without installing anything on your hard disk.

- **Testing:** You can test a computer with Linux before purchasing it.

- **Portability:** You can move your Linux from computer to computer easily. You can bring your Linux with you and use it wherever there's a computer. You can use your office application wherever you are. Or you can use the Live CD for demonstration or training purposes.

Some Live CDs include installation software. You can boot Linux from the CD and try it out. Then, if you like it, you can install it on your hard disk from the running Linux.

The following are some popular Live CDs:

- **Knoppix:** A Debian-based distribution with excellent hardware detection. Knoppix provides the KDE desktop and many applications, including Konqueror Web browser, OpenOffice, GIMP, and many more. With decompression, Knoppix holds 2GB of software. www.knoppix.com (Typing www.knoppix.org gets you a German Web page.)

- **Mandrake Move:** Provides a complete Mandrake Linux system on a bootable CD. Applications enable you to create and edit office documents, listen to music, access the Internet, and more. Data and configuration files can be stored on a USB key for use with the CD. In addition, Mandrake Move enables you to read data from another CD. www.mandrakesoft.com/products/mandrakemove

- **MEPIS:** Provides a bootable CD as the installer. You can boot and run MEPIS from the CD to try it out. The bootable CD includes an installer, so you can install Linux onto your hard disk from the same CD. MEPIS was the first to combine a Live CD with an installer. www.MEPIS.org

Summary

The Linux operating system that's installed on your computer is a collection of many programs, called a distribution, put together by a group or a company. All distributions contain a core set of essential components, necessary for Linux to run your computer. However, most distributions include more than the bare essentials. They can differ on the number of applications included, installation procedures, system utilities, levels of support, and other factors.

Distributions are available via a download from Web sites or on CDs. The downloadable software consists of CD images that you write to CD. You then install Linux from the CDs you created. Some distributions provide boxed sets with CDs and manuals.

Fedora Core, the successor to the very popular Red Hat Linux, is the main distribution discussed in this book. Its strengths are strong support, graphical installation procedures and administrative utilities, and easy software updates. Fedora is not available in a boxed set. You must download it yourself or purchase it from vendors that download and create CDs for you. No manuals, but documentation is available on your system and at the Web site.

In addition, the Mandrake and SuSE distributions are described in this book. Both emphasize ease of installation and use. These three distributions are oriented toward desktop computer users and provide installation procedures similar to Windows installation procedures. Other popular distributions are Slackware, Debian, MEPIS, Xandros, Linspire, and Gentoo, described briefly in this chapter. Live CDs that enable you to run your computer from the CD are also available. Many, many distributions are available. More complete coverage of distributions is available at www.distrowatch.org, which maintains a database of 320 distributions.

Choosing a distribution is your first step. Next, you need to get ready to install your chosen Linux. You need to be sure you have the necessary computer resources, obtain the Linux software, and decide on the type of installation you want. Chapter 3 provides the information you need to prepare for installation.

▌▌ CHAPTER 3 ▐▐

Getting Ready to Install Linux

Some thought, and perhaps some work, is necessary to prepare for Linux. Before you begin the installation of Linux, you need to do the following:

- **Check your hardware:** Linux requires certain minimum hardware resources. In addition, Linux needs to communicate with your hardware, such as your monitor and your mouse. You can check your hardware to ensure that it's compatible with your Linux distribution.

- **Obtain the Linux software:** The easiest way to obtain Linux is to purchase it. When you purchase a Linux distribution, CDs with Linux ready to install arrive on your doorstep. On the other hand, the quickest way to obtain Linux is to download it from the distribution Web site. However, then you must copy the downloaded files onto a CD.

- **Plan your preferred computer system:** Linux can be installed alone on your computer or can be installed together with another operating system, such as Windows.

- **Prepare your computer for multiple operating systems:** If you plan to run more than one operating system, you need to prepare separate sections of the hard disk, called partitions, for each operating system.

- **Set up your computer to boot from the CD drive:** To install Linux from the CDs, you need to boot your computer from the CD drive. You need to determine whether your computer can boot from the CD. If it doesn't, you can change its settings so that it does boot from the CD. Or, you can boot from a floppy disk.

Hardware Requirements

Linux requires certain hardware resources. Different Linux distributions have different requirements. Some Linux distributions were developed specifically to be installed in a very small space or on old or unusual computers. However, this book provides information for complete Linux distributions, including desktops and general applications, such as office or graphics applications. Therefore, the hardware considerations discussed in this section refer to complete Linux distributions, such as Fedora, Mandrake, and SuSE. General requirements are as follows:

- **Computer type:** Pentium class computer equivalent to Pentium II with a speed of 400MHz or better.

- **Memory:** The memory requirements suggested by Fedora are a minimum of 192MB with 256MB recommended. SuSE gives 128MB as the minimum with 256MB recommended. Mandrake gives 64MB as the minimum, with 128MB or more recommended.

- **Hard disk space:** As with most software, most Linux distributions get larger as they improve and add features. For instance, Mandrake 9.2 requires 100MB for a minimum installation, with 1GB recommended; whereas Mandrake 10 requires 500MB, with 1GB recommended. It's best to check the Web site for the hard disk requirements of the Linux distribution and version you want to install.

  The number and type of packages is also a consideration. A minimum installation may not include space for all the packages you need. In fact, some minimal installations are so stripped down that they are barely usable. Even a usable installation can provide different package sets with installation. For instance, Fedora allows you to select an installation type during the install process. The Personal Desktop type installs fewer packages than the Workstation type. Thus, Personal Desktop requires 2.3GB, whereas Workstation requires 3GB. For most purposes, you should try to allow at least 2GB if possible.

  In addition, you need to include some extra space in your installation. You may want to add packages later. You also need room for the data you add. And Linux requires some empty space (5 %) for its own use.

Hardware Compatibility

The Linux operating system is a collection of programs that run a computer. To perform its job, it needs to communicate with the computer hardware so that it can store information on the hard disk, display information on the screen, send data to the printer, and perform other tasks. Thus, Linux needs to know what type of hardware is on your system so that it can communicate with the hardware.

In the early days of Linux, the person installing the software needed to provide Linux with the hardware information it needed, which meant that the person needed to be knowledgeable about the hardware. Consequently, Linux developed the reputation of being difficult to install, not to be attempted by a novice. However, in recent times, this is no longer the case. Extensive hardware expertise is no longer required.

Recent Linux installation procedures can identify the hardware in your computer quite accurately by probing the computer. Occasionally, if your hardware is very unusual or very new, the installation procedure might not be able to recognize it. You can check any hardware for compatibility at the distribution Web site before you start the installation. Fedora, Mandrake, and SuSE maintain databases where you can search for your hardware to see whether it's compatible (hardware.redhat.com; cdb.suse.de/; www.linux-mandrake.com/en/hardware.php3).

You can be doubly prepared during installation if you gather information about your hardware, in case you need it. The best solution is to gather the manuals for your hardware, such as the manual for your monitor and modem. If you don't have the manuals, you can usually get the information you need in one of the following ways:

- **From Windows:** If you are installing Linux on a computer that already has Windows installed, you can find the name of your hardware from the Windows Control Panel. For instance, in Windows XP, go to `Start->Control Panel->Administrative Tools->Computer Management->Device Manager`. You see a list of hardware on your computer. You don't need to know what all those things are. But, if you click modem or mice, it will list what kind of modem or mouse you have. If you double-click the specific modem name, it gives you a screen showing the properties of the hardware.

- **From the Web:** Go to the Web page for the hardware manufacturer, find the model that matches yours, and look at the specification page for the product.

Purchasing Linux

The easiest way to obtain Linux is to purchase it. In fact, the very easiest way to obtain Linux is to purchase a computer with Linux already installed. Although it's certainly not as easy to buy a computer with Linux installed as to buy one with Windows installed, it's possible. Some companies that sell Linux workstations are Monarch Computer Systems (www.monarchcomputer.com) and Penguin Computing (www.penguincomputing.com). Laptops can also be purchased with Linux installed at these companies and at Emperor Linux (www.EmperorLinux.com), which specializes in selling laptops.

More often, you want to install Linux on a computer you already own—one with no operating system or with Windows already installed. To purchase Linux, order it from the distribution Web site or from a Web site that distributes Linux software CDs. You can purchase Linux in two varieties:

- **Boxed sets:** Some Linux distributions are available in boxed sets, similar to Windows software, that can be purchased from the distribution company, usually on the company Web site. The CDs are packaged in a nice box, along with their manuals and other documentation. When you purchase a boxed set, you usually receive technical support as part of the purchase. Prices begin around $30. The following are some Linux distributions available in a boxed set:

  - Mandrake (www.mandrakesoft.com/products), starting at $49.90

  - SuSE (www.suse.com/us/private/index.html), starting at $29.95

  - Slackware (store.slackware.com), $39.95

- **CDs:** You can order just CDs, the same CDs you would have if you downloaded the CD image (ISO image) files and copied them onto CD yourself. For a reasonable price, you can purchase the CDs and save yourself the trouble. If your Internet connection is dial-up, downloading can be a long and painful process. A 650MB ISO image can take 27 hours to download. The Fedora distribution is only available this way; a boxed set is not available. Some distributions available in boxed sets are also available as CDs only. Two places where you can purchase Linux CDs are as follows:

  - **www.cheapbytes.com:** Sells many Linux distribution CDs. Also sells other products.

  - **www.easylinuxcds.com:** Offers many different Linux distributions. Also sells training CDs.

Downloading Linux

The quickest way to obtain Linux is to download it. The files you download are CD images, also called ISO images. After downloading, you copy the images onto CDs and install Linux from these installation CDs. For example, to download Fedora, follow these steps:

1. Go to fedora.redhat.com/download/.

2. Scroll down the page to the heading Downloading the ISO Images.

3. Click the link: http://download.fedora.redhat.com/pub/fedora/linux/core/2/i386/iso/.

4. Download the files with names ending in disc*n*.iso, where *n* is a number. These are the ISO images for the CDs. For example, these are the files for Fedora Core 2:

   FC2-i386-disc1.iso

   FC2-i386-disc2.iso

   FC2-i386-disc3.iso

   FC2-i386-disc4.iso

5. Write the four ISO images to four separate CDs. The exact procedure for writing the CDs depends on the software you use to write CDs. Read the software manual to see how to write ISO images.

You now have the installation CDs from which you can install Linux. The installation instructions are provided in Chapter 4.

You can also install Linux from a DVD using a similar procedure. Download a DVD image, rather than the CD images. DVDs hold more information, so you will download fewer files (probably one), but it will be much larger, up to 4GB.

Most Linux distributions provide a Web site where you can download ISO images. For example, the download location for Mandrake is www.mandrakelinux.com/en/ftp.php3 and for Debian is www.debian.org/CD/http-ftp/.

SuSE has an unusual download procedure. You install Linux directly from the SuSE Web site using FTP. The Web site is www.suse.com/us/private/download/suse_linux/.

NOTE

Downloading Linux is not feasible if you are using a dial-up connection. A single ISO image for one of the installation disks can take as long as 27 hours to download at dial-up speeds.

Planning Your Computer System

Linux can be installed alone on your computer or can be installed together with another operating system, such as Windows. If it's installed with another operating system, you see a menu when you start your computer that enables you to choose which operating system you want to boot. This type of system is called a dual-boot system, or multiple-boot if you have more than two operating systems. Your first decision is whether you want Linux running alone on your computer or together with another operating system. Reasons for running more than one operating system include the following:

- To learn both systems.

- To learn Linux without giving up Windows.

- To use operating system specific applications. Application software can't run on both Windows and Linux, although some software has two versions—one that runs on Linux and one that runs on Windows. You may want to use one application that runs on Linux and another that runs on Windows.

- To test applications on both systems. If you develop a computer application, you can test it to see whether it runs on both systems.

A dual-boot system has the following disadvantages:

- Slower to boot up. It goes through the process of displaying the boot menu each time.

- Less disk space for each operating system.

- More maintenance required. An operating system requires maintenance, such as updating to newer versions and updating software. Two systems require more maintenance work than one system.

- More organization required. If you work on two different systems, you need to organize your work so that you have what you need where you need it. Invariably, the file you need for one application is stored under the other application.

If you plan to have only Linux installed on your computer, your preparation is easy. You don't need to prepare your hard disk at all. If you plan to run Linux together with another operating system, you need to prepare your hard disk. See the next section for information on running Linux and Windows together.

Running Linux with Windows

You can install both Linux and Windows on your computer, although only one operating system is running the computer at any given time. A menu is displayed when your computer starts, allowing you to select which operating system to boot. Each operating system is installed in a separate section of your hard disk, called a partition.

To install Linux with Windows on your hard drive, you need to have Windows already installed in a partition and enough free space on your hard disk for Linux. Thus, Windows needs to be installed first. When Windows is installed, you can install it in a partition that does not take up your entire hard disk, leaving enough room for Linux. The Windows installation instructions will tell you how to do this. For example, when installing Windows XP on a hard disk with no existing version of Windows, you will see a screen that displays the existing partitions, giving you choices where Windows can be installed. The only partition is probably "unpartitioned space" showing your entire hard disk. Select the choice "Create a new partition from unpartitioned space." When the new partition is displayed, select a partition size that is smaller than your hard disk, leaving room for Linux.

When you install Windows 2000 or XP, you can select the type of file system for the Windows partition. NTFS and FAT32 are the most common types. Although NTFS has many advantages (such as, better security and efficiency), it has disadvantages in a dual-boot system with Linux. At this time, it's difficult for Linux to read/write an NTFS file system, preventing file sharing between the partitions. In addition, NTFS file systems can't be resized easily if you should want to make room later for another partition. For a dual-boot Linux system, FAT32 may be preferable.

If Windows is already installed on your computer taking up the entire hard disk, you need to resize the Windows partition to a smaller size to make room for Linux. You can do this with a utility on the Linux CD called FIPS. However, FIPS cannot resize a Windows XP NTFS partition. As of this writing, the solutions are to purchase Partition Magic, which can resize it, or to install Mandrake Linux, which can resize the Windows partition during installation, making room for itself. Another suggestion is to install an additional hard disk and install Linux there. If the partition is not a Windows XP NTFS partition, see the section "Making Room for Linux Before Installation" in this chapter.

If you don't know whether you have one or two hard disks or how your hard disk is partitioned, you can use Windows Administrative Tools to look at your hard drive, as described in the following section, "Examining Your Hard Drive."

Examining Your Hard Drive

If you don't know which partitions are available, you can use Windows Administrative Tools to find out. On Windows XP, select `Start` -> `Control Panel` -> `Administrative Tools` -> `Computer Management` -> `Disk Management`. The window shown in Figure 3-1 displays, showing the hard disks and their partitions.

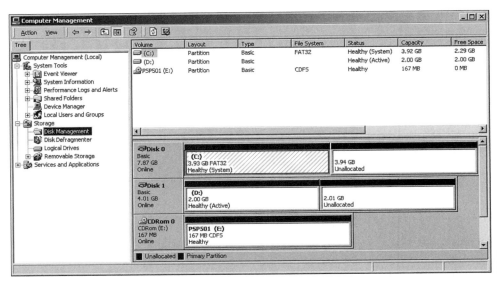

FIGURE 3-1 Disk partition information in Windows 2000.

The display in Figure 3-1 shows two hard disks (C and D) and one CD drive (E). Each hard disk has one partition and some unallocated space. On drive C, the partition is 3.93GB, formatted with a FAT32 file system. The unallocated space is 3.94GB. Linux could be installed in the unallocated space on drive C.

Notice in the top panel that the partition on drive C shows a capacity of 3.92GB, with 2.29GB of free space. If it was necessary, the partition on C could be resized smaller without losing any data because 2.29GB contain no data.

NOTE

When Linux is installed, it's usually installed into more than one partition, facilitating some Linux security features and techniques. The installation procedure for most distributions creates the Linux partitions in the unallocated space during installation.

Making Room for Linux During Installation

If your Windows partition leaves no room for Linux, you need to resize the Windows partition, splitting some of its unused space into a partition for Linux. Mandrake and SuSE (but not Fedora) can resize the Windows partition during the installation procedure.

Before resizing the partition, you need to defragment the Windows partition, moving files to the beginning of the partition. In Windows 2000/XP, select:

```
Start->Programs->Accessories->System Tools->Disk Defragmenter
```

For your NTFS file system, the Windows swap file (virtual memory) may remain at the end of the partition. You can temporarily shut down your virtual memory while installing and start virtual memory again after the installation. In addition, it's a good idea to back up your data before resizing the Windows partition. Just in case something goes really wrong.

Mandrake installs easily with Windows. During the installation procedure, Mandrake displays a screen asking where Linux should be installed. Select:

```
Use the free space on the Windows partition
```

This selection causes Mandrake to resize any Windows partition, even NTFS partitions, to make room for itself. After this procedure, the Windows partition is smaller.

SuSE allows you to partition manually. During the installation procedure, a screen is displayed showing suggested partitions. Select:

```
Create custom partition setup
```

A screen displays where you select a hard disk for the Linux installation. If the hard disk contains a Windows partition and not enough room to install Linux, a screen displays asking whether to delete or resize the Windows partition. When you select "Resize Windows partition," SuSE displays a screen that allows you to select the new size for the partitions.

Making Room for Linux Before Installation

You can resize your Windows partition when installing some Linux distributions, but not others. For instance, Mandrake and SuSE can make room for Linux during installation, but Fedora cannot. When you can't resize during installation, you need to resize the Windows partition before starting the installation. It's best to get a copy of Partition Magic for this purpose (www.symantec.com/partitionmagic/).

In some cases, you can use the FIPS utility to resize the Windows partition. However, often FIPS is not successful because of unmovable blocks in the Windows partition.

NOTE
Be sure to defragment and back up your hard disk before starting installation, as discussed in the previous section.

FIPS is on the Linux installation CD, probably in dosutils\fips20, but it may be in a different directory. You need to copy it onto a floppy disk that you can boot to resize the partition:

1. Open the Command Prompt window.

2. If your CD drive is D and your floppy disk is A, type:

   ```
   copy D:\dosutils\fips20\*.* A:
   ```

3. After you have made the floppy disk, shut down your computer.

4. Turn on your computer, booting from the floppy.

5. Type: FIPS. FIPS displays a list of partitions, asking which one to split.

6. Enter the partition number of the Windows partition.

7. FIPS asks whether you want to make a copy of your boot sector. Type Y. Put in a second floppy and type Y again. Press <Enter>.

8. FIPS displays your partitions. Use the arrow keys to change the size of the partitions to make room for Linux. When the size is correct, press <Enter>. At this point, nothing is actually written to the hard disk. You can still change your mind.

9. Type Y to write the partition scheme to disk. Now your hard disk is changed.

FIPS cannot resize a Windows XP NTFS file system. If your Windows partition is Windows XP NTFS, you can install Mandrake, which can resize NTFS file systems during installation, or you can purchase a commercial product that can resize NTFS file systems, such as Partition Magic. Or you can add a hard disk to your system where Linux can be installed.

Booting from the CD or from a Floppy

To install from the CDs that you have purchased/written, you need to boot from your CD drive. Most computers are set up so that they try to boot in the following order:

1. **From the floppy:** If a bootable disk is in the floppy drive, the computer boots from the disk.

2. **From the CD drive:** If a bootable CD is in the drive, the computer boots from the CD.

3. **From the hard drive:** If no floppy or CD is found, the computer attempts to boot from the hard drive.

Test whether your computer boots from the CD by putting a CD in the drive and turning on the computer. If your computer ignores the CD and boots from the hard drive, the boot order may be different, with the hard drive coming before the CD drive. The boot order can be changed using the setup program. The manual for your motherboard explains how to use the setup program. In general, you enter the motherboard setup program when your computer first boots by pressing a specific key, such as the Del key. Instructions, such as "Press Del to enter Setup," display on the screen. Enter the boot options menu and change the order, usually using the tab or arrow keys. Be sure to save the new settings when leaving the setup program.

Some older computers or laptops may refuse to boot from the CD, requiring you to make a boot floppy to start the installation. Most distributions provide a method for making a boot floppy on a Windows system; the procedure may differ, however, so read the documentation for information. To make a boot floppy for Mandrake:

1. Start rawwritewin. The program is located on the first CD in the directory dosutils. Click the program or type its name in a command prompt window. A user interface appears after a short wait.

2. Select Image File. In most cases, the image file should be ..\image\cdrom.img.

3. Put a floppy disk into the floppy drive.

4. Make sure the floppy disk selected is correct. \A: is usually correct.

5. Click Write.

After creating the floppy, you can boot your computer with the floppy, which starts the installation. The installation will then continue using the CDs.

NOTE

Fedora Core 1 provides a very similar procedure. However, starting with Fedora Core 2, the dosutils directory is no longer provided on the CDs.

Summary

Some thought, and perhaps some work, is necessary to prepare for Linux.

- Check your hardware to be sure your CPU is powerful enough, that you have enough memory, and that you have enough hard disk space. You also need to check that your hardware, such as video card, monitor, modem, printer, etc. are compatible with Linux.

- Obtain the Linux distribution you plan to install. Either purchase or download it.

- Decide whether to install Linux alone on your computer or together with another operating system, such as Windows. You can install each operating system on a separate section of the hard drive, called a partition.

- Prepare your hard disk for the system you plan to install. If you plan to install Linux alongside Windows, Windows needs to be installed first. Use Windows to examine your hard disk to see whether a partition exists suitable for installing Linux. If not, you can make room for Linux before installation or during installation.

- Set up your computer so that it boots from the CD drive.

When your computer is ready for Linux, install using the instructions in Chapter 4.

▌▌ CHAPTER 4 ▐▐▐

Installation

Installing software involves more than copying the software onto a hard disk. The software must be configured with the information it needs to perform its job. An operating system is complex software, which requires considerable information to perform its job. Most software, including operating systems, comes with an installation program. To install the software, you run the installation program, which asks questions and installs the software, configuring it with the information obtained during the installation procedure.

If you have installed software on a Windows machine, you know that the installation procedure asks you questions, such as where you want the software installed and what is your registration number. After you answer the questions, the installation program installs the software based on the information you provided.

Most Linux distributions come with an installation program that installs the software based on information obtained during the installation procedure. Information is obtained both by probing the computer hardware for information and by asking questions.

The installation procedures for Fedora, Mandrake, and SuSE, the three major Linux distributions discussed in this book, have been developed and refined to be easy to use. Installation for these distributions is described in detail in this chapter.

Installation Overview

The Linux installation procedure performs two tasks:

- Gathers information
- Installs Linux

To install correctly, the Linux installation procedure needs the following information:

- **Local information:** The language the user prefers to use. The local time zone.

- **Hardware information:** Linux communicates with the computer hardware—to display information on the monitor, to send documents to the printer, to store data in a file on the hard disk, to send information via the modem, etc. To communicate correctly, Linux needs to know which hardware is installed, including the type of monitor, type of modem, type of printer, and so on.

- **Where to install Linux:** Is Linux to be installed on the entire hard disk or only part of it? Is Linux sharing the hard disk with another operating system? Is this a new installation or is it replacing a previous Linux installation? The options for installing Linux are discussed in Chapter 3.

- **Accounts:** Linux requires users to have accounts before they can use the computer. The necessary accounts are created during installation. Accounts are discussed in Chapter 8.

- **Software:** Which software packages to install. Most distributions come with hundreds or thousands of packages. Not all the packages need to be, or even should be, installed.

- **Network settings:** To communicate across a network, Linux needs to know what type of network and network connection is to be used. Networks are discussed in detail in Chapter 16.

Any Linux distribution needs this information to install Linux. In olden days, the person installing Linux needed to provide the information. Thus, the person needed to be knowledgeable, especially about the hardware. Over time, many Linux distributions have developed installation procedures to make the installation process much easier. The installation procedure can obtain much of the information needed by probing the computer hardware and settings.

The three distributions (Fedora, Mandrake, SuSE) discussed in this book provide installation procedures that are quite easy to follow. The three distributions take different approaches to collecting information.

- **Fedora:** The installer steps through each bit of information needed, asking questions if it needs to—a screen for the keyboard, a screen for the mouse, etc.

- **SuSE:** Begins by probing the computer, gathering information, and making estimates for all the settings. It shows the estimated settings in a screen. You can accept or change the settings.

- **Mandrake:** Asks questions one by one like Fedora. However, at the end of the questions, a screen is displayed showing the settings, similar to the SuSE screen, giving you the opportunity to change any settings.

After the information is collected, the software is installed. Installation consists of the following:

- Configuring the software based on the information gathered
- Copying the programs to the appropriate locations on the hard disk.

Fedora and Mandrake copy all the software packages at once. SuSE installs a basic system, reboots, and then uses the basic system to install the remaining software.

The Linux installation may take an hour or more, depending on the distribution and the amount of software installed. It's okay to let the installation wait in the middle of installation, but if you stop the process, for instance by shutting off your computer, you will have to start over from the beginning.

The following pages describe the installation procedures for Fedora, Mandrake, and SuSE in detail.

Starting the Fedora Installation Procedure

Put the first installation CD (Disk 1) or DVD in the CD or DVD drive and turn on the power to your computer. The computer will boot from the CD and display the installation start screen. (If your machine doesn't boot from the CD, see Chapter 3.)

FIGURE 4-1 The opening screen in Fedora.

Press <Enter> to begin the graphical installation procedure. Fedora performs a few tasks, displaying its progress in a plain screen as shown in Figure 4-2. You don't need to respond to or understand the lines on the screen.

```
JFS: Disk quotas dquot_6.5.1
Dquot-cache hash table entries: 1024 (order 0, 4096 bytes)
SELinux:  Registering netfilter hooks
Initializing Cryptographic API
Limiting direct PCI/PCI transfers.
pci_hotplug: PCI Hot Plug PCI Core version: 0.5
ACPI: Processor [CPU0] (supports C1, 8 throttling states)
isapnp: Scanning for PnP cards...
isapnp: No Plug & Play device found
Real Time Clock Driver v1.12
Linux agpgart interface v0.100 (c) Dave Jones
```

FIGURE 4-2 A transitional screen in Fedora.

Before proceeding any further, Fedora provides an opportunity to test the installation CDs. It's not necessary to test them, but it's wise. If you are in the middle of the installation and a CD is unusable, it brings the installation to a halt. Figure 4-3 shows the CD test screen.

If you elect to test the CD, the media check continues for some time. When it is done, you see a screen like Figure 4-4.

FIGURE 4-3 The CD test screen in Fedora Core 2.

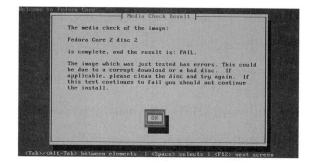

FIGURE 4-4 The CD test result screen in Fedora Core 2.

The result screen displays PASS or FAIL. If your CD fails, try cleaning the CD or just testing it again. Sometimes a CD that fails on the first try is actually okay. Press <Enter> for
OK and the screen in Figure 4-3 displays again, allowing you to test another CD (or the
same one again). After you have tested all the CDs you need to test, select Skip to continue with the installation.

Fedora displays a few more lines. Then the welcome screen is displayed.

FIGURE 4-5 The welcome screen in Fedora Core 2.

The Fedora installation procedure provides buttons on each screen to proceed to the
Next screen, when ready, or go Back to the previous screen.

Collecting Hardware Information for Fedora

Fedora gathers the hardware information it needs to install Linux. As part of the installation procedure, it probes the hardware to determine the mouse, keyboard, and monitor types. Fedora may or may not need to display a screen for a hardware item, depending on the results of the probe. The following screens may be displayed:

1. **Language:** Selects the language for the installation screens. If the highlighted language isn't correct, highlight the correct language.

2. **Keyboard:** Selects the keyboard layout. One layout is highlighted. Select a different layout if preferred.

3. **Mouse:** Fedora highlights a mouse name and is almost always right. If the selected mouse isn't correct, highlight the correct mouse.

4. **Monitor:** Fedora displays a screen to select the monitor. The monitor identified by the installation procedure is highlighted.

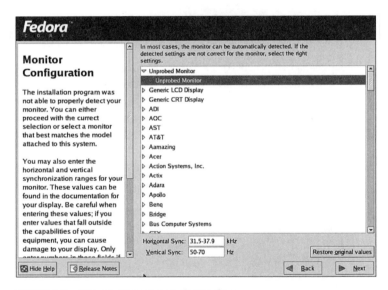

FIGURE 4-6   The monitor screen in Fedora Core.

In Figure 4-6, the program was unable to identify the monitor, so it highlights a generic choice. If the correct monitor is not highlighted, find your monitor in the list. Selecting the triangle by a manufacturer drops down a list of models. If you can't find the correct model, you can enter some specifications (Horizontal Sync, Vertical Sync) that allow Fedora to display correctly to your monitor. You can find the specifications in your monitor manual or on the manufacturer's Web site.

Selecting the Installation Type for Fedora

If the installer finds Fedora on your hard disk, it asks whether you want to upgrade or install a new version. The instructions in this chapter are for a new installation.

A Linux computer can serve many purposes. The next screen displayed allows you to select a type of installation for your computer. The choices are shown in Figure 4-7.

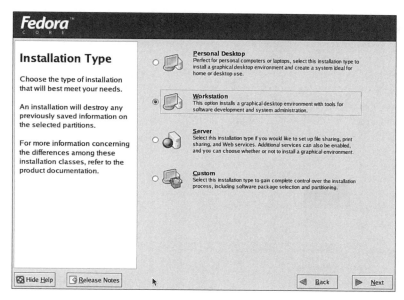

FIGURE 4-7 Installation type screen in Fedora Core 2.

Select one of the following choices:

- **Personal Desktop** provides a desktop and a selection of desktop applications. It includes office applications. This choice removes all existing Linux software on your hard disk, but leaves any Windows software in place.

- **Workstation** includes the applications provided by Desktop and adds tools for software developers and system administrators.

- **Server** is not designed for desktop use. This choice will remove all other software, including Windows, from your hard disk.

- **Custom** allows you greater flexibility, but you must know what you are doing.

In the remainder of the Fedora instructions, the choices are based on a Workstation installation. If you choose another type, you may see small differences in the screens displayed.

Selecting Where to Install Fedora

The next screens allow you to select where Fedora will be installed. If you are installing Fedora by itself onto a machine that currently has no operating system, you probably want Fedora to use the entire hard disk. If you already have an operating system on your computer (either Linux or Windows), Fedora can replace the current operating system or coexist with it, each operating system having its own section of the hard disk, called a *partition*. Using multiple operating systems is discussed in Chapter 3. In addition, Fedora needs to divide its partition into subpartitions. You have the opportunity to tell Fedora how to organize its partition.

The first partitioning screen offers the choice to partition automatically or manually, as shown on the right. Unless you have a specific need to partition manually, such as a very unusual purpose for your computer, select Automatically. You must be fairly knowledgeable to partition manually.

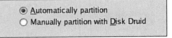

If you select automatic partitioning, the screen in Figure 4-8 displays.

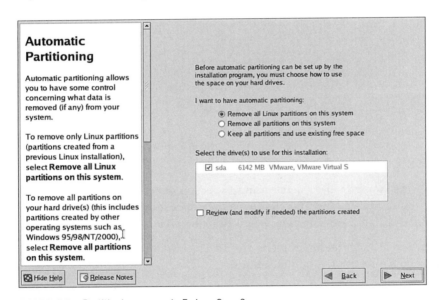

FIGURE 4-8   Partitioning screen in Fedora Core 2.

Different choices may be offered depending on what is currently on your hard disk. If you select Remove all partitions, all data is erased, including any Windows partitions. The list box in the screen shows the hard disk where Fedora will be installed. If you have more than one hard disk, be sure the correct one is checked. Possible entries in the list include the following:

- **hda:** Your first hard disk

- **hdb:** Your second hard disk

- **sda:** Your first SCSI drive

- **sdb:** Your second SCSI drive

The boot loader determines what operating systems can boot your system. Fedora uses the GRUB (Grand Unified Boot Loader) boot loader, but you can choose to use LILO (Linux Loader) instead. Figure 4-9 shows the boot loader installation screen.

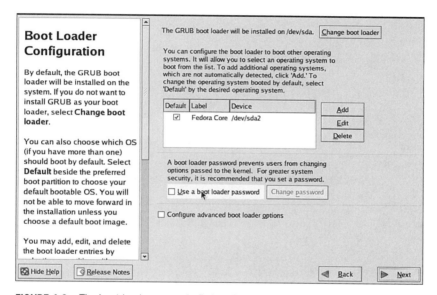

FIGURE 4-9   The boot loader screen in Fedora Core 2.

Unless you have a specific reason, use GRUB. If an operating system is currently installed on your hard disk, such as Windows, it will show up in the list. After your system is installed, each time you turn on or reboot your computer, GRUB displays a menu of operating systems for you to select. If you don't select one, the default operating system will start after a short pause (often 10 seconds). Be sure you check the Default box for the operating system you want to start automatically.

For most systems, it's not necessary to use a password for your boot loader.

Collecting Network Information for Fedora

The next screens allow you to configure your network. These screens only appear if the Fedora installer detects a network card in your computer. If your computer has no network card, Fedora skips these screens. Figure 4-10 shows the first network screen.

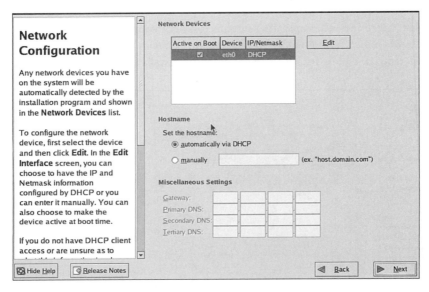

FIGURE 4-10   Network configuration in Fedora Core 2.

The network connection hardware detected by the Fedora installer is shown in the list at the top of the screen. This figure shows one network connector, eth0. Two settings are configured:

- **Active on Boot:** The network connection is activated when your computer starts.

- **IP/Network:** Each network connector has an address, called an IP address, that allows the network to locate the computer and transfer information to it. The IP address can be set automatically by DHCP, or you can enter an IP address manually.

Settings can be entered or changed by highlighting the network connector and clicking Edit. If you are on a company network, the network administrator can tell you which settings to use. Most DSL or cable modem connections use DHCP. If you don't know which settings to use, just accept the Fedora defaults. These settings can be changed after your system is installed.

A firewall is included with Fedora. A firewall helps protect your computer from outside access. The firewall screen is shown in Figure 4-11.

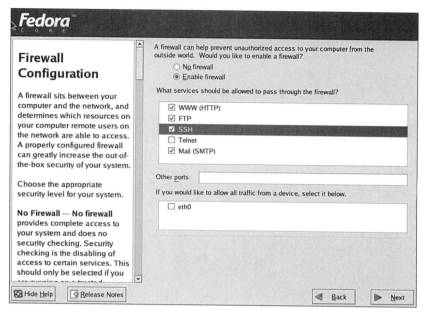

FIGURE 4-11   Firewall configuration in Fedora Core 2.

First, at the top of the screen, select whether to turn your firewall on. If you turn it on, select which services are allowed to pass through your firewall.

Languages and Time Zone for Fedora

Linux can support more than one language. At this point, you can select the language(s) for Linux to use on your computer in the screen shown in Figure 4-12.

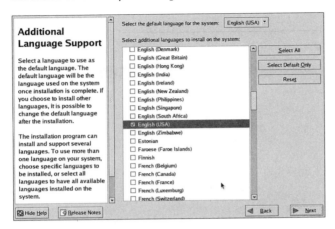

FIGURE 4-12   The language screen in Fedora Core 2.

At the top of the screen, select the language to use by default. If you want other languages to be available on your system, check them in the list of languages. After the system is installed, you can change to any language that you select in this screen.

Select your time zone in the screen shown in Figure 4-13.

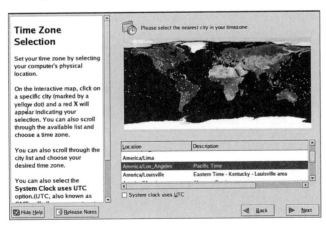

FIGURE 4-13   The time zone screen in Fedora Core 2.

Select the city nearest your location to select your local time zone. You can click the map or select from the list of cities.

Creating the Root Account for Fedora

Users must have an account to use Linux. When you boot, your first screen will ask you to log in to an account. A root account is required. The root user is also often called the super user. Other user accounts are usually installed as well. Accounts are discussed in detail in Chapter 8.

In this screen, shown in Figure 4-14, you create the root account. Other user accounts are created later.

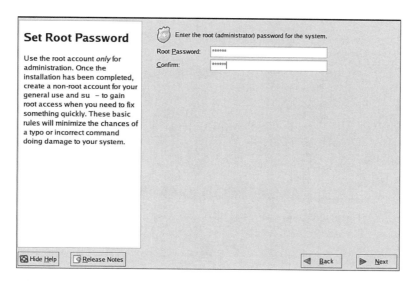

FIGURE 4-14   Root password screen in Fedora Core 2.

Type a password for the root account. Type the same password twice, to be sure that you don't make a mistake. It's extremely important that you remember this password. You can't make any changes to your Linux system without using the root account. Even if you install user accounts later and you can log in to a user account, you can't do many things that need to be done unless you can use the root account.

Choose your password to be as secure as possible, easy to remember but not to guess:

- Use at least 8 characters.
- Use one or more of each of the following: uppercase letters, lowercase letters, numerals, and punctuation marks.
- Don't use a word that is in the dictionary.
- Don't use a name, phone number, or date.

Selecting Packages to Install on Fedora

The software screen lists the packages Fedora intends to install. The list depends on the type of installation you selected earlier. The workstation software list is shown on the top. You have the choice to install the suggested list of software or modify the software list, removing or adding the names of packages to be installed. If you select the option to Customize software packages, shown on the bottom, the screen in Figure 4-15 will display, giving you the opportunity to add or remove packages.

Desktop shell (GNOME)
Office suite (OpenOffice.org)
Web browser (Mozilla)
Email (Evolution)
Instant messaging
Sound and video applications
Games
Software Development Tools
Administration Tools

◉ Install default software packages
○ Customize software packages to be installed

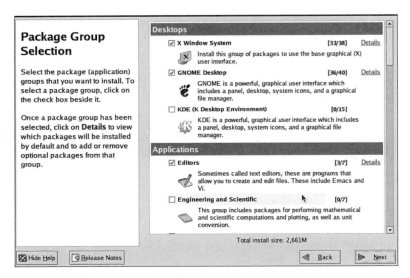

FIGURE 4-15   Package selection in Fedora Core 2.

The package selection screen shows groups of software that you can check or uncheck for installation. For instance, the GNOME desktop is the default for Fedora. You can see in Figure 4-15 that GNOME is checked and the KDE desktop is not checked. If you're new to Linux, you may want to try out both desktops to see which you like. Check by KDE to install the KDE desktop along with the GNOME desktop.

Some software listed is in categories containing more than one package, such as Editors. Clicking Details displays a screen showing exactly which packages are in the category, allowing you to pick and choose.

The choices made here are not the final word. You can add and remove software at any time after Fedora is installed.

Installing the Fedora System

Until now, Fedora has been gathering information; your hard disk is unchanged. The next part of the installation procedure copies files onto your hard disk, changing your hard disk. Fedora displays a warning screen, shown in Figure 4-16.

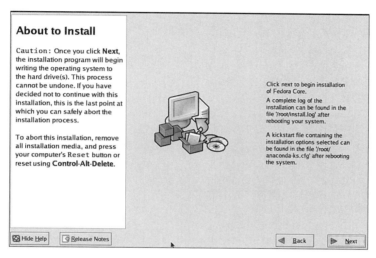

FIGURE 4-16   The warning screen in Fedora Core 2.

The installation procedure is as follows:

1. Formats the hard disk, displaying a status bar as it progresses

2. Displays a list of the CDs required for the installation

3. Installs the software, reporting its progress as shown below

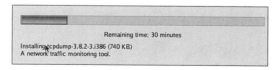

4. Requests a different CD when it needs one, as shown below

5. Performs some post-installation configuration

When the software installation is complete, Fedora displays the screen in Figure 4-17.

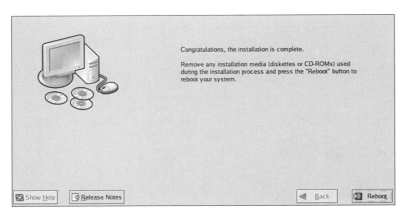

Congratulations, the installation is complete.

Remove any installation media (diskettes or CD-ROMs) used during the installation process and press the "Reboot" button to reboot your system.

FIGURE 4-17   Installation complete in Fedora Core 2.

To use your new Fedora system, you need to reboot. Remove the CD or DVD from the CD or DVD drive and click Reboot. After rebooting, Fedora displays the boot loader menu shown in Figure 4-18. Only one system is shown—Fedora. If you have another operating system (e.g., Windows) installed, select the system you want to boot.

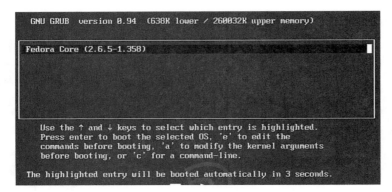

FIGURE 4-18   The boot loader menu for Fedora Core 2.

Select Fedora Core to boot into your new Fedora Linux system.

Starting the Mandrake Installation Procedure

Put the CD or DVD in the CD or DVD drive and turn on the power to your computer. The computer will boot from the CD or DVD and display the installation start screen. (If your machine doesn't boot from the CD/DVD, see Chapter 3.)

The opening screen for Mandrake is shown here:

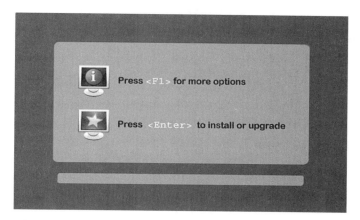

FIGURE 4-19   The start screen for Mandrake 10.

Press <Enter> to begin the graphical installation procedure, which starts as follows:

1. Performs a few tasks, displaying its progress as shown below. You don't need to respond to or understand the lines on the screen.

2. Loads the install program into memory, displaying a status bar as shown below.

Collecting Information for Mandrake

Mandrake gathers the information it needs to install Linux. As part of the installation procedure, it probes the hardware to determine the mouse, keyboard, and monitor types. If it is unable to identify the hardware, it displays a screen requesting information. However, Mandrake is particularly good at identifying hardware and seldom needs to display hardware screens. The following screens display:

1. **Language:** If the selected language is incorrect, highlight the correct language. Click the triangle by a category entry to see a drop-down list of languages.

2. **License agreement:** Mandrake displays a license agreement. You must click Agree before you can proceed.

3. **Type:** If Mandrake finds another Linux on your hard disk, a screen is displayed where you can select a New installation or to Upgrade the existing Linux.

4. **Security level:** Mandrake allows you to select a security level. The Standard security level is sufficient for most purposes. Enter an email address for the person who should be informed of security problems.

5. **Selecting where to install Mandrake:** Linux can be installed alone on your hard disk or share your hard disk with other operating systems, each with its own section of the hard disk, called a partition. Depending on what is currently on your hard disk, Mandrake offers 2 or more of the following choices:

   - **Use free space:** Installs Mandrake on free, unused space on your hard disk. This is the choice if no operating systems are currently installed.

   - **Use existing partition:** Select this choice if you want to install Mandrake on existing Linux partitions.

   - **Use the free space on the Windows partition:** If your computer is currently running the Windows system only, Mandrake can create a Linux partition on the hard disk using part of the Windows space. The Windows partition will be smaller after Linux is installed.

   - **Erase entire disk:** Replace all current operating systems, including all data on the hard disk.

   - **Remove Windows:** Replace the current Windows partition, erasing all data in the process.

   - **Custom disk partitioning:** Allows you to create partitions manually. Unless you have a specific need to partition manually, such as a very unusual purpose for your computer, don't select this option. You must be fairly knowledgeable to partition manually.

Selecting Packages to Install on Mandrake

The Mandrake screen for selecting package groups to install is shown in Figure 4-20.

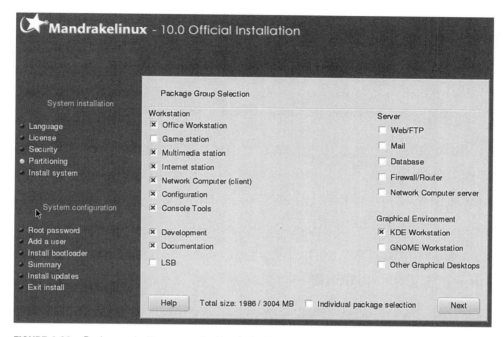

FIGURE 4-20   Package selection screen for Mandrake 10.

Checks are shown by the package groups Mandrake plans to install. You can check additional groups or uncheck groups. For instance, if you are new to Linux, you might want to check the GNOME desktop so Mandrake will install both KDE and GNOME, allowing you to try both before you decide which you prefer to use.

A line at the bottom shows you the "Total size" of the packages checked so that you can be sure you have enough disk space available.

If you check Individual package selection and click Next, Mandrake will display a screen that allows you to select individual packages, rather than groups of packages.

Unless you are really sure you need something that's not included in Mandrake's displayed list, it's usually best to accept Mandrake's choices. You can always add or remove software later, after your Linux system is installed. You don't need to decide now.

Installing the Mandrake System

Until now, Mandrake has been gathering information; your hard disk is unchanged. The next part of the installation procedure copies files onto your hard disk, changing your hard disk. While installing the software, Mandrake displays a progress screen, similar to the screen shown in Figure 4-21, showing the time remaining.

FIGURE 4-21   Installation progress screen for Mandrake 10.

Depending on how many packages you selected to install, the installation might require more than one CD. Mandrake will request another CD when it needs one, as shown in Figure 4-22.

FIGURE 4-22   The change CD screen for Mandrake 10.

Creating Accounts for Mandrake

Users must have an account to use Linux. A root account, often called the super user, is required. At least one other account is also required. Accounts are discussed in detail in Chapter 8. The user account creation screen is shown in Figure 4-23.

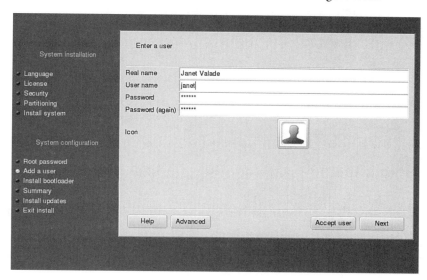

FIGURE 4-23 Account creation screen for Mandrake 10.

Mandrake first creates the root account. The screen to create the root account does not include the Real name and User name fields, because the account is necessarily named root. Type a password for the root account. Type the same password twice, to be sure that you don't make a mistake. It's extremely important that you remember this password. You can't make any changes to your Linux system without the root account.

Select your passwords carefully to maintain the security of your system. Passwords should be at least 8 characters, have a mix of letters and numerals, and should not be words that are found in the dictionary.

After you create the root account, you must create at least one user account for your own use. You can create as many accounts as you want. You should create an account for each person who is going to use the computer.

Pressing Accept user displays the screen again so you can enter another user account. When you have created all the accounts you need, press Next.

A screen asks whether you want to automatically log in to an account. In general, for security reasons, it's better not to select this feature.

Configuration Summary for Mandrake

At this point, Mandrake displays a screen showing a summary of the current configuration settings, as shown in Figure 4-24.

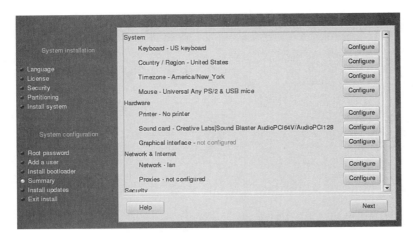

FIGURE 4-24   Configuration summary for Mandrake 10.

If anything on this screen is incorrect, press Configure to change it. For instance, the time zone is listed as America/New_York. If this is not correct, press Configure and select a different time zone, such as Los_Angeles for the Pacific time zone.

Notice this screen states that the graphical interface is not configured. It must be configured to use a desktop. Pressing Configure allows you to select your monitor from a list and to set the screen resolution you want to use.

When you are satisfied with the configuration in the summary screen and click Next, Mandrake provides the opportunity to update your packages. Unless you just downloaded Mandrake with the most recent packages, updating is a good idea. You need to be connected to the Internet to update.

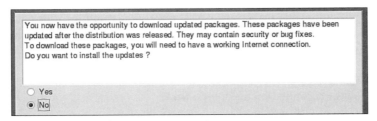

FIGURE 4-25   Update packages screen for Mandrake 10.

Finishing Mandrake Installation

Mandrake displays the screen in Figure 4-26 to show the installation is done.

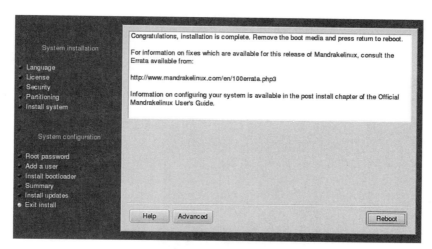

FIGURE 4-26   The installation done screen in Mandrake 10.

To use your new Mandrake system, you need to reboot. Remove the CD or DVD from the CD or DVD drive and click Reboot. After rebooting, Mandrake displays the boot loader menu shown in Figure 4-27. Unless you have a reason to select one of the other choices, select linux. If you have another operating system (e.g., Windows) installed, it is listed and you can select the system you want to boot.

FIGURE 4-27   The boot loader menu for Mandrake 10.

Starting the SuSE Installation Procedure

Put the CD or DVD in the CD or DVD drive and turn on the power to your computer. The computer will boot from the CD or DVD and display the installation start screen. (If your machine doesn't boot from the CD/DVD, see Chapter 3.)

The opening screen for SuSE is shown here:

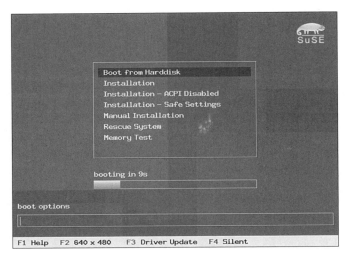

FIGURE 4-28   The start screen for SuSE 9.0.

The SuSE start screen offers several options. Boot from Harddisk is selected by default and will start unless you select another option. Notice the status bar that says "booting in 9s" (9 seconds).

Use the down-arrow key (↓) to highlight Installation. Press <Enter> to start. The installation procedure begins by performing a few tasks, displaying its progress as shown in Figure 4-29.

```
ide1 at 0x170-0x177,0x376 on irq 15
ide-floppy driver 0.99.newide
ide-floppy driver 0.99.newide
md: md driver 0.90.0 MAX_MD_DEVS=256, MD_SB_DISKS=27
md: Autodetecting RAID arrays.
md: autorun ...
md: ... autorun DONE.
NET4: Linux TCP/IP 1.0 for NET4.0
IP Protocols: ICMP, UDP, TCP, IGMP
IP: routing cache hash table of 2048 buckets, 16Kbytes
TCP: Hash tables configured (established 16384 bind 32768)
```

FIGURE 4-29   The transition screen for SuSE 9.0.

You don't need to respond to or understand the lines on the screen.

Configuration Settings for SuSE

The installation program for SuSE is YaST (Yet another Setup Tool). The current version is YaST2. The first graphical screen displayed is the language selection screen shown in Figure 4-30.

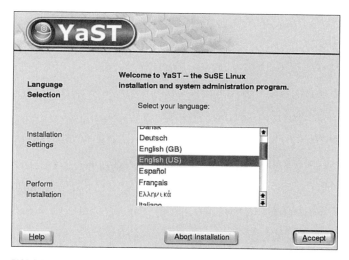

FIGURE 4-30   The language screen for SuSE 9.0.

If YaST detects a SuSE Linux system on your hard disk, a screen is displayed allowing you to select the type of installation, with the following choices:

- **New installation:** Replace existing Linux system, including all data.

- **Update an existing system:** Update existing Linux system, keeping data in place.

- **Repair installed system:** If current Linux system won't boot, this option tries to diagnose and fix the problem.

- **Boot installed system:** Boots the Linux system found on the hard disk.

- **Abort installation**

Check an option and click OK.

If no current Linux is detected on your hard disk, YaST assumes "New installation" and skips the installation type screen.

YaST probes hardware and settings to estimate the installation settings. A screen showing the probed settings displays, as shown in Figure 4-31.

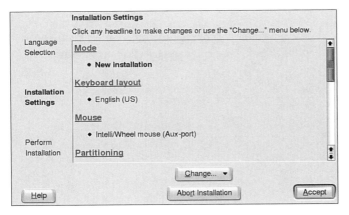

FIGURE 4-31 The settings summary screen for SuSE 9.0.

Any settings can be changed by clicking the setting name, such as Mode or Mouse. The settings shown are as follows:

- **Mode:** New installation or upgrade.

- **Keyboard Layout:** Language for the keyboard layout.

- **Mouse:** Type of mouse. If incorrect, you may be unable to use your mouse. You can use <Tab> to move to Mouse, click it, and select the correct mouse.

- **Partitioning:** Linux can be installed alone or share your hard disk with other operating systems, each with its own section of the hard disk, called a partition. SuSE selects the installation partitions based on what's currently on your hard disk. You need to be pretty knowledgeable to change the default selections.

- **Software:** List of software to be installed. Changing the software selections is discussed in the next section.

- **Booting:** Menu that will be displayed when your computer boots. You need to be pretty knowledgeable to change the default settings.

- **Time Zone:** Local time zone

- **Language:** Language used on your Linux system.

When the settings are correct, click Accept.

Selecting Packages to Install on SuSE

The summary screen shows the packages selected for installation, as shown on the right. If you click Software, you see the choices shown in Figure 4-32.

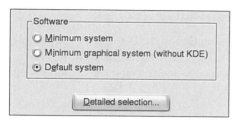

Software

- Default system
- + Help & Support Documentation
- + KDE Desktop Environment
- + Office Applications
- + Graphical Base System

FIGURE 4-32   The system types for SuSE 9.0.

If you select either Minimum or Minimum graphical system, your Linux system will not include a desktop, so Default is usually best. To change the package selection for the Default system, click Detailed selection to see the screen in Figure 4-33.

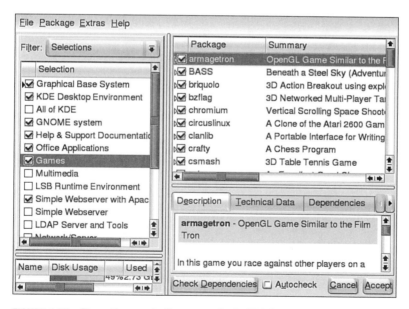

FIGURE 4-33   The software selection screen for SuSE 9.0.

The software selection screen in Figure 4-33 contains the following three selection panels:

- **Package groups** (upper left): Selected groups of software packages are checked. Check or uncheck groups to change package selections. For instance, KDE is the default desktop. However, if you are a new Linux user, you may want to try both KDE and GNOME before deciding which desktop you prefer. You can check GNOME and both KDE and GNOME will be installed.

- **Packages** (upper right): The individual packages for the highlighted group are listed in this panel. For instance, in Figure 4-33, Games is highlighted in the left panel. In this panel, you can check and uncheck individual game packages.

- **Package descriptions** (lower right): The description of the highlighted individual package in the right top panel is displayed in this panel. For instance, in Figure 4-33, the package Armagetron is selected in the top panel, and its description is displayed in this panel.

When you have selected the packages you want installed, click Accept.

The packages selected are installed during the Linux installation procedure. If you are sure which packages you need, it's convenient to install them when installing the system. However, this selection is not final. It's easy to install or remove software packages after your Linux system is installed. Adding and removing software is discussed in Chapter 10.

Installing the SuSE System

When all the settings in the summary screen (Figure 4-31) are correct, click Accept. Up to this point, SuSE has been gathering information, making no changes on your hard drive. Now it begins installing the system, making changes on your hard disk. Before it starts, it displays the warning screen shown in Figure 4-34.

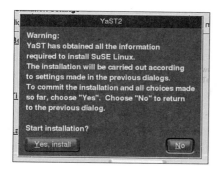

FIGURE 4-34   The installation warning screen for SuSE 9.0.

SuSE installs the system in 3 steps:

1. Installs a basic system, displaying its progress as it proceeds. Notice it displays the needed disk space in the upper-right panel.

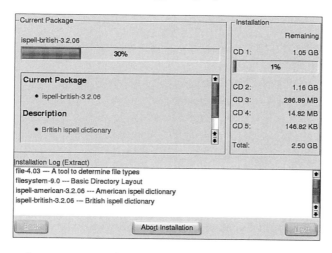

2. Reboots:

followed by

```
Restore device permissions                    done
Setting up the CMOS clock                      done
Setting up timezone data                       done
Setting scheduling timeslices                  unused
Setting up hostname 'linux'                    done
Setting up loopback interface                  done
```

3. Uses the basic system to install the remaining packages, requesting a new CD when needed.

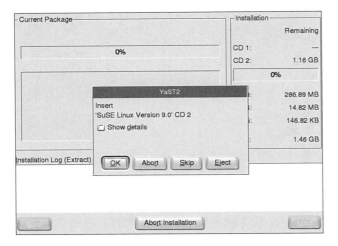

After installing all the software, SuSE installs the root account that is required for your Linux system, as shown in Figure 4-35.

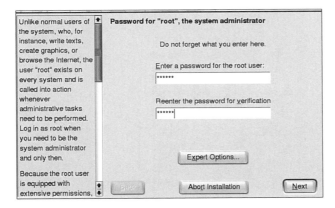

FIGURE 4-35 Root account installation for SuSE 9.0.

Type a password for the root account. Type the same password twice, to be sure that you don't make a mistake. It's extremely important that you remember this password. You can't make any changes to your Linux system without using the root account. Even if you install user accounts later and you can log in to a user account, you can't do many things that need to be done unless you can use the root account.

Configuring the Installed SuSE System

The next screens add network connections and user accounts to your Linux system:

1. **Network Settings:** Suggested settings are shown in a screen similar to the summary screen in Figure 4-39. You can change the settings by clicking Change. If you are on a company network, the network administrator can tell you which settings to use. Most DSL or cable modem connections use DHCP. If you don't know which settings to use, accept the SuSE suggestions or check Skip Configuration. These settings can be changed later, after your system is installed.

2. **Network Configuration:** If you set up a network connection in screen 1, the network is configured, displaying its progress in a screen with a status bar.

3. **Network Test:** Tests the network. If the connection is okay, any available software updates are downloaded.

4. **Authentication Method:** Offers two methods for authenticating users. In most cases, Stand-Alone is the correct choice. If you are using NIS or LDAP, check Network Client.

5. **Add User:** You can create new user accounts. Type the password twice. For security reasons, the password does not display on the screen.

6. **System Configuration:** Configuration is written to the system, displaying its progress in a status bar.

7. **Release Notes:** Displays release notes for you to read.

8. **Hardware Configuration:** Suggested settings are shown in a screen similar to the summary screen in Figure 4-31. You can change the settings by clicking the name of the item you want to change, such as graphics card or printer.

Finishing SuSE Installation

When YaST is finished displaying the configurations screens, it displays the Installation Completed screen, as shown in Figure 4-36.

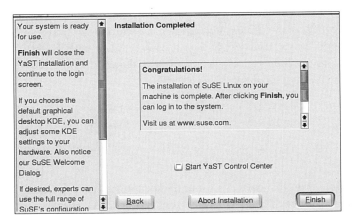

FIGURE 4-36   Installation Completed screen for SuSE 9.0.

Click Finish. The system displays some lines on the black screen and then displays the login screen, shown in Figure 4-37.

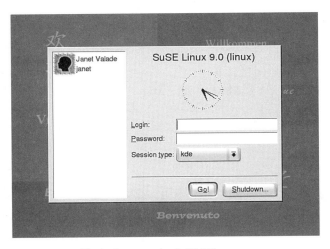

FIGURE 4-37   The login screen for SuSE 9.0.

Click an account, such as janet in the login screen, type your password, and click Go!. If you don't want to use the KDE desktop, click the arrow and select another desktop, such as GNOME, from a drop-down list.

Summary

Installing Linux involves more than copying the software onto a hard disk. It must be configured with the information it needs to perform its job. Linux distributions come with an installation program that asks questions and installs the software, configuring it with the information obtained during the installation procedure. Information is obtained both by probing the computer hardware for information and by asking questions.

To install correctly, the Linux installation procedure needs local information (e.g., language, local time zone), hardware information (e.g., manufacturer, model), where to install Linux, which software packages to install, network settings, and other information. In recent years, Linux distributions have developed installation procedures that greatly reduce the information you need to supply. Linux can obtain most of the information by probing the hardware.

The Linux installation may take an hour or more, depending on the distribution and the amount of software installed. It's okay to let the installation wait in the middle of installation; however, if you stop the process (for instance, by shutting off your computer), you will have to start over from the beginning.

The three distributions (Fedora, Mandrake, SuSE) discussed in this book provide installation procedures that are quite easy to follow. This chapter provides detailed steps for installing these three Linux distributions.

After Linux is installed, you can log on and begin using your new system. Chapter 5 describes the interfaces you can use to work on your new Linux system.

Interacting with Linux

L inux is an operating system. It transforms a collection of electronic parts into a usable tool that takes your instructions and executes them—stores information in files, sends data to the printer, displays information on the screen, starts applica- tion software, and performs many other tasks. Linux provides two basic types of interface for you to use to get your computer work done:

- **Graphical user interface:** A graphical user interface (GUI) in which you select menu items and click icons to accomplish your computer tasks. If you come from a Windows background, you are familiar with a GUI.

- **Command-line interface:** A text interface in which you type commands that Linux executes. If you come from a UNIX background, you are familiar with a command- line interface (CLI). Or, if you have worked in DOS or at the command-line prompt on a Windows computer, you have some experience with a CLI.

When you work on your computer, the interface provides the communication between you and the Linux kernel, the part of Linux where the low-level work takes place. The kernel communicates directly with the hardware to save files on the hard disk, send data streams to the printer, send information out onto the network, and other basic tasks. Your instructions are accepted by the interface, processed, and passed into the kernel.

The Graphical User Interface on Linux

The graphical user interface (GUI) provides graphical images on the screen that can be selected using the mouse. The most familiar computer GUI is a windowing system. Many windows can coexist on the screen, with independent tasks being performed in each window. The user can open, close, move, resize, and otherwise manipulate the windows.

The desktop environment so familiar to Windows users is a windowing system that's intended to represent the top of your office desk. When your computer starts, you have an empty working surface. The tools you need to perform tasks are available on the desktop, such as icons and menus, tool trays, a clock, a calculator, and other tools. You can open whichever application you need on the working surface. In fact, you can open as many applications as you need, simultaneously, in different windows.

Linux offers two popular desktop environments:

- **GNOME:** GNU Network Object Model Environment (GNOME) is open source software, a project that's part of the GNU project. The first public version, GNOME 1.0, was released in March 1999.

- **KDE:** K Desktop Environment (KDE) is free, open source software produced by the KDE project. The first public version, KDE 1.0, was released in July 1998.

Because both emulate a desktop, they are similar in many ways. Both desktops provide the following:

- A work surface with icons on it.

- A bottom panel with icons that start applications or menus.

- Many applications, such as email software, browsers, file editors, etc.

- A menu for starting applications, almost identical to the Windows Start menu.

- Virtual desktops. That is, alternative desktops. You can have one virtual desktop set up with the tools for one project, such as icons, menus, and open software, and another virtual desktop set up with the tools for a different project. Then, you can switch between desktops, depending on which project you're working on. You can have several virtual desktops.

- Configuration tools that enable you to change and control much of the look and feel of the desktop

- Administrative tools for managing your system.

The differences between GNOME and KDE are mainly in the administrative utilities, the tools for configuring the desktop, and the default applications chosen for installation with the desktop. For example, both KDE and GNOME provide a Paint program, but it is not the same Paint program. Another example is that KDE ships with a word processor called KWord, whereas GNOME ships with AbiWord, but both provide access to OpenOffice.

Almost all Linux distributions provide GNOME or KDE. Some distributions allow you to choose which desktop to install while installing Linux. Many install both, allowing you to choose your desktop when you log in. Which you use is mainly a matter of personal preference. You may want to try both before you decide.

Some software packages only run under one desktop, GNOME or KDE. However, some packages designed for one desktop also run under the other desktop. And some packages are shipped with both desktops, such as the GIMP. When GNOME and KDE are both installed, all packages shipped with both are installed, forming a single pool of software packages. The desktop provides access to any package that can run with it. For instance, if a GNOME package can also run under KDE, the KDE start menu will show the package, even though the package actually shipped with GNOME.

Other GUIs

Many other GUIs in addition to KDE and GNOME are available. Linux epitomizes flexibility and configurability and gives choices whenever possible. Almost all Linux distributions include GNOME and KDE, but many include other GUIs as well. For instance, Mandrake includes a desktop called IceWM that is smaller and faster than GNOME or KDE.

Most users install desktops other than the big two for special purposes only, such as when installing Linux on a machine with limited resources—a situation calling for a GUI that uses less disk space and/or memory. Of course, some people choose to use a different GUI just because they like it. Your Linux GUI can be quite elaborate and individualistic if you want to spend the time customizing it. In the future, when you are a Linux guru, you may want to look into other GUIs.

GNOME

GNOME (GNU Network Object Model Environment), a popular desktop environment, is shown in Figure 5-1.

FIGURE 5-1   GNOME desktop in Mandrake 9.1.

Notice the blank work surface, icons on the desktop, and a panel at the bottom. The first icon at the left of the panel shows a foot (the GNOME logo). This icon opens a menu of applications (a menu that looks very similar to the start menu on Windows). Because the desktop is provided by Mandrake in their distribution, the icons and panel contents are customized by Mandrake, as seen by the Mandrake Welcome icon (big yellow star) on the desktop.

The GNOME project is supported by Red Hat. The default desktop for Red Hat and Fedora is a customized version of GNOME called Bluecurve GNOME. Bluecurve GNOME has a red hat logo for the start menu icon, rather than the GNOME foot logo. And, of course, Bluecurve GNOME doesn't have a Mandrake Welcome icon.

The KDE desktop shown on the next page (Figure 5-2) is very similar. It too has a work-space, icons, and a panel. The difference is mainly in the icons on the desktop and the organization of the panel. Using the desktop is discussed in Chapter 6.

KDE

KDE (K Desktop Environment), the most popular desktop environment, is shown in Figure 5-2.

FIGURE 5-2 KDE desktop in Mandrake 9.1

Notice the blank work surface, icons on the desktop, and a panel at the bottom. The first icon at the left of the panel shows a big K, the KDE logo. This icon opens a menu of applications (the menu looks very similar to the start menu on Windows). Because the desktop is provided by Mandrake in its distribution, the icons and panel contents are customized by Mandrake, as seen by the Mandrake Welcome icon on the desktop.

Although GNOME is the default desktop for Red Hat and Fedora, a customized version of KDE, called Bluecurve KDE, is also provided with their distributions. Bluecurve KDE has a red hat logo for the start menu icon, rather than the K logo. And, of course, Bluecurve KDE doesn't have a Mandrake Welcome icon.

The GNOME desktop shown on the previous page (Figure 5-1) is very similar. It too has a workspace, icons, and a panel. The difference is mainly in the icons on the desktop and the organization of the panel. Using the desktop is discussed in Chapter 6.

The Command-Line Interface on Linux

The command-line interface (CLI) is a text environment in which you type commands for Linux to execute and Linux displays text messages in response. In the CLI, you use the keyboard, rather than the mouse, to send instructions to Linux. When you are working with the CLI, you are interacting with a program called a shell. The shell accepts your commands, processes them, and passes them into the kernel, the part of Linux where the basic computer work takes place. Linux offers a choice of several shells, but this book provides information only for Bash, the most popular Linux shell.

Linux can boot directly into a command-line environment. You see a screen that is mainly empty, waiting for your input. Rather than seeing a login window, you type your account ID and password on a blank command line. In this type of setup, you use the CLI exclusively. Users with this type of setup don't generally use the desktop at all.

Often, users want to use the GUI most of the time, but use the CLI for certain tasks. These users set up Linux to boot in to the desktop. Whenever they want to use the CLI, they can open a CLI window.

The desktop is easier to use than the CLI. On the desktop, you select tasks from menus. In the CLI, you need to type the command. It's up to you to know which command, how it's spelled, what arguments and options produce the desired effects, and how to interpret the text output. However, the CLI has some advantages that make its use attractive in some situations:

- **Faster execution:** The GUI brings with it a certain amount of overhead, such as drawing graphics on the screen, which takes time. When you type commands directly into the CLI, commands execute faster without the GUI overhead.

- **Shorter command entry:** In some cases, typing a command takes less time than navigating through menus. Often, file management and other system tasks can be entered more quickly at the command line than by using menus. In addition, the CLI allows you to chain commands together, resulting in a single output, in a way not possible in menus.

- **Fewer resources:** The GUI requires disk space, memory, and other computer resources. When running Linux on an underpowered computer, running without the GUI might be necessary.

- **More functionality:** Some commands and options to commands are not available on a menu. They can only be executed from the command line.

Using the command-line interface is discussed in detail in Chapter 7.

Choosing the Interface

The installation procedure for most Linux distributions provides the opportunity for you to select the software you want to install. In general, there's a default set of applications, or perhaps different sets of applications, that you can choose from. In addition, you probably have the opportunity to include or remove any applications from the set being installed.

During Fedora installation, for example, a screen is displayed that lists the default set of packages, including GNOME, to be installed. The screen gives you the choice to install the default set or to customize the software packages to be installed. If you select customize, a screen allows you to check and uncheck software packages. GNOME is checked by default. You can check KDE in addition to GNOME or instead of GNOME. You can even uncheck both.

If you installed GNOME or KDE, your system boots to the installed desktop. If you installed both, most distributions provide the opportunity to select which desktop you want when you log in. If neither desktop was installed, your computer will enter the command-line environment when you log in.

If your computer boots into a GUI and you want to boot into the CLI, or vice versa, you can change the default boot interface by editing a file called inittab. Linux reads this file for instructions when it starts up. You need to locate this file, probably in /etc. Chapter 9 tells you how to find files. To change your interface, you need to edit the following line in inittab (Chapter 18 discusses editing text files):

```
id:n:initdefault:
```

n is a number that causes Linux to boot in to the GUI or the CLI; 5 signals the GUI and 3 signals the CLI. Change n to the number for your preferred default interface.

Summary

Linux is an operating system—software that runs your computer. When you work on your computer, the interface provides the communication between you and the Linux kernel, the part of Linux where the low-level work takes place. The kernel communicates directly with the hardware to save files on the hard disk, send data streams to the printer, send information out onto the network, and other basic tasks. Your instructions are accepted by the interface, processed, and passed into the kernel. Linux provides two types of interface that you can use to send instructions: a graphical user interface (GUI) and a command-line interface (CLI).

The GUI provides graphical images that can be selected with the mouse. One popular GUI is a desktop, made popular by Windows. A desktop is designed to represent the top of your office desk—a work space with tools on it. Linux offers two popular desktop environments: GNOME (GNU Network Object Model Environment) and KDE (K Desktop Environment). Because both emulate a desktop, they are similar in many ways. Both resemble Windows and provide the same features, such as windows, icons, menus, etc. The differences between GNOME and KDE are mainly in the administrative utilities, the tools for configuring the desktop, and the default applications chosen for installation with the desktop. Which desktop you use is mainly a matter of personal preference. You may want to try both GNOME and KDE before you decide. Using a desktop is discussed in Chapter 6.

The CLI is a text environment. You type commands for Linux to execute and Linux displays text messages in response. When you are working with the CLI, you are interacting with a program called a shell. The shell accepts your commands, processes them, and passes them into the kernel. Using the command-line interface is discussed in detail in Chapter 7.

Linux can open a desktop at startup or boot directly in to a command-line environment. Most users prefer Linux to start with a desktop. When the user wants to use the command line, he or she opens a CLI window.

## CHAPTER 6

Using Your Desktop

L inux provides two basic types of interface for you to use when working with your computer: GUI (graphical user interface) and CLI (command-line interface). An overview of the interface types is provided in Chapter 5. In this chapter, the most common type of interface, a GUI called a desktop, is discussed in detail. The CLI is discussed in detail in Chapter 7.

Linux can start without a desktop, but most users prefer to have Linux start with a desktop. The installation instructions provided in Chapter 4 result in a desktop opening at startup. A desktop interface functions as the top of your desk, supplying an empty working surface and a set of tools.

Different distributions provide different desktops, but most provide KDE (K Desktop Environment) and/or GNOME (Gnu Network Object Model Environment)—the Big Two of Linux desktops. The default desktop differs by distribution. For instance, Fedora defaults to GNOME, and Mandrake/SuSE defaults to KDE. However, you can change the default once you decide which desktop you prefer.

KDE and GNOME are open source software, each developed in a project of its own. New versions are released independently of Linux releases or the release of any specific Linux distribution. As a result, different distributions include different KDE and/or GNOME versions. In addition, KDE and GNOME are very configurable. Almost everything about them can be changed. Consequently, KDE and GNOME don't look exactly the same in different distributions or versions of distributions.

When using this book, remember that your KDE or GNOME may not look exactly like the book. Most of the figures in the book are Fedora Core 2 (KDE 3.2/GNOME 2.6) or Mandrake 10 (KDE 3.2/GNOME 2.4). Your version may be older or newer. Because your KDE and GNOME may not always look and behave exactly as shown in the book, it's best to consider the instructions in this chapter as suggestions, rather than an exact map. It provides clues to the most likely places to find configuration tools, but not necessarily a detailed route.

This chapter describes the contents of your desktop and how to use them. Then, when you are comfortable with the default appearance and behavior of your Linux, you find out how to change everything.

Logging In

To access your desktop, you must log in using a Linux account. When you power on your computer, the process goes as follows:

1. The computer boots up.

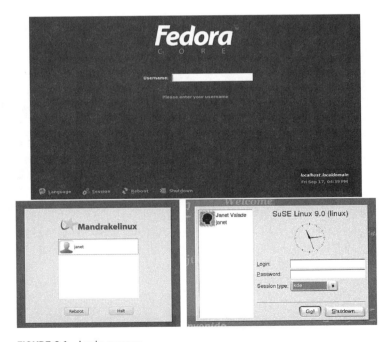

2. The computer prompts you to log in.

3. You log in to an account, typing your password.

4. The desktop displays.

After the computer boots (Step 1), you see a login screen. The login screens for Fedora Core, Mandrake, and SuSE are shown in Figure 6-1.

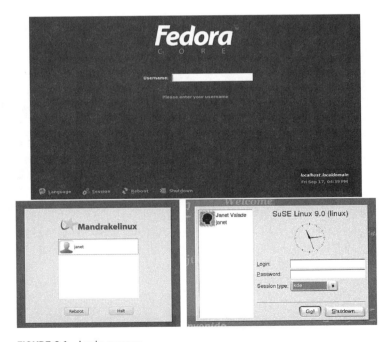

FIGURE 6-1 Login screens.

Notice that Mandrake and SuSE give you a choice of accounts. In this case, only one account (janet) is available. If more accounts were installed, they would also be on the login screen. Accounts are discussed in Chapter 8.

Select an account by clicking it. In SuSE, the account name appears in the Login field. Type the password in the Password field and click Go! to log in. In Mandrake, a second screen appears, as shown in Figure 6-2.

FIGURE 6-2 Second login screen for Mandrake.

Type in the password and click Login to log in.

Fedora requires you to type the name of the account. When you type the account name and press <Enter>, the username field changes to the password field, asking for the password. Type the password and press <Enter> to login in.

Many Linux distributions allow you to select which desktop to use when you log in. Of course, you can only select among the desktops that you installed. KDE and GNOME are discussed in this book, but other desktops are available and were possibly installed by default 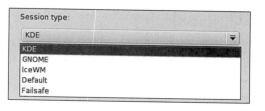 during installation. For instance, notice in Figure 6-2 that the Mandrake login screen has a button to select Session type. If you click the button, a drop-down list appears, shown on the right. The default desktop is KDE, but you can change it. GNOME is shown in the list because it was specifically added during the installation, as shown in Chapter 4. Failsafe starts Linux without a desktop, just with the CLI, discussed in Chapter 7.

Notice that all three login screens in Figure 6-1 provide a button (Shutdown, Halt) that allows you to stop the login if you want.

Your First Login

The first time you log in to your system after installation, Linux may require some post-installation setup. For example, Fedora creates a user account when you first log in to your new system. Mandrake and SuSE create user accounts during installation, but Fedora only creates a root account, waiting until now to create a user account.

The first time you log in to Mandrake, it runs a procedure called Mandrakefirsttime Wizard. The first screen introduces the wizard, stating that it will help you:

- Configure the basic setup of your desktop in a very few steps.
- Register your product in order to easily open a Mandrakeclub account and to benefit rapidly from all its products and services.

The next screen in the wizard displays a Choose Desktop button. When you click it, a list of possible desktops drops down. KDE is the default, but you can select another. After you select a desktop, a screen allows you to select one of several themes. A theme is a unified set of colors and images that integrate all parts of the desktop into a single look and feel, including the window borders, fonts, icons, etc. A demo screen shows the appearance of the default Galaxy 2 theme. If you check a different theme, the appearance of the demo screen will change, showing the new theme. When the demo shows the appearance you like best, click Next.

The Mandrakefirsttime Wizard also helps you set up and configure a Mandrakeclub account. Mandrakeclub offers software downloads, forums, special discounts, and other benefits for a small monthly fee. The first month is free so you can try it out.

When the wizard finishes, the desktop displays with a welcoming message. Click Close to close the welcome message without closing the desktop. Uncheck "Open this window on startup" at the bottom of the welcome message when you no longer want to see this screen every time your computer starts.

During your first login, SuSE also displays a welcome message with links to the SuSE home page.

Anatomy of a Desktop

Most desktops have common basic components, as shown in Figure 6-3. This desktop should look fairly familiar to Windows users.

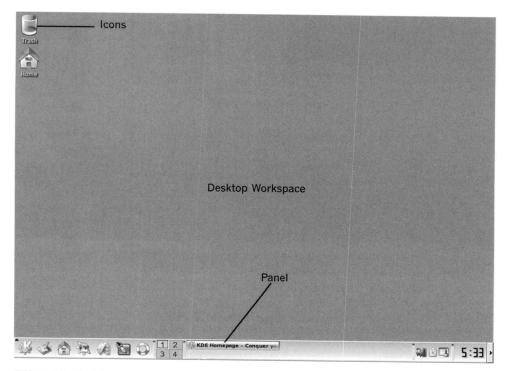

FIGURE 6-3 Desktop.

The desktop workspace contains icons, in this case two icons, that perform actions when clicked, just as Windows desktop icons do. You can customize the desktop—adding, removing, and rearranging icons. Handling icons is discussed later in this chapter.

The panel (also sometimes called kicker) is the bar across the bottom of your desktop. The panel can be moved to the left, right, or top. You can have more than one panel.

In Figure 6-3, the left side of the panel contains several icons. You can customize these icons—adding and removing them from the panel. To the right of the icons is a four-button pager—buttons that you can click to open alternative virtual desktops, explained later in this chapter. To the right of the pager is a section, called the taskbar, where application buttons appear when an application is running. To the right of the taskbar are icons for useful system tools. A clock displays on the far right of the panel. You can reorganize the panel—adding, removing, moving the objects on it.

KDE and GNOME Desktops

The two most popular desktops, KDE and GNOME, are discussed in this book. KDE and GNOME look very similar. Figure 6-4 shows the KDE and GNOME desktops provided by Fedora.

FIGURE 6-4   KDE and GNOME desktops for Fedora.

KDE and GNOME for Fedora are very similar. Both have "trash" and "home" icons, but GNOME has two additional icons. The panel has the same icons. One reason both look so similar is that both desktops are very customizable. Thus, the Fedora desktops are both configured in a manner deemed useful by the Fedora developers. Desktops configured for different distributions can be customized differently, but still are very similar. KDE desktops distributed with Fedora and Mandrake are shown in Figure 6-5.

FIGURE 6-5   KDE desktops for Fedora and Mandrake.

The two KDE desktops have different icons, with Mandrake providing several more. The panel is different. For instance, the leftmost panel icon for Fedora is a red fedora. Yet, the basic anatomy is the same.

The Panel

The panels for the desktops are shown in Figure 6-6. The KDE panel is the top panel; the GNOME panel is the bottom panel.

FIGURE 6-6 KDE and GNOME panels for Fedora.

The panels have the same five components, from left to right:

- **Icon bar:** The section on the left that contains application icons. It's also called the application launcher. Clicking an icon starts an application. Moving the mouse pointer over an icon displays the application name in a tool tip.

- **Pager:** The four-paned window that switches between virtual desktops.

- **Taskbar:** A section that contains items for any open applications. The KDE panel shows one application open—X Settings. The GNOME panel shows two open applications—OpenOffice and the Mozilla browser. Clicking an application on the panel opens it if it is minimized and brings it to the top of the open applications on the desktop.

- **System tray:** The section on the right that contains icons for useful system applications that you access directly on the panel, rather than open in a window. The clock is farthest on the right. If you move the mouse pointer over the clock, the date displays in a tool tip. If you click the clock, a one-month calendar displays. You can move forward or backward through the calendar in monthly or yearly jumps. If you right-click on the clock, a menu displays that allows you to perform tasks, such as adjusting the date and time and changing the way the time displays. This type of application is called an applet.

- **Panel-hiding button:** The little arrow on the end(s) of the panel. Clicking the arrow causes the panel to slide off the desktop, leaving only a little arrow that you can click to bring the panel back onto the desktop.

Notice that the leftmost icon is the red fedora that opens the main menu, discussed earlier in this chapter.

Working on the Desktop

The desktop is a workspace with some tools sitting on it. When you want to perform a task, you start an application that opens in a window on the desktop. You can open many windows at once, each performing different tasks, using the same or different applications.

Your desktop offers many features to assist you. Many of the following features will be familiar to Windows users:

- **Icons:** You can click icons on the desktop or panel to start applications or go to locations. In most distributions, the desktop icons activate with a double-click and panel icons activate with a single-click. However, this is configurable and some distributions start desktop icons with a single-click. You can add, remove, or reorganize icons on the desktop or panel, discussed later in this chapter.

- **Menus:** Linux provides a main menu and many component-specific menus. You can add, remove, or edit menu items. When you install a new application, a menu item is usually added to the main menu.

  - **Main menu:** Contains available applications and utilities as main menu items or items on submenus, similar to the start menu on Windows. The main menu is opened by clicking an icon on the panel, usually the leftmost icon. The main menu icon is a large K for KDE and a foot for GNOME. However, distributions often use their own logo as the main menu icon, such as the red hat logo on the Fedora panel and the green dragon head on the SuSE panel.

  - **Component-specific menu:** Menus specific to a component open when you right-click the component. If you right-click on the desktop background, you see one menu; if you right-click on the panel, you see a different menu. If you right-click an icon, you see another menu still. And if you right-click inside an open window, you see still another menu. The menus contain selections that are specific to the object.

    In many menus, one letter is underlined in the menu selection. You can type the letter, rather than highlight and click, to select the menu item. Some menus show shortcuts for their actions, such as <Alt+F9>. This means you can press <Alt+F9> without opening the menu and the action is performed.

- **Tool tips:** Information that displays when you move the mouse pointer over an object and hold it a for a short time, called hovering. You can turn tool tips on and off.

- **Windows manipulation:** Windows can be moved, minimized, maximized, resized, moved out of the way, or closed.

  - **Move:** Click the top bar of the window and drag the window around the desktop using the mouse. Or click the button in the upper-left corner and select move.

  - **Resize:** Drag the sides or the corners of the window using the mouse. To maximize the window to full-screen size, click the middle button in the upper-right corner.

  - **Move out of the way:** Double-click the title bar of the window. The window rolls up like a window shade. To unroll it, double-click the rolled up window. Click the - button in the upper-right corner to minimize the window. If your panel has the Show desktop icon, click it to minimize all open windows at once. If the Show desktop icon isn't present, you can add it to the panel, as described later in this chapter.

  - **Close:** Click the x button in the upper-right corner or select close from the upper-left drop-down menu.

- **Look and feel:** The look and feel of the Linux desktop is very configurable. For instance, the desktop background displays a default appearance provided by the distribution. The background for Fedora, Mandrake, and SuSE is blue. Fedora and Mandrake include logos on the background. However, you can change this background to any color, pattern, design, or picture that you want.

  You can change the appearance of all elements of the desktop, such as the window borders and title bar and the panel. Linux users often configure their desktop with a theme—a unified set of colors and images, even sounds, that integrate all parts of the desktop into a single look and feel. Some themes are included with your distribution that you can use. Others are available for download from the Web. Some people develop their own theme.

  Some behavior of desktop components can also be changed. For instance, icons can be configured to activate with a single-click or a double-click. Windows can become active when clicked or when the mouse pointer passes over them. Tool tips—information that displays when the mouse pointer passes over a component—can be turned on or off.

Remember that almost everything is configurable. This section describes the usual behavior of desktop components. However, most appearance and behavior is configurable. Any distribution might decide to configure their desktop differently. A previous user of your system might have changed some features. If the behavior of your system is different from the description in this chapter, you can change it to your preferred appearance or behavior. Configuring Linux is described later in this chapter.

Configuring the Desktop

You can change many settings for both the desktop and the panel. In fact, many people go to great lengths to express their creativity with their desktops. Some creative desktops can be seen at www.lynucs.org/index.php?p=featured.

Almost everything about your desktop is configurable. Some changes are made in desktop and panel menus and some on the main menu. In some cases, a setting can be changed by more than one method. In general, KDE and GNOME provide different, although often similar, procedures for configuring your desktop.

Specific instructions for the most frequently changed settings are provided in this chapter. However, space is not available to provide instructions for all possible desktop configurations. If you want to make a change to your desktop and don't find instructions in this book, it doesn't mean the change isn't possible. It probably is.

In KDE, many changes can be made in the KDE Control Center, accessed from the main menu, either directly or through the Preferences submenu. When you start the KDE Control Center, you see a screen similar to the screen shown in Figure 6-7.

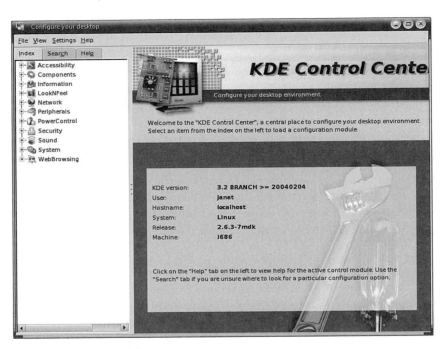

FIGURE 6-7 KDE Control Center.

Most of the configuration for your desktop appearance and behavior is found by clicking Look and Feel in the left pane above.

GNOME doesn't have a single application like the KDE Control Center. Instead, it provides separate menu items. The menu items are usually in a single menu category, such as Preferences in Fedora or System Configuration in Mandrake. The GNOME configuration menu items for SuSE are shown in Figure 6-8.

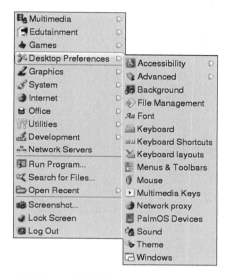

FIGURE 6-8   GNOME desktop preferences.

In this figure, the Desktop Preferences main menu item displays the submenu of configuration tools.

The remainder of this chapter describes how to change some settings for your desktop. The following settings are discussed:

- **Background:** Desktop background and background of the panel. Change the color or use a picture as a background.

- **Icons:** Add or remove desktop icons and panel icons.

- **Fonts:** Change the font style and size.

- **Screen saver:** Set the screen saver and the time delay.

- **Panel:** Change length, width, and location. Reorganize objects on the panel.

Both KDE and GNOME desktop configuration are covered.

Changing the KDE Background

You can change the background of the desktop and the panel. The backgrounds can be a solid color, a pattern, or a picture stored in a file. Files are discussed in Chapter 9, graphics in Chapter 13.

To change the desktop background, right-click the desktop and select Configure desktop. A screen displays with choices in the left panel. Click Background. Figure 6-9 shows the configuration window that displays.

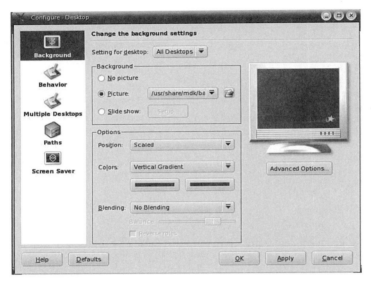

FIGURE 6-9 Background configuration window.

When you make changes, the picture of a screen shows what your selection will look like. The Apply button in the lower-right corner changes your desktop to its new appearance before you leave the configuration window, so you can try different looks.

To use a picture for your background, check Picture, as shown in Figure 6-9. Use the drop-down list to select from a list of available pictures. Or use the Browse button to the right of the drop-down list to navigate to a picture file.

To use colors, rather than a picture, for the background, check No picture. If you click the Colors button, a drop-down list of color options appears, such as horizontal gradient. If you click the Pattern option, a Setup button appears that, when clicked, displays a screen with a list of patterns you can select. The screen includes an Add button that lets you enter a path to a graphics file containing a pattern.

You can select one or two colors for your background. If you select two different colors, they serve as the endpoints for a vertical or horizontal background gradient.

To select a color, double-click a color button. In the color selection screen, shown on the right, you can select a color by clicking it or by setting the values specifically, such as setting the numbers for R, G, and B. The color you have selected displays in the lower box, so you can see when you get a color you like.

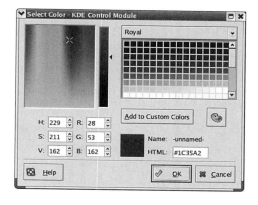

To change the panel background, right-click the panel (an empty space on the panel, not a button) and select Configure Panel. Click Appearance in the list of icons in the left pane. If the Appearance icon doesn't appear in the list, an Appearance tab should be available if you click Layout. A screen similar to Figure 6-10 displays.

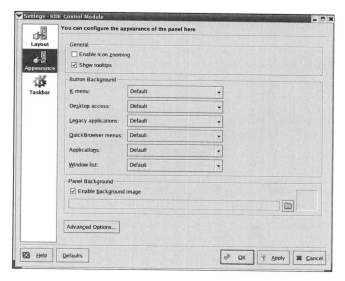

FIGURE 6-10 Panel background window.

You can configure the background of each component separately, such as the main menu (K menu) or the application icons, by choosing a background from the drop-down list for the specific item.

You can add a background to the entire panel by checking "Enable background image." You can type a path to the picture or use the folder button on the right to browse to the picture file. Any graphic file can provide the background for your panel. Files are discussed in Chapter 9. Graphics are discussed in Chapter 13.

Changing the GNOME Background

You can change the background of the desktop and the panel. The backgrounds can be a color or a picture stored in a file. Chapter 9 discusses files, Chapter 13 graphics.

The desktop background can be set to any solid color or color style, such as a vertical or horizontal gradient, or to use a picture as a background. To change the background, right-click the desktop and select Change desktop background. The screen in Figure 6-11 displays, showing two background choices—no wallpaper and a picture.

FIGURE 6-11 Background configuration screen.

In the figure, a picture in a file named default.png is selected for the desktop background. To use a different picture for your background, you need to add it to the selections shown on the screen. Some pictures are usually available for you to choose or you can add your own pictures.

To add a picture, click Add wallpaper, which displays a file selection window similar to file selection screens in Windows (Windows Explorer)—directories highlighted in the left pane and files listed in the right pane. The files listed contain any graphic files made available in the Linux distribution. You can select one of these files or use your own file. To use a file of your own, add it to the directory shown or navigate to a file in a different location. Saving and finding files are discussed in Chapter 9.

When the file you want is selected, click OK to return to the main background configuration screen. The picture you selected is added to the list of background choices in the window.

For a color background, highlight No Wallpaper in the window, which shows the current color—blue. Use the drop-down list and the color button in the Desktop Colors section to set the color background.

The drop-down list offers three background styles: solid color, vertical gradient, and horizontal gradient. Clicking the color button displays the color selection screen in Figure 6-12.

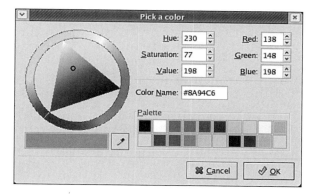

FIGURE 6-12   Color selection screen for GNOME.

To select a color, click the color you want. Or type in the color values, such as a number for Red, Green, and Blue. The lower-left color bar previews the color currently selected. When you are satisfied with the color selected, click OK to return to the main background configuration window.

When you are satisfied with your background selections, click Close in the main configuration window.

To change the panel background, click the panel and select Properties. In the Properties window, click the Background tab to display the three background choices.

- **None:** The panel uses the same color as other elements of the desktop. This is the default.

- **Solid Color:** Sets the panel to a solid color. Click the color bar to select a color. Use the slider to make the panel more or less transparent.

- **Background Image:** Uses a picture for the background of the panel. The text box requires the path to the file that contains the picture to use for the background. Type the path or use the Browse button to navigate to the file.

When you are satisfied with the settings, click Close.

Setting Fonts

You can change the size and style of the fonts used on your desktop. In the main menu, select KDE Control Center. In the index, click LookNFeel->Font. The window in Figure 6-13 opens. Click Choose to select the font size and style.

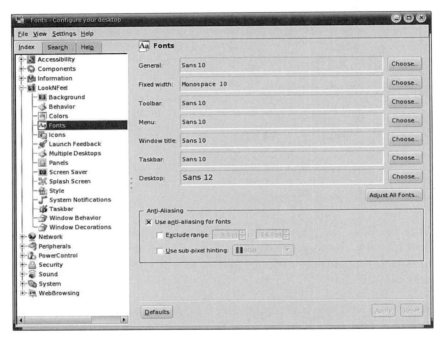

FIGURE 6-13 Font selection screen.

In GNOME, click the main menu icon. Select Preferences->Font. The screen on the right opens, showing the current fonts. To change one of the fonts, such as the Desktop font, click the name of the font. A screen will display that allows you to select the font, size, and style, such as bold or italic. When you select font settings in this screen, a preview of the font is shown, so you can see what your selections look like before pressing OK to save them.

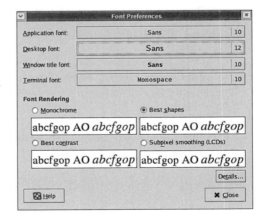

When you are satisfied with your settings, click Close.

Setting the Screen Saver

Linux includes a screen saver—a screen that replaces your work screen when you don't type anything or move the mouse for a period of time. Pressing a key or moving a mouse returns your work screen. You can set the look of the screen saver and the length of no-activity time that must occur before the screen saver starts running.

On KDE, right-click the desktop and select Configure Desktop, which displays a screen with a list of icons in the left panel. Click Screen Saver, which displays the screen shown in Figure 6-14.

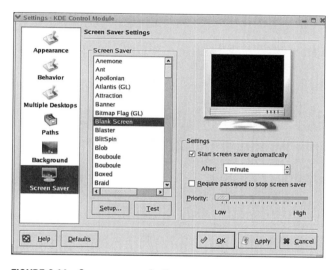

FIGURE 6-14 Screen saver selection.

Select a screen saver from the list, which previews on the image of a computer terminal. Some screen savers can be changed, such as changing the color of "Blank Screen." To configure the specific screen saver you have selected, click Setup. Click Test to test the screen saver before clicking OK to save the settings.

Using a screen saver is optional. On the right, the Settings panel allows you to check or uncheck "Start screen saver automatically." You can change the amount of time before the screen saver starts running.

For GNOME, click the main menu icon. Select Preferences. Select Screen Saver from the submenu. A similar screen displays that allows you to select a screen saver or to select several screen savers that run consecutively. You can select the amount of time before the screen saver starts and, if more than one is chosen, select the amount of time each is run before the next is started.

Organizing the Desktop

Your desktop can be organized to suit your individual work style. Quick access to applications is provided through icons on the desktop. Application icons on the panel provide access when the desktop is covered by open windows. Many useful utilities can reside on the panel, such as the clock and an icon that minimizes all windows at once. Icons for locations, such as Home, or files, such as todo, are also handy.

You can drag applications and locations onto the desktop or panel. Find the application and highlight it on the menu. Or open the directory. Then use the mouse to drag the application or directory to the desired location.

In addition, a menu of items specifically for use on the panel is available. Right-click directly on the panel and select Add or Add to panel to see items such as Accessories or Amusements. Highlight the desired item on the menu or submenu and drag it onto the panel.

You can drag the icons on your desktop wherever you want them. You can also arrange all icons at once from the desktop menu. In GNOME, right-click the desktop and select Clean Up by Name to arrange the icons in alphabetic order starting from the upper-left corner. From the KDE desktop menu, select Icons to line them up vertically or horizontally or to sort them by name, size, or type.

To move objects on the panel, right-click the icon and select Move. Drag the object to its new panel location using the mouse. On the KDE panel, some objects, such as the taskbar and the pager, are moved using menus specific to the object.

FIGURE 6-15   Section of KDE panel.

If you click the small arrow to the left of the taskbar, a menu specific to the entire taskbar opens with items that you can select, including Move Taskbar.

In Figure 6-15, a side pointing arrow is located on the end of the panel—the Panel-hiding button. Clicking the button hides the menu; clicking again brings it back. This button is not always included on the panel. To add the Panel-hiding button in KDE, right-click the panel and select Configure Panel. Click the Hiding tab. Check "Show left panel-hiding button" and/or "Show right panel-hiding button." To add the buttons in GNOME, right-click the panel and select Properties. Check "Show hide buttons" and "Arrows on hide buttons."

Changing the Panel Location and Size

The size and location of the panel can be changed. In KDE, right-click the panel and select Configure Panel, which displays the screen in Figure 6-16.

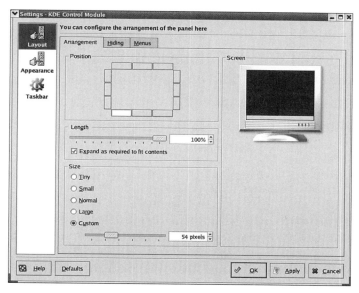

FIGURE 6-16 Panel configuration screen for KDE.

The computer terminal in the Screen section previews the current settings. Any setting change is shown immediately in the preview screen. The panel in this figure is shown across the entire bottom. In the Position section, the lower-left square is selected. Click a different square to move the panel. Move the slider to change the length of the panel. The current setting for Size is a Custom size of 54 pixels. The size refers to the height or width of the panel. Use the slider to change the custom size or check a different size (e.g., Small or Tiny). Click OK to keep the new settings.

For GNOME, right-click the panel and select Properties. The screen shown on the right displays. The Orientation button allows you to select Top, Bottom, Left, or Right. You can select or type the number of pixels for the size.

Click Close when you are satisfied with the settings.

Configuring Multiple Virtual Desktops

Not only does Linux allow you to configure almost everything about your desktop, it also allows you to have multiple desktops, each configured differently. You can have one desktop that you use for your financial work and another configured for use on your art projects. The desktops can have different applications available, with any other configuration changes that are appropriate for the desktop functionality.

Multiple desktops are also called virtual desktops. The section of the panel related to virtual desktops is shown in Figure 6-17.

FIGURE 6-17   Section of KDE panel.

The object with four squares, called the pager, represents the virtual windows available. Square 1, representing desktop 1, is white, meaning that desktop 1 is currently in use. Notice that desktop 2 and desktop 4 show open applications, whereas desktop 1 and desktop 3 do not. The taskbar shows two open applications, which represents the applications on all windows. Click a numbered square to go to a specific desktop. Click an application button on the taskbar to go to the application wherever it's open. If it's open on a different desktop, the desktop opens.

Applications can be moved easily from one desktop to another. When you click the upper-left corner arrow in an open application, you see a menu that includes the items shown in Figure 6-18.

FIGURE 6-18   Section of KDE panel.

Select the appropriate item to move the application from desktop 1 to another desktop or all desktops.

Although the pager shows four desktops, you can actually have more if you need them. To set up more desktops, right-click on the desktop and select Configure Desktop. Select Multiple Windows from the left pane. The window in Figure 6-19 opens.

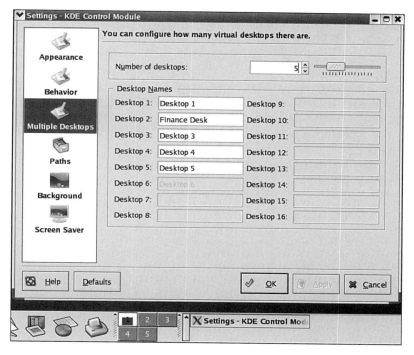

FIGURE 6-19 Section of KDE panel.

In this figure, five desktops are available. Notice that the pager shows five desktop squares—window 1 active with an application open.

Use the Number of desktops field at the top of the screen to change the number of desktops available. You can type a name for a desktop if you want, to help organize your desktops. The name will display in a tool tip when you move the mouse pointer over the pager square.

Logging Out

Powering off your machine without logging out and shutting down properly can cause problems. Linux may be in the middle of some background activities necessary to run your computer and may not be able to finish its tasks.

To log out, select Log Out on the main menu or on the desktop menu displayed when you right-click on the desktop. In most cases, a window with at least three choices displays, similar to the SuSE window shown in Figure 6-20.

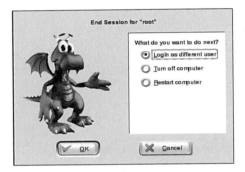

FIGURE 6-20 SuSE logout window.

One choice is usually Log Out, or in this case Login as different user. Selecting this choice logs out this session, but displays a login screen so you can log in as a different user (or with a different desktop). Linux is not shut down. A second choice restarts (reboots) the computer. Linux is shut down but restarts itself without your assistance.

A third choice is Shut Down, or Turn off computer. This closes down everything. The computer may power itself off or display a message that it is ready to be powered off.

Power down is not necessary. Linux can run indefinitely without problems. It saves you the trouble of the shutdown/boot process between uses. Saves time and some say it is better for the computer. If you are reluctant to leave the computer on because it's possible for someone else to access it, you can lock the screen so that no one can use it without the password. To lock the screen, select Lock screen from the main menu. If anyone tries to use the computer with a locked screen, a password prompt displays and the computer can't be used until the password is entered.

Summary

Linux provides two basic types of interface for you to use when working with your computer: GUI (graphical user interface) and CLI (command-line interface). This chapter describes how to use the GUI. The following information is available in this chapter:

- How to log in
- What is on your desktop
- The similarities and differences between the two major desktops—KDE and GNOME
- The organization and components of the panel at the bottom of your desktop
- How to use your desktop features
- How to configure your desktop
- How to log out

This chapter describes how to work on your desktop. The next chapter (Chapter 7) explains how to work at the CLI.

Using the Command Line

The command line is a blank line where you type a command. No icons, no menus, no buttons. Well, not totally blank. A few characters, called the system prompt, display at the beginning of the line, followed by a blinking square, called a cursor. If you haven't worked in DOS or at the command prompt in Windows, a command-line interface (CLI) may be new territory for you.

The blinking cursor signals that the shell is waiting for you to type a command. The shell, a computer program, provides the interface between you and the part of Linux that executes the command—the kernel. The shell provides the command line where you enter the command, accepts your input, interprets it, processes it, and executes the resulting command. Several shells are available for Linux. The default shell is called Bash. Bash stands for Bourne again shell, because Bash is a descendent of an earlier shell called the Bourne shell. Only the Bash shell is discussed in this book. You are unlikely to need to use a different shell unless you become a system administrator or an advanced programmer.

The shell communicates with the kernel, the core of Linux. All the computer magic occurs in the kernel. It's the kernel that transfers data to and from the peripherals (printer, screen, mouse), writes files to the hard disk, sends data across the network, and all the other low-level tasks that make a computer work. It is not the function of this book to explain the workings of the kernel. Perhaps some of you will delve into this magic after you learn the basics, but most of you will not.

Many Linux users can perform all their required tasks from the desktop, without using the command line. However, working directly in the shell is almost always faster. In addition, the command line provides more functionality. Some tasks that are difficult or impossible to accomplish from the desktop become simple when working in the shell. Even for parallel functions, commands often have many more options, providing more functionality than the desktop feature that performs a similar function. System administrators and programmers need to work in the shell frequently. After you become familiar with the shell, you may find it faster and easier to work in the shell for many of your tasks.

Many of the command descriptions in this chapter refer to files and directories. If you aren't familiar with these terms, they are explained in detail in Chapter 9.

Entering Commands

To use the command line, you can open a terminal window, also sometimes called the console, in which you can work directly in the shell. This is similar to opening a DOS or Command Prompt Window in Windows.

Some distributions provide an icon on the panel that you can click to open a terminal window. The icon includes a monitor screen. Others don't provide a terminal screen icon. Usually the desktop menu (right-click on the desktop) includes an item to open the terminal window. You can always find it on the main menu, either as a main menu item or on a submenu under system.

The terminal window displays the system prompt, followed by the cursor, showing that it's waiting for you to enter a command.

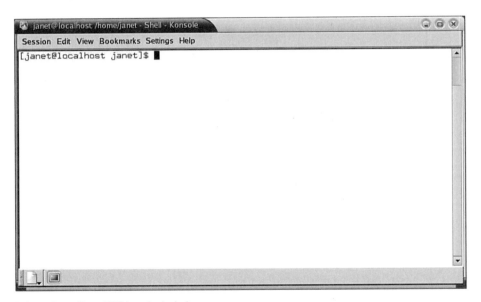

FIGURE 7-1   Open KDE terminal window.

When you type a command and press <Enter>, the command executes.

The system prompt is configurable. Different distributions of Linux set different system prompts during installation. It might be as simple as $, or contain added useful information. The system prompt in Figure 7-1 provides extra information—the current account (janet@localhost) and directory (janet). This prompt is set during the installation of Fedora, Mandrake, and other distributions.

Entering a Single Command

Occasionally, you may want to enter a single command, such as a command to start a program or application. A Run option is provided on the start menu, similar to the Run option in Windows, that is a shortcut for entering a single command. When you select the Run option from the menu (Shortcut: <Alt+F2>) a window opens where you can enter a command.

The dialog box for KDE, shown on the left, provides a text box where you can enter the command and a Run button that executes the command.

The Run dialog box in Gnome, shown on the right, provides a list of available applications, allowing you to select one instead of typing the name of the application, and a button that allows you to browse for a file to be run by the program or an application that you start. You can, of course, type in a command if you want.

If you want to execute a command that produces output, you need to check "Run in terminal," an option that opens a window where the output displays. (In KDE, click the Options button to see the "Run in terminal" check box.)

For example, the sort command shown in the KDE dialog box above does not reformat the information in the file. Instead, it outputs the information from the file in sorted order. Thus, to see the information in sorted order, you need to check the "Run in terminal" box, which opens a window where the sorted output displays.

Command-Line Syntax

Type commands on the command line, following the command prompt. When you press <Enter> after typing the command, the command is executed. While the command is executing, no system prompt displays. When the command finishes running, the system prompt displays, indicating that the shell is ready to accept another command.

Tip: While a command is executing, you can stop it by pressing <Ctrl+c>.

A command consists of the `command`, `options`, and `arguments` in the following format:

`commandname options arguments`

where

- *Commandname* is the name of the command.
- *Options* are keywords that affect command execution. Options consist of one character, preceded by a hyphen (-), or a character string, preceded by two hyphens (--). The hyphens tell the shell that the next characters are an option. For most commands, options are optional.
- *Arguments* are information that the command uses during execution. For instance, a command may process a file, so that you need to pass the name of the file as an argument. You can pass as many arguments as the command needs. Not all commands require arguments. Some commands that require arguments can use default values when you don't pass the arguments. If an argument includes spaces or special characters, enclose it with quotes on the command line, so that the shell knows it's one argument, rather than two.

The following command shows a command name, an option, and an argument:

`ls -l /home/janet`

The `ls` command lists the files in a directory. The argument is a path to a directory; the files in the directory specified by the argument (janet) are displayed on the screen. However, `ls` is a command that doesn't require an argument, using a default when you don't pass an argument. If you don't include a directory name, the `ls` command lists the files in the current directory.

The -1 is one of many options you can use with the ls command to determine the information displayed and its format. The -1 option produces output with more information than the standard ls output. The output from the standard command, without the -1, is the following list of files in the directory /home/janet:

```
ls /home/janet
text.txt
text2.txt
```

while the output from the ls command with the -1 is longer, as shown below:

```
ls -1 /home/janet
-rw-r--r--  1  janet  janet  50 Apr 25 11.09  test.txt
-rw-r--r--  1  janet  janet  52 Apr 25 11.15  test2.txt
```

You can enter more than one option as follows:

```
ls -ld /home/janet
```

You can enter more than one command, separated by a semicolon (;), as follows:

```
ls /home/janet; ls /home/kim
```

Tip: You can enter commands that are more than one line long. Type a backslash (\) at the end of the line, before pressing Return, and the second line will be treated as a continuation of the first line.

Creating Shortcuts for Long Commands

You might have a long command that you type often. If so, you can create a short alias for the long command, so that you don't have to type the long command every time you need it. You can type the short alias instead.

For instance, the following command creates the alias listall—an alias for the four ls commands:

```
alias listall='ls /home/janet; ls /home/kim; ls /home/george; \

ls /home/sam'
```

You can now type listall to display the files in all four directories.

Redirecting Input and Output

Often commands need to receive input from the keyboard and/or send output to the screen. Whenever data is moved from one program or device to another, it is transferred in a stream. When a program runs, it is connected automatically to an input and an output stream: `stdin` and `stdout`. By default, `stdin` is connected to the keyboard and `stdout` is connected to the screen. You can redirect `stdin` and `stdout`.

The `ls` command outputs a list of files to `stdout`, which by default is connected to the screen. You can change the output location using the redirect metacharacter—the greater than sign (>), as follows:

`ls > dirlist`

The list of files is redirected to a file called dirlist and does not display on the screen. If dirlist doesn't exist, it's created. If dirlist exists, it's replaced. If you don't want to overwrite the file, you can append the output to the existing file, by using >>, instead of >. Or, you can set `noclobber`, a shell option that stops file overwriting, printing an informative message instead, such as "Can't overwrite existing file," as follows:

`set -o noclobber`

The redirect metacharacter for `stdin` is the lesser than sign (<). For example:

`mail < message`

The `mail` command inputs the text from the file named message, rather than from the keyboard, and sends the message via email.

A third stream called `stderr` is connected to running programs. Error messages use the `stderr` stream, which is connected by default to the screen. When you redirect output using `>`, `stderr` is not redirected; it still displays on the screen. To redirect `stderr`, use a command similar to:

`ls &> dirlist`

Now, both the list of files and any error message are sent to the file dirlist.

Sometimes you want to connect `stdout` on one program directly to `stdin` on another program. Making this type of connection is called piping and is done using the metacharacter `|`. Suppose you want to send a list of all the files in your directory directly to the printer. You can use the following command:

`ls | lpr`

Running Commands in the Background

Some commands take a long time to finish executing. For instance, the following command stores the name of every file on your computer in the file allfiles:

```
ls -lR / > allfiles
```

This command can tie up your command line for a long time until it completes the job. If you don't want to wait for a command to finish, you can execute the job in the background, allowing you to enter other commands while your first command is executing. You can start the command in the background by adding an ampersand (&) to the end of the command, as follows:

```
ls -lR / &
```

A number is assigned to background jobs in consecutive order. The job number displays when the command is submitted and used to monitor the status of the background job.

You can also send a job that is already running to the background, as follows:

```
Ctrl-z
bg
```

The first line suspends the job. The second line starts the job in the background.

You can list the jobs that are running by typing:

```
jobs
1 ls -lR /
```

You can bring any job into the foreground with the command:

```
fg jobnumber
```

For example:

```
fg 1
```

Editing the Command Line

Several command-line features assist you with entering commands. For instance, wildcards are available, the same wildcards that you can use with Windows. The asterisk (*) can be substituted for a string of characters and a question mark (?) can be substituted for a single character. Thus, the following command lists all filenames that include var and end with a single character:

```
ls *var?
xvar1
Study_varA
```

File and directory names are completed for you when you press the Tab key. As soon as you have typed enough of the name so that it refers to only one file, press the Tab and the remainder of the filename is filled in on the command line.

The shell stores a history of the commands you enter. You can see it by typing history, which lists the commands, adding a line number at the start of each line.

You can repeat commands using commands that begin with an exclamation point:

- !! Repeats the last command entered.

- !string Type an exclamation point, followed by one or more letters that begin a command. The last command that begins with the letters is repeated. For instance, if you type !c, the last command that begins with c is repeated.

- !n Type the !, followed by a line number. The command shown on that line number in the history list is repeated. For instance, if you type !6, the command on line six of the history is repeated.

You can also repeat a command using the up-arrow key. Each time you press <up arrow>, the previous command displays. Continue to press <up arrow> until you reach the command you want to repeat.

You can edit the previous command and reenter it using ^old^new. The following command will replace string1 with string2 in the first command that just executed:

```
srot test.txt
^ro^or
```

As shown, you accidentally typed srot, when you meant to type sort. The second line tells the shell to re-enter the command, changing ro to or.

Command-Line Help

Linux provides several commands that give help with the details of its many commands:

- **help:** Gives a list of the shell commands, a subset of Linux commands including `cd`, `alias`, `bg`, `jobs`, and others. Type `help` *commandname* for details.

- **man:** The man (manual) pages document all the programs on Linux. To see the details of any command, type `man` *commandname*. If you don't know the name of the command you want, you can search all the descriptions using the `-k` option. For example, if you type `man -k copy`, a list of all commands that have copy in their description displays.

- **info:** A program that displays online documentation via a hierarchical menu of topics that you can select. In addition, related information is hyperlinked. Info often contains information that is more complete, with more conceptual information, than the man pages. When you type info with no arguments, the top-level menu displays. If you know a topic name, you can type `info` *topicname*.

- **help option:** Many programs have an option that displays information about using the program. It's worth a try to type the program name, followed by either `-h` or `--help`. For instance, typing `info --help` displays a brief help file.

Man pages are divided into numbered sections, based on the type of command, such as executable programs, system calls, or games. Most of the commands you are interested in while learning Linux are in section 1—Executable programs or shell commands. If you specify the section number, the `man` command does not need to search all the man pages, only one section, speeding the command considerably. For instance, you might use the following command to look up all the available options for the `ls` command:

```
man 1 ls
```

When software is installed on Linux, the associated help, man, and/or info files are installed in the appropriate location. The `man` command looks for files in a specific directory, in subdirectories for each section. To see where the man pages are located, type `manpath` at the command line.

Some Useful Commands

The tables below list some of the most useful Linux commands. The tables show the command name, what the command does, and where to find more information. In addition, sort and grep, two of the more flexible commands, are documented in this chapter to show the use of complex commands.

Linux commands can be used on the command line or in shell scripts, programs that perform tasks in the Linux shell. Creating shell scripts is discussed in Chapter 19.

TABLE 7-1   Some Useful Linux File Management Commands

Command	What it does	Details in
cat	Display contents of a file.	Chapter 9
cd	Change current directory.	Chapter 9
chgrp	Change the group owner for a file.	Chapter 9
chmod	Change the permissions of a file.	Chapter 9
chown	Change the owner of a file.	Chapter 9
cp	Copy file or directory.	Chapter 9
diff	Compare the contents of two files.	Chapter 9
diff3	Compare the contents of three files.	Chapter 9
find	Find a file on your hard disk.	Chapter 9
grep	Find a file with specified contents.	Chapter 9
less	Display the contents of a file on the screen, one page at a time.	Chapter 9
ls	List the file names of files in a directory.	Chapter 9
mkdir	Create a new directory.	Chapter 9
mv	Change the location of a file. Can be used to change the name of a file.	Chapter 9
pwd	Show the path to the current directory.	Chapter 9
rmdir	Remove a directory.	Chapter 9
touch	Update the last access/modification dates of a file.	Chapter 9

TABLE 7-2 Some Useful Linux Account Management Commands

Command	What it does	Details in
env	Set or display environmental variables.	App B
groupadd	Add a new group.	Chapter 8
groups	Display the list of existing groups.	Chapter 8
passwd	Change your password.	Chapter 8
quota	Display used and available disk space for account.	App B
su	Change to the super user or another user account.	Chapter 8
unset	Remove an environmental variable.	App B
useradd	Add a new user account.	Chapter 8
userdel	Delete a user account.	Chapter 8
whoami	Display the current account.	Chapter 8

TABLE 7-3 Some Useful Linux Print Job Management Commands

Command	What it does	Details in
lpr	Send a file to the printer queue.	Chapter 14
lprm	Remove a file from the printer queue.	Chapter 14
lpq	Display information about the jobs in the queue.	Chapter 14

TABLE 7-4 Some Miscellaneous Useful Linux Commands

Command	What it does	Details in
whereis	Find the location of a program.	App B
tar	Put files into and retrieve files from an archive file.	Chapter 10
ftp	Transfer files from one computer to another.	App B
clear	Clear the screen.	App B
date	Display the current date and time.	App B
gzip	Compress files.	App B
gunzip	Uncompress files.	App B

The sort Command

If you want to sort the contents of a plain text file, you can bring it into your word processor and sort it. However, Linux has a sort command that is much faster and often easier to use. The command to sort a file named unsorted.txt is:

```
sort unsorted.txt
```

The unsorted and the sorted contents of the file are below:

Unsorted	Sorted
Little Boy Blue	Jack Horner
Jack Horner	Little Bo Peep
Little Bo Peep	Little Boy Blue

This is the simplest form of sort, which is sufficient for many needs. In addition, the sort command has several options which affect the sorting procedure. Table 7-5 shows the most useful options.

TABLE 7-5 Options for the sort Command

Option	What it does
-ofilename	Save the output in the specified file.
-r	Sort in reverse order.
-u	Remove identical lines.
-k	Specify which key to sort on.
-t	Define a character to separate the keys in the text line.

More complicated sorts are possible using the -k and -t options. These options allow you to specify exactly which text in the line to sort on, rather than just sorting from the beginning of the line. For instance, you could use the following command:

```
sort –k2 –t" " unsorted.txt
```

The -t defines an empty space to be the character that separates the keys. The -k2 specifies key 2 as the key to sort on. Thus, sort will sort the lines based on the second word in the line: The output for this sort is:

```
Little Bo Peep
Little Boy Blue
Jack Horner
```

The grep Command

The grep command is so beloved by Linux users that it has its own t-shirts. The grep command finds files that have specified contents and outputs each line that it finds. The general format for the grep command is:

grep *options pattern files*

where:

- *pattern* specifies the text string to search for. *pattern* can be a literal string, such as abc or xxx. *pattern* can also be a regular expression, a pattern to be matched, such as any uppercase character or any word that begins with Q. Regular expressions are discussed in Appendix A.

- *files* specifies the files to search for the string. *files* can specify filenames (using wildcards if needed) or a directory.

For example, the following is a simple grep command with its output:

```
grep "Mary Poppins" *
file1.txt:I like Mary Poppins!
file7.txt:Mary Poppins is a great movie.
```

The command looks in all the files in the current directory for the string, Mary Poppins. Lines containing the search string display, with the filename prepended. You can use a path (such as /home/janet) instead of *, to specify a directory and all the files in that directory are searched.

The grep command has many options, some of which are shown in Table 7-6.

TABLE 7-6   Options for the grep Command

Option	What it does
-c	Output the number of lines found, rather than the lines themselves.
-i	Ignore upper- and lowercase when matching.
-l	Output the names of files with matches, rather than the actual lines.
-n	Include the line number of the match: file1.txt:16:Text on line.
-r	Check all subdirectories in the specified directory.
-v	Output all lines that don't match.
-x	Output a line only when the pattern matches the entire line.

Configuring the Terminal Window

You can configure the terminal window to your liking. You can change the colors, the font size, the opening window size, the sounds, and other characteristics of the terminal window. Both KDE and Gnome allow configuration, but the method used to make changes differs.

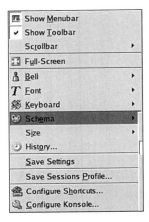

The KDE terminal window has a menu across the top. The Settings drop-down menu where you can change your window settings is shown on the right. You can show or hide the Menubar (top) and the Toolbar (bottom). You can have the Scrollbar on either the left or right side. You can change the window size to full screen or can use the Size menu item to specify a window size. If you select Font, you see a menu that allows you to change the font size. History allows you to set options for your history—the list of commands that you have executed. Schema, the highlighted item, allows you to set the text and background colors.

If you select Save Settings, the settings currently in effect are saved. When you next open a terminal window, these settings will still be in effect.

Gnome offers the same options, but through a different mechanism. Gnome lets you set a profile. Select edit->profile on the terminal menu and you see the panel to the right.

Notice the tabs for General, Title, Colors, Effects, and Scrolling. Clicking the tab allows you to set the options for the profile. You can have different profiles and change the profile as desired. The default profile is in effect, unless you change to a different profile.

Summary

Linux provides two basic types of interface for you to use when working with your computer: GUI (graphical user interface) and CLI (command-line interface). This chapter describes how to use the CLI, including how to do the following:

- Enter commands
- Redirect input and output
- Run commands in the background
- Get help with commands
- Configure the terminal window

In addition, a summary of useful commands is provided. The sort and grep commands are described in detail as examples of command use.

In the next chapter, the management of Linux accounts is described. Methods for managing accounts using the desktop and using the CLI are described.

CHAPTER 8

Linux Accounts

Linux is a multi-user operating system—a system that allows many users to work on the same computer, at the same time. For this to work, each user's work must be kept separate. One user can't be allowed to interfere with another's work, either accidentally or with evil intentions. A system that allowed your rival to delete the report you spent weeks writing would not be very popular. Linux accounts keep users' work private and protected.

A Linux system basically consists of files and processes. All information is organized into files and each file is owned by an account, protected from other accounts. All work done on your computer, including the invisible work that keeps your computer running, is done in a process—a program that is running. A program is run by an account. Consequently, you can do nothing on Linux without an account.

You may be the only person working on your computer. If so, user accounts may seem unnecessary to you. Nevertheless, you can't work on Linux without an account. So, at least one account is required. Accounts help protect you from unauthorized access from the Internet, as well as unauthorized access from your desk chair.

You will see accounts on your system that you didn't create. These are special accounts that run system and application processes. Some are created during installation. Others are created by the installation process when you install a software application. However, these are not accounts that you are likely to need to log in to. Only a system administrator is likely to need to understand or work with special accounts.

Account Types

All accounts are not equal. Each account has a set of privileges—a set of actions it is allowed to perform. There are two types of accounts:

- **Root:** The root account, called the super user, is allowed to do anything. It can access every file, directory, and program on the system. Every Linux system must have a root account.

- **User:** User accounts are more restricted. Unless given additional permissions, user accounts can only access directories and files and run programs that were created using the account itself.

During installation, a root account, and probably one or more user accounts, were created and given passwords. Don't forget the root password. You must use the root account to make changes to the system. Root can add new accounts at any time.

It is wisest to log in to and use your user account most of the time. In fact, don't use the root account unless you really need to. The root account has unlimited power that allows you to make disastrous mistakes.

User accounts can be temporarily given root privileges. If you need to perform a task that requires root privileges while logged in to your user account desktop, you can enter the root password and perform the task. For instance, if you open `main menu->System Settings` and select `Users and Groups` or `Root Password` while logged in to your user account, you will be prompted with the window shown in Figure 8-1.

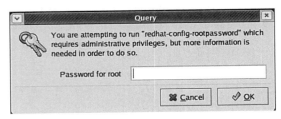

FIGURE 8-1   Root password prompt.

When working in the shell in a terminal window, you can change from one account into any other account, as long as you know the password. Change account using:

`su accountname`

Unless you are logged in to root, you will be prompted for a password. Root can `su` to any account without needing a password.

Groups

Each account is assigned membership in a group when it is created. Privileges assigned to a group are available to all accounts in the group. An account can belong to more than one group at a time.

Groups are a useful way to grant privileges to an account. For instance, suppose you have a program, called destroy, that only certain people should use. You can set up this program so it's available for use by people in the expert group, but not by all users. When you install a new account that needs to run the destroy program, you assign the account to the expert group. If you install a new program, destroy2, for the use of this group of people, you set up the new program so that only the expert group can run it.

At least one group must be assigned to each account when it's created. A group must exist before any account can be assigned to it. Linux allows you to set a system default group that is assigned to each new account. Some Linux systems assign the same group, usually named users, to all new accounts. The user group has no extraordinary privileges. Other Linux systems assign an individual group to each new account. For instance, when Fedora creates a user account, it also creates a group with the same name and assigns the group to the new account. Thus, the account janet belongs to the group janet. The group janet has no extra privileges.

Linux installs several groups by default. Root is one group installed by Linux; the root account is a member of the root group. If a new account is assigned to the root group, the new account will have the same privileges that are assigned to root.

You can create groups for your own purposes. Group names should represent the purpose of the group, such as the sales group or the mail group. Group names are limited to 16 or fewer characters.

Groups allow privileges to accounts by means of file permissions. File permissions are discussed in Chapter 9.

Account Information

You can look at and/or edit account information. On Fedora, select main menu->System Settings->Users and Groups to get the window shown in Figure 8-2.

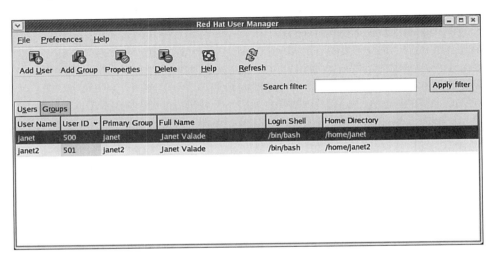

FIGURE 8-2 Account management window.

Highlight an account and click Properties. The window in Figure 8-3 opens.

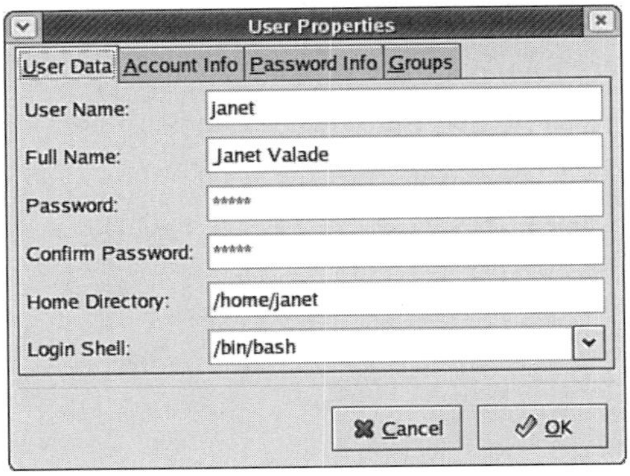

FIGURE 8-3 Account management window.

The home directory is a section of the file storage space that belongs to the account. No other user can access the home directory unless the account owner allows them to. Well, no one except root. Root can go anywhere and do anything. The most common location for the home directory is /home/*accountname*.

Click tabs in the window to see additional information about the account. Figure 8-4 shows the Account Info and Password Info screens.

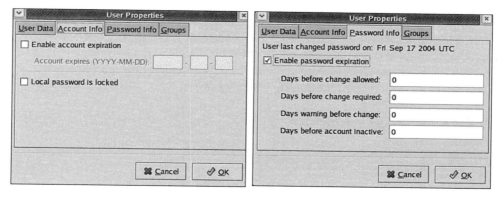

FIGURE 8-4 Account and Password Info screens.

The Account Info screen allows you so enter an expiration date for the account. The Password Info screen allows you to set a password expiration date, forcing the user to change the password periodically. Both settings improve the security of systems that have a large number of users.

The Groups screen provides a list of all the existing groups on the system. Groups that the account is a member of are checked. You can check or uncheck any groups if needed. The groups shown in the figure were set up by Fedora during installation. It would be unwise to uncheck any group that Fedora checked.

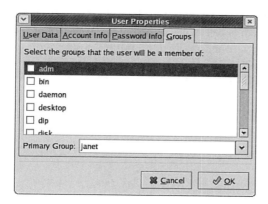

FIGURE 8-5 List of groups.

Most distributions have similar utilities to manage accounts. SuSE has YaST, accessed at main menu->Control Center. Mandrake has a Control Center at System->Configuration->Configure your computer. Click System to see Users and Groups.

Adding Accounts

New accounts are added using the utility discussed in the previous section, the utility used to look at and change account information. On Fedora, select main menu->System Settings->Users and Groups to get the window shown in Figure 8-2. To add a new account, click Add User. The window in Figure 8-6 opens.

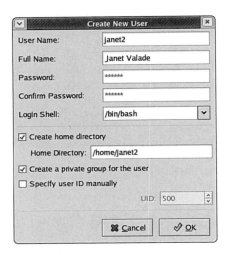

FIGURE 8-6   Create New User window.

Fill in the information for the new account. Account names must be less than 33 characters and can't begin with a number. The system enters defaults for the Login Shell and the Home Directory. When you click OK, the new account is added. A group is created with the account name. Other systems, such as SuSE, create user accounts with a general group, such as User, rather than with a private, individual group.

New accounts can also be created from the command line in a terminal window. While logged in as root (or su to root), type:

```
useradd janet3
```

The new janet3 account doesn't have a password yet. Next, type:

```
passwd janet3
```

You will be prompted for the password, as follows, and again to double-check:

```
Changing password for user janet3
New password:
```

Passwords

Passwords are important to the security of your Linux system. They protect you from unauthorized use both from your terminal and from the Internet. Your root password is particularly important. In general, make your password difficult for someone to guess, but easy for you to remember. Some suggestions for creating passwords are:

- Use a mixture of characters, including uppercase letters, lowercase letters, numbers, and punctuation.

- Use at least 8 characters.

- The starting letters of a favorite saying make a password that's hard to guess. For instance, Take me out to the Ball Game! becomes TmottBG!.

- Substitute numbers for letters, such as 1 (one) for l (L) or 0 (zero) for o (oh). For instance, Tm0ttBG!.

Some practices to avoid are:

- Don't use any word that can be found in a dictionary. Cracking software can try dictionary words one by one.

- Don't use dates. It's a common practice and there are a limited number of possibilities. In addition, birthdays can be discovered.

- Don't use any part of your name.

- Don't use your children's or pets' names. Someone who knows you might guess these.

- Don't write your password down and paste it to the front of your terminal. Or any variation of this. Use a password you can remember.

- Don't tell anyone your password. If someone needs to use your computer, create a new account for him or her to use.

Group Information

Some groups are created when your Linux system is installed. In addition, each Linux distribution provides a default group when an account is installed. The default for some distributions is a general group that all accounts belong to, such as users. The default for other distributions, such as Fedora, is a private group for each account, given the same name as the account, such as the janet group for the janet account.

You can see the available groups and their members using the account management utility discussed earlier in this chapter—the utility used to look at and change account information. On Fedora, select main menu->System Settings->Users and Groups to get the window shown in Figure 8-2. Click the Groups tab. The window in Figure 8-7 opens.

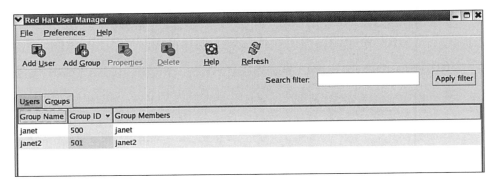

FIGURE 8-7   Display of group information.

The groups that are not system groups are displayed. To see all the groups, including system created groups, click Preferences and select Filter system users and groups to turn the setting off (the checkmark by the setting means that it's on).

You can reorder the list by clicking the title bar. For instance, clicking Group ID reorders the group ID list to descending order, rather than the ascending order shown in the figure.

Adding Groups

To add a group, use the account management utility discussed earlier in this chapter—the utility used to look at and change account information. On Fedora, select main menu-> System Settings->Users and Groups to get the window shown in Figure 8-2. Click the Groups tab. Click Add Group. You see the window in Figure 8-8.

FIGURE 8-8   Add groups dialog window.

Type the name for the new group and click OK. Group names must be less than 17 characters and may not begin with a number. The new group will be added to the window in Figure 8-7, with no group members listed. To add accounts to the group:

1. Click the Accounts tab.

2, Highlight an account.

3. Click Properties.

4. Click the Groups tab.

5. Check the box by the new group in the list of groups.

New groups can also be created from the command line in a terminal window. While logged in as root (or su to root), type:

```
groupadd sales
```

To add a user to a group, type:

```
groupmod -G group user
```

where group is the name of the group and user is the account name, for example:

```
groupmod -G sales janet3
```

Forgotten Root Password

Forgetting your root password is not an insurmountable problem. You can enter a new root password by booting your computer in single user mode. This is a special mode of operation, used mainly by system administrators for specific tasks. You can use this mode to recover from a lost root password.

You enter single-user mode when the system is starting, from the boot loader screen. The Fedora boot loader screen is shown in Figure 4-18. Notice that it includes some directions: 'e' to edit the command before booting. To enter single-user mode:

1. While the boot loader screen displays, press <e>. The contents of a configuration file are displayed, similar to the following example.

```
root (hd0,0)
kernel /vmlinuz-2.4.22-1.2115.nptl ro root=LABEL=/ rhgb
initrd /initrd-2.4.22-1.2115.nptl.img
```

2. Use the arrow keys to move to the kernel line.

3. Press <e> to edit the line.

4. Add the word single to the end of the line, as follows, and then press <Enter> to save the change:

```
grub edit> kernel /vmlinuz-2.4.22-1.2115.nptl ro root=LABEL=/ rhgb single
```

5. Press <b> to boot.

In Mandrake, you can enter single user mode by choosing Failsafe at the boot loader. For other distributions, read the documentation. If you use LILO instead of GRUB, type linux single at the boot prompt.

When your system finishes booting, it displays a prompt. If it asks for a login, enter root. At this point, you can change your root password. Type:

```
passwd root
```

Enter the new password twice when prompted. Then type:

```
reboot
```

to reboot your computer in its normal mode—multi-user mode.

Summary

Linux is a multi-user operating system. Linux accounts keep users' work separate from each other, private and protected. All information is organized into files and each file is owned by an account, protected from other accounts. Consequently, you can do nothing on Linux without an account.

All files are owned by an account and by a group. Permission to look at, modify, or run a file is assigned to the user, to the group, and to all users. This system of permission is what protects each user's work and information.

This chapter explains how to do the following:

- Check and change account information, such as username, home directory, and group membership
- Add accounts
- Add or modify passwords. Provides rules for secure passwords
- Add groups
- Set a new root account password

The next chapter explains how to set and change file permissions. It also explains how to create, move, rename, delete, and otherwise manage files.

## CHAPTER 9

File Management

All information on Linux is organized into files. All information, without exception. A file is the mechanism that Linux uses to store information. You are most likely to need to know about and manage files that contain the following types of information:

- **Data files:** Files that contain information stored on the computer. Two types of data files are:

  - **Application-specific files:** Information created by a specific application, stored in a format that only the application can interpret. Creating, changing, storing, or printing the data file must be done using the application. The documents created by many word processing applications are stored in an application-specific file.

  - **Text files:** Information stored in a common computer format (ASCII) that most applications can read. Linux system commands can read and modify the file. Your word processor allows you to specifically save your file as text, even though the default is an application-specific file.

- **Programs and applications:** Files that contain instructions. When you run a program, Linux reads the instructions in the file and performs the tasks as directed.

- **Image files:** Files that contain pictures. You need to use software that understands graphic content to see or modify these files. Graphics files are described in Chapter 14.

- **Configuration files:** Files that contain information used by an application to perform its work. For instance, the settings for your desktop are stored in a configuration file. When your desktop starts, it reads the file to see what color the background is, what kind of fonts to use, etc.

In many cases, you create and manipulate data using an application. The application manages the files; you only need to know the data filename. However, on occasion, you need to work with files directly. This chapter describes how files are stored and how to create, copy, move, delete, and otherwise manage them.

File Organization

Files are organized into directories, also called folders. Windows users are probably familiar with folders. A directory can contain files and other directories, as many as needed. A directory can even be empty, containing no files or directories.

> **NOTE**
> Because all information on Linux is stored in files, a directory is actually a file that contains the information needed to access the files assigned to it.

Directories are organized in a hierarchy on your hard disk, called a file system. Although technically the directories can be named and organized in any manner desired, most Linux systems are organized in the accepted Linux way. The top directory is called root, designated by a forward slash (/).

When a user account is created, it's assigned a home directory. For instance, the account janet is assigned a home directory named janet. Home directories are located in a directory named home in the root directory— /home. Many directories are in the /home directory, one for each user account, such as:

```
/home/janet
/home/kim
/home/theboss
```

The directory names above include the names of the directories above them. This designation is called the path. /home is the path from root to janet. If a file named test is in the directory janet, the path is /home/janet, so that the complete name to locate the file is /home/janet/test.

The home directory for the powerful root account is separate from other users, in /root.

You can use shortcuts in the path. A dot represents the current directory; two dots represent the one immediately above the current directory. For instance, in the directory /home/janet, the dot directory is janet and the dot dot directory is home.

The location of a file in the file system includes the path. You can have two files with the same name as long as they are located in different directories.

The entire path from the root directory is called the absolute path. It refers to the total path needed to locate the file—the path from / to the file. A file can also be located by its relative path—the path from the current location to the file. For instance, if you are located in the /home directory, the relative path to the file test is janet/test—the path from /home to the file.

Shortcuts are useful in relative paths. For instance, if you are located in /home/janet, the path to /home/kim can be specified as ../kim.

File Information

Each file has properties. For some specific uses of a file, you may need to know information about it:

- **Name:** String of characters that identifies the file.
- **Location:** Path to the file.
- **Size:** Number of bytes. A byte usually holds a character.
- **Owner/group:** The name of the user account and the group that own the file. Groups are explained in Chapter 8.
- **Date created/accessed/modified:** The date/time the file was created, last accessed, or last modified.
- **Permissions:** Settings that determine who can access the file. Permissions are discussed in detail later in this chapter.
- **Type:** Format in which the file is stored, such as text file or a program file.

You can look at the file information from:

- **Desktop:** A file manager application allows you to look at and manage files.
- **Command line:** Many Linux commands are available for file management.

The file manger for KDE is Konqueror. To examine files, Konqueror serves as a file browser, allowing you to navigate through the file system, looking at files and file information (similar to Windows Explorer). Konqueror also serves as a Web browser.

On your KDE desktop, if you click an icon that is a directory, such as home, Konqueror opens and displays the contents of the home directory. Some Linux distributions also have a menu item for home. You can find Konqueror on the main menu or a system sub-menu. Some distributions have the Konqueror icon on the desktop or panel.

In this chapter, file management instructions for the desktop are given using Konqueror. You can use Konqueror on your GNOME desktop, as well as on KDE, as long as you selected KDE, as well as GNOME, during installation. GNOME has its own file manager called Nautilus, so if you click the home icon on GNOME, Nautilus opens, not Konqueror. However, often Konqueror is on the GNOME menu.

If Konqueror eludes you on the desktop and menus, you can select Run from the main menu, type Konqueror, and click Run on both KDE and GNOME.

Examining Files from the Desktop

The Konqueror file browser is shown in Figure 9-1. It's open in the home directory of a user on a Fedora Core 2 system—opened from the KDE desktop by clicking a home icon or Home on the menu.

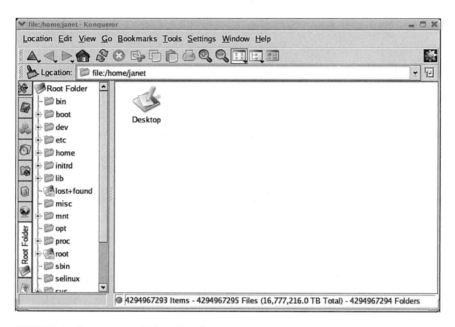

FIGURE 9-1   Konqueror on Fedora Core 2.

The Location field, above the main sections, shows the current directory path: /home/janet. The large pane on the right shows icons for the files in the directory, in this case just one entry: Desktop. If you double-click an icon for a folder (such as Desktop), you move into the folder and see its contents; if you double-click an icon for a file, the file opens in its associated application (discussed later in this chapter).

A row of buttons down the left side of the window controls the contents of the left pane. In this case, the root folder button is open, so the root folder contents are shown in the left pane. Clicking a folder in the left pane moves you into the folder directory.

You can also move around the file system with the up, back, and forward arrows on the toolbar. You can return to the home directory by clicking the home icon on the toolbar.

If you click View->Show Hidden Files, many additional files display. These are system files, files that keep your account running properly. It's best to leave these files alone until you are fairly knowledgeable.

To see file information, right-click the file icon and select Properties.

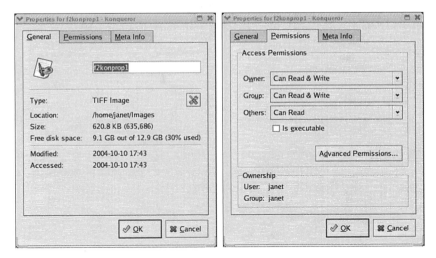

FIGURE 9-2 File information.

The window on the left shows the filename, type, location, size, and dates modified and accessed. In addition, the total disk space and the available disk space for the Linux file system are shown.

The window on the right opens if you click the Permissions tab. The permissions, the owner, and the group for the file are shown. You can change the permissions from this screen. Changing permissions is explained later in this chapter.

Figure 9-1 shows the directories and files as icons. You can change the file listing display style. Click View->View Mode and select from the list shown on the right. The Tree view is the view shown in the left pane of Figure 9-1. The Detailed List view is useful. It displays a text listing for each file and directory with most of the file information in one summary line, as shown in the format below. This listing shows the filename, size in KB, type, date/time last modified, permissions, owner, and group.

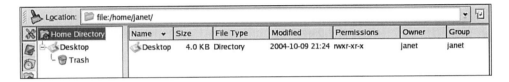

An explanation of the permissions notation is provided in the "File Permissions" section of this chapter.

Examining Files from the Command Line

To use the command line, open a terminal window. You see the home directory of the account you are using. To see a listing of the files in the directory, use the ls command, as follows:

```
ls
Desktop      Images      test.txt
```

The output shown just lists the names. Some distributions output color-coded listings to show the type of files, such as blue for directories. Others show a forward slash (/) after the names of directories, as shown in the following output:

```
ls
Desktop/     Images/     test.txt
```

To see more information about the files, use the options of the ls command. All the options are documented in the man page for ls, accessed by typing:

```
man ls
```

One useful option is -l to get a long listing, as follows:

```
ls -l
drwx------   3  janet  janet  4096  Oct   2  13:21  Desktop/
```

The first character is d for directory. A file would show a - for the first character. The next 9 characters are the permissions, as explained in the "File Permissions" section of this chapter. The first janet is the user owner. The second janet is the group owner. 4096 is the file size. Oct 2 at 13:21 is the date/time the file was last modified. Desktop is the filename.

You can use ls to list the contents of a directory by specifying its name, as follows:

```
ls /home/robert
Desktop      mysecretstuff
```

Actually, you can only look at the contents of the robert directory if you have permission to do so. If you don't have permission, you see an error message such as:

```
ls:   /home/robert:  Permission denied
```

You can save the directory listing in a file, rather than display it to the screen, with the following command:

```
ls > dir_listing
```

The list of files is stored in a text file named dir_listing in the same format that it would be displayed on the screen. You can look at the file or print it.

The files and directories listed using the ls command don't include system files unless you use the -a option. On Linux, system files are named with a dot (.) as the first character, such as .bash_history, which contains a history of your commands. These files make your system behave properly. In general, it's best to leave these system files alone until you are fairly knowledgeable.

When you use the -a option, your file listing includes . and .., representing the current directory (.) and the directory above the current directory (..), also called the parent directory.

To move through the file system, use the cd command. The following are valid cd commands:

```
cd /home/janet     (moves to /home/janet)
cd ..              (moves up one directory)
cd                 (moves to your home directory)
```

Most Linux distributions provide you with a prompt that displays which directory you are in. However, if you don't know which directory, you can always type:

```
pwd
```

It displays the path to the current directory.

If you provide ls or cd with a directory or filename that can't be found, you will see a message similar to the following:

```
No such file or directory
```

For instance, if you want to change to the directory /home/janet, you can type the following relative path if you are in the /home directory:

```
cd janet
```

However, if you are in a different directory, you will get the "No such file or directory" message.

File Permissions

Because Linux is a multi-user system, directories and files need to be protected from unauthorized use. Each directory and file has associated permissions, settings that determine who can access the file and what they can do with it.

Permissions to the file are given to three types of user accounts:

- **Owner:** The account that owns the file
- **Group:** Members of a group that owns the file
- **All users:** All accounts on the system

Users can be given permission to do one or more of three things to the file:

- **Read:** Look at the contents of the file
- **Write:** Save the file to the hard disk
- **Execute:** Run the file or enter the directory

The permissions can be given in any combination. For instance, file1 might have permission as follows:

- **Owner:** Read, write, execute
- **Group:** Read, execute
- **All users:** Read

The owner can look at, edit, save, and run the file. Members of the group can only look at and run the file, but they can't change it. Everyone on the system can look at the contents of the file. Remember that a directory is simply a file, so directories can be given the same type of permissions as a file.

File permissions are often displayed in a shorthand format as follows:

rwxr--r--

The r, w, and x stand for read, write, and execute, as described earlier in this section. The 9 characters shown represent three groups of three: rwx and r-- and r--. The first group displays the permissions for the owner, the second is the permissions for the group, and the third is the permissions for everyone. Thus, in this case, the owner can read, write, and execute the file, but the group and all users can only read the file, not write/execute it. Only the owner or the root account can change file permissions.

Changing Permissions

You can change the permissions for a file using the Properties screen shown in Figure 9-2. To open the permission screen, right-click the file to be changed and select `Properties`. Then, click the `Permissions` tab.

The screen shows the permissions for each of the three types of accounts. If you click the button for a particular account type, you see three choices: `Forbidden`, `Can Read`, and `Can Read & Write`. If you want to give execute permission to the file, check the Execute box. When the settings are right, click `OK`.

On the command line, the `chmod` command is used to change the permissions. The format is one of the following:

```
chmod accounttypes+permissions filename
chmod accounttypes-permissions filename
chmod accounttypes=permissions filename
```

The three account types are indicated by letters: u for user (owner), g for group, o for others, and a for all account types. The three permissions are r, w, and x, as discussed previously. The three symbols that assign permissions are + (plus) to add permissions, - (minus) to remove permissions, and = (equal sign) to set new permissions. Thus, one command might be:

```
chmod g+w file1
```

The command gives write permission to the group for a file named file1. It doesn't change any other permissions for the file. If the group already had read permission, it still has read permission. Another command might be:

```
chmod g-w file1
```

The command removes write permission to the group for the file without changing any other permissions for the file. Another command might be:

```
chmod go=x file1
```

The command gives execute permission to group and all accounts on the file. Group and all other accounts are not given read or write permissions. Because u was not specified in this command, the permissions for the owner are not changed. You can set all permissions at once using:

```
chmod a=r file2
```

The a means all users—all three account types. All user accounts on the system can now look at the contents of file2. However, they can't write or execute it.

Managing Owners and Groups

Permissions to your files are given to the owner, the group, or all accounts. You may want to transfer a file you created to another owner. More often, you want to change the group for a file as a way of allowing specific users to access it.

On many systems, when a file is created, the group for the file is the same name as the owner who created it. For instance, a file created by janet may belong to the janet group. If you give permissions on the file to other accounts by adding them to the janet group, you allow them access to *all* files you create. A better solution is to create a new group, add the members you want to be able to access the file to the new group, and change the group for the file. Then, if you give write permission to the group for the file, all group members (but not all accounts) have write permission.

On some systems, the group for a user account is one general group that includes all user accounts. You need to set your permissions on your file with that in mind. To limit the access to your file, you can change the group.

You can change the owner or group of a file at the command line using one of the following commands that change the owner and group of file2:

```
chown salesmanager file2    (changes owner to account salesmanager)
chgrp sales file2           (changes group to sales)
```

If you are in the Konqueror file manager, you can use the Run Command item in the Tools menu to quickly execute a single command. Or open a terminal window with Tools->Open Terminal.

A group must exist before you can give it ownership of a file. Creating groups is done using the User and Groups utility discussed in Chapter 8. To create a group on Fedora, select main menu->System Settings->Users and Groups to get the window in Figure 8-2. Click Add Group. Type the new group name in the dialog box. Click OK. Or create a group, much more quickly, at the command line by typing:

```
groupadd groupname
```

To add an account to a group, in the Users and Groups window, highlight an account and click the Group tab. Check the box by a group name to add the account to the group. Or use the command-line command:

```
usermod -G groupname username    (notice the uppercase G)
```

The account you use to change owners and groups must have the power to change them. If you see a message like "Operation not permitted," the account can't make the change you entered. Changing to the root account (su root) solves the problem.

File Types

Although Linux handles other types of files (such as block device), this chapter only discusses ordinary, also called normal, files and symbolic links. Ordinary files include data, configuration, text, graphics, directories, and other files. Links are filenames that only point to another file. Ordinary files are categorized by the information they contain. Linux desktops and applications recognize file types by the filename extension, just as Windows recognizes .doc extensions as MS Word files.

File extensions are associated with an application. When you double-click a file, the file extension determines which application the file is opened in. A document with an .sxw extension is opened in OpenOffice. New applications usually create associations for their file extensions during installation.

You can change the associations manually if necessary. To add or edit an association, highlight a file with the extension, right-click, and select `Edit File Type` to see the screen on the right. The top pane shows .HTML, .htm, and .HTM should be opened using Konqueror. Click `Add` to add an extension using a pattern, such as `*.abcdef`. Linux extensions can be any number of characters, not just three.

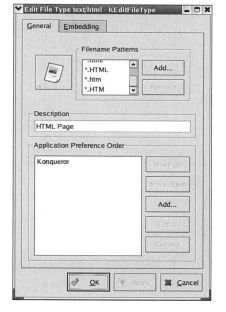

More than one application can be listed in the lower pane. For instance, you could add Mozilla before Konqueror. The file is opened in Mozilla if possible; if not, the file opens in Konqueror. Clicking the `Add` button displays a list of applications to select from.

Whereas desktops and applications recognize extensions, Linux doesn't. It looks inside a file to determine file type. You can use the `file` command at the command line to see the actual file type, regardless of the extension, as follows:

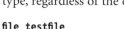

```
file testfile
testfile: ASCII text
```

The `file` command has a very large list of file types it recognizes. In general, files with "text" in the file type, such as "c program text," can be looked at and edited with Linux tools. Data is a file type used when Linux can't recognize a more specific type.

Finding Files

Linux has excellent file-finding utilities for both the desktop and the command line. On the KDE desktop, open the main menu and select Find Files. Or in Konqueror, click Tools and select Find Files. The screen in Figure 9-3 opens with blank fields.

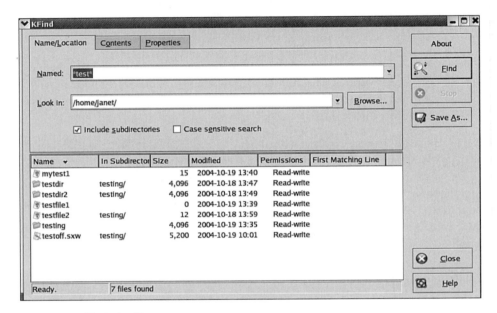

FIGURE 9-3 File-find utility.

Typing *test* for the filename finds all files with test anywhere in the name, because * is a wildcard meaning any string of characters. Typing or browsing to /home/janet starts the search in the janet directory. "Include subdirectories" is checked. When you click the Find button, files display in the bottom pane. Four directories and four files are found. Two of the files and two of the directories are in the testing subdirectory.

Clicking the Contents tab displays a screen where you can select the type of file and the file contents to search for, such as a string such as "Hello World." Clicking the Properties tab allows you to search by last access date, file size, owner, or group. When you click Find, the parameters set in all three tabs are used in the search. GNOME has a search utility with very similar functionality, also accessed from the main menu.

From the command line, you can use the find command to find files by filename or properties and the grep command to find files by content. The find command syntax is:

find *pathname conditions*

pathname specifies the directory where the search should start. It's common to use dot to mean the current directory and subdirectories or / to search the entire file system. *conditions* sets the search parameters. Many conditions are available. You can use more than one in a command. Some useful conditions are shown in Table 9-1.

TABLE 9-1 Parameters for Use with the find Command

Parameter	Means	Example
-print	Display the matches on the screen.	-print
-name *filename*	Pattern to match filenames.	find . -name "*test*"
-group *name*	Files own by the specified group.	find . -group janet
-user *name*	Files owned by the user.	find . -user janet
-atime +*n*|-*n*|*n*	Last access time is more than, less than, or exactly n days ago.	find . -atime +5
-ctime +*n*|-*n*|*n*	Last changed time is more than, less than, or exactly n days ago.	find . -ctime -5
-size *nc*	Files n characters long.	find . -size 100c
-empty	Files that are empty.	-empty

For example, the following command searches the entire file system for all files beginning with chapter, owned by janet, and last accessed less than 3 days ago.

```
find / -name "chapter*" -user janet -atime -3
```

The grep command searches the contents of files. It has the general format:

```
grep options pattern files
```

grep searches the contents of the specified files for the *pattern*. It outputs any matches found. The *options* specify the operation of grep, such as -c, which instructs grep to output a count of matched lines, rather than the entire line, and -v, which outputs the lines that don't match, rather than the lines that do match. The pattern can be a string of characters or a regular expression—a pattern used to match strings, such as all words that begin with uppercase *A* or all lines that contain a number. Regular expressions are explained in Appendix A. The grep command is explained in more detail in Chapter 7 and in Appendix B.

Creating Directories, Files, and Links

You can create new directories, files, and links from your desktop using Konqueror. In Konqueror, navigate to the directory that is to house your new item. Click Edit and select Create New. A menu of items you can create is opened, including:

- **Directory:** Type the directory name.

- **HTML File:** Type the filename. The new file contains skeleton HTML code.

- **Text File:** Type the filename.

- **Link to Application:** Similar to a Windows shortcut. Clicking the link starts the application. In the first screen displayed, type the name of the link. Then select the Execute tab. In the Execute screen, type the command to start the application or click the Browse button to select the application.

- **Link to Location:** Shortcut to a location. When you click the link, the location opens in Konqueror. In the screen displayed, type a filename for the link. Type the URL to the location or click the Browse button to navigate to the URL.

Names can be up to 255 characters. Linux accepts almost any character in a filename, but some characters have a special meaning to the Linux shell and complicate your life when used in a filename. It's best to use only letters, numbers, underscores, hyphens, and dots in filenames. Upper- and lowercase letters are not the same (file1 is not File1). Filenames don't need to have an extension, although many applications use specific extensions. Technically, the dot is just another character, so you could name a file something like file.test.mine. Special system files have names that begin with a dot, so don't use a dot to begin filenames for other types of files.

You can create a directory in any directory where you have write permission using the command line mkdir command:

mkdir *path/dirname*

If your path includes directories that don't yet exist, you can create them in one command with the -p option, as follows:

mkdir -p /usr/local/newparent/mydir

If newparent doesn't exist, it's created, then mydir is created inside newparent.

Files can be created by applications, such as a word processor. File editors create and edit plain text files, as Notepad does on Windows. Links can be created at the command line using the ln command (see Appendix A).

Copying, Renaming, and Moving Files

Konqueror allows you to copy, rename, and move directories and files. When you copy or move a directory, all its contents are copied or moved as well.

Highlight a directory or file icon to be copied or moved. Use the `Ctrl` key or the `Shift` key with the mouse to select more than one icon. Right-click your highlighted icon(s) and select `Cut` or `Copy` to put the file(s) onto the clipboard, similar to the Windows clipboard. You can then `Paste` the file(s) wherever it's needed. Select `Rename` to give the file a new name. `Copy to` and `Move to` provide a list of directories where you can create a new copy of the file. Select `Copy Here` when in the target directory.

You can also copy or move a file or directory by dragging it to a new location. For instance, you can highlight a file icon in the right pane of Konqueror and use your mouse to drag it to any folder icon in the left pane of Konqueror. Or to a directory that's open in another window. Or to an application that's open in another window.

You can copy, rename, and move directories and files at the command line using the `cp` and `mv` commands. To copy or move a file, type:

```
cp path/sourcename path/targetname      (copies a file)
cp -r path/sourcename path/targetname   (copies a directory)
mv path/sourcename path/targetname      (moves a file or directory)
```

After a `cp` command, two copies of the directory or file exist, with two different names. After a `mv` command, the source directory or file is gone, only the new copy, *targetname*, exists. Thus, `mv` functions as a rename command. The basic rules are:

- If *targetname* doesn't exist, a copy of *sourcename* is created and given the name *targetname*.

- If *targetname* exists and is a file, it is overwritten if *sourcename* is a file, but not copied at all if sourcename is a directory.

- If *targetname* exists and is a directory, a copy of *sourcename* is written into *targetname* and given its original name

To copy or move files, your account needs to have write permissions to the directory where you are copying or moving the file or directory.

Viewing and Editing Text Files

Text files are files that contain only text characters, with no formatting information. Text files contain information stored in ASCII code, a code that is understood by most applications. HTML files, program source code, and many Linux configuration files are stored in text files. Although you can view and edit the contents of text files with a word processor, it's generally quicker and simpler to open them in a text editor—an application that has only the features necessary to edit text. Some text editors are:

- **Kate:** A simple basic text editor with a GUI interface, very similar to Notepad. Kate is discussed in full detail in Chapter 18.

- **KWrite:** A text editor similar to Kate, with a few more useful features, such as a spell checker. KWrite is the default text editor for KDE. When you double-click a text file, it opens in KWrite.

- **Emacs:** A popular editor, developed by GNU, with advanced features for programmers.

- **vi:** A command-based text editor, suitable for use at the command line. vi is installed on every Linux and UNIX system, regardless of what other text editors are installed. vi is described in detail in Chapter 18. Many Linux distributions provide an updated version of vi called vim. Any commands that work in vi also work in vim.

You can look at the contents of a file at the command line without opening the file in a text editor with the command:

cat *filename*

The entire file contents display on the screen at once. You can display the contents one screen at a time with the following command:

less *filename*

Output pauses after one screen displays. Press <spacebar> to display the next page. Press <q> to quit the command, stopping the output.

Linux provides two applications for automating repetitive text editing:

- **sed:** A powerful, fast search and replace utility. Your search term can be a pattern (regular expression, discussed in Appendix A). sed can process many large files in seconds.

- **gawk:** A simple, limited purpose scripting language. gawk processes each line in the file, rearranging, removing, and/or adding text as directed.

Deleting Files and Directories

To delete a file or a directory when in Konqueror, highlight the icon and right-click. Select either Move to Trash or Delete. Move to trash is the safer option because the file can be retrieved from the trash can so long as the trash hasn't been emptied. Files that are deleted are not retrievable.

Konqueror also allows you to delete a file or directory by using your mouse to drag it into the trash can on your desktop.

To delete a file from the command line, type:

rm *filename*

You can use wildcards (e.g., ch* or ch?) to delete more than one file at a time. Be very cautious when using wildcards. Linux allows you to issue a command like the following:

rm *

It deletes all the files in the current directory. It's easy to make a disastrous mistake using wildcards. Listing the files with the wildcard, such as with:

ls *

shows the files that will be deleted. It's worth a few seconds to be careful.

To remove a directory, use the command:

rmdir *dirname*

However, *dirname* needs to be empty. If it's not, you will get an error message and it won't be deleted. You can remove all the files and issue rmdir again. Or, you can use the rm command, as follows:

rm -r *dirname*

This will remove *dirname* and all its contents, including all nested directories. This command deserves a caution. Be sure you know what's in the directory and that you want to delete it all before issuing this command.

To delete files, you must have write permissions on the directory containing the files. You don't need to have write permissions on the files themselves. However, if you don't have write permissions on the file you are deleting, you will be asked whether you really want to delete the file. If you answer yes, the file is then deleted.

Summary

All information on Linux is organized into files. All information, without exception. Some files you might need to know about and manage are data files, programs, image files, and configuration files. Although you usually create and manage files with applications, on some occasions you need to create, copy, move, delete, and otherwise manage files directly.

Files are located in directories, also called folders, organized in a hierarchical file system. Each account has a home directory where it can store files. Each file is uniquely identified by an absolute file path, which lists all the directories between / (the top directory called root) and the file.

Each file has properties, such as its name, location, size, and date created. Each file is protected by a system of permissions that define whether only the user owner, the group owner, or anyone can access it and what each can do with it.

You can create and delete files. You can examine and change the properties and permissions of a file from the desktop or from the command line. You can edit file contents using text editors. This chapter explains how to do the following:

- Examine and change file permissions
- Examine and change owners and groups
- Associate file types with applications
- Find files
- Create directories, files, and links
- Copy, rename, move, and delete files and directories
- Edit the contents of text files

Chapter 10 discusses programs and applications. In particular, you find out how to install and update software on your Linux system.

Applications and Programs

A ll information on Linux is organized into files. Programs and applications are no exception. Programs are files that contain instructions that Linux follows to perform tasks. Applications are one or more programs that perform work. The word processing document that you create is stored in a file. The word processing application that you use to create and store the file is also stored in a file—a program. Or more likely, many programs working together.

A program can be quite simple, with one instruction that tells Linux to display "Hello World" on the screen. An application may be quite complex, such as a word processing application. The word processing application programs contain the instructions that tell Linux what to do when you click a button or type a word. When you click Save, the application tells Linux to store the document in a file. The instructions may be complex, with many tasks being performed at once, but the principle is the same as the simple program that displays Hello World. The program contains instructions that Linux follows.

This chapter discusses programs and applications. Information on running programs, starting applications, and managing software applications is included.

Programs

Programs are files containing instructions that the computer executes. However, computers require instructions in machine language, not in a language that humans use. The solution is interpreters and compilers—programs that translate a human-readable file into machine language that the computer can execute.

Programming languages are the languages that humans use to write programs. Programming languages differ. Each has a very detailed syntax that allows a compiler to recognize its instructions and convert them to machine language. Some popular languages for writing programs are C, C++, Java, and Perl.

The program file that contains the instructions written in a programming language is called the source code. The source code is converted by a compiler or interpreter specific to the language. Interpreters convert the program and execute it immediately. Compilers can save the program in machine language so that the program doesn't have to be converted again every time it runs. The saved program is a binary file (a file the computer understands), called the executable. Some compilers understand more than one language.

Programs in executable files are run by typing the program name. The name includes the path. For instance, a program you write and compile in your own directory runs when you type:

```
./programname
```

Programmers will find an open source C and C++ compiler developed by GNU available on most Linux systems. A simple command that compiles a C program is:

```
gcc -o myprogram myprogram.c
```

The -o option provides a name for the executable file. The source code is in the file myprogram.c. After gcc compiles it, you can type ./myprogram to run the program. The compiler has many options. Type man gcc to see more information about using the gcc compiler.

Most Linux systems also include Perl and Python, two open source languages. Many system administrators use Perl to write programs to manage their Linux systems. Shell scripts are also frequently used by system administrators. Shell scripts, discussed in Chapter 19, are programs containing Linux commands.

Programs can't execute unless their permissions include x for the account types that are to execute them. Even the owner can't execute a program without x permissions.

Linux Commands

Linux commands are programs, developed by GNU or other projects, and included with the Linux distribution. You can see some Linux commands by typing:

`ls /bin`

The output includes many of the Linux commands you use. For instance, the `ls` command used above to see what's in the bin directory runs a program stored in the bin directory, as shown in the output from the `ls` command. The commands are binary files. To see the file type, enter:

file /bin/ls
`/bin/ls: ELF 32-bit LSB executable, Intel 80386 version...`

This is an executable file. If you tried to display it on the screen with something like `cat /bin/ls`, the output would be garbage.

You can run this program by typing `ls` at any command line. You don't need to use the path because the program is on the system path. When you type any command at the command line, Linux searches the system path and executes the first program it finds that matches the command you typed. You can see the system path by typing:

echo $PATH
`/usr/kerberos/bin:/usr/local/bin:/usr/bin:/bin:/usr/X11R6/bin:/home/janet/bin`

The system path is a series of directory paths, separated by colons (:). Notice that the directories are named bin, which stands for binary. The name is not required, just customary. Different distributions use different paths. This is the path for a Fedora user account. The root account has a different path, including directories containing system administration commands. The following is the path for a SuSE user account:

`/home/janet/bin:/usr/local/bin:/usr/bin:/usr/X11R6/bin:/bin:/usr/games:opt/gnome/bin:/opt/kde3/bin:/usr/lib/java/gre/bin`

You can add commands to your Linux system by copying a program into any directory on the system path. You can add commands you write and compile yourself or commands you download from the Internet. It's customary to put commands added by the user into /usr/local/bin or /usr/bin. SuSE provides a default bin directory in the home directory that can be used for commands you want to run yourself or perhaps permit only to a few other accounts.

Linux commands can be saved in a file called a shell script. When the script runs, it executes the commands, one by one. Shell scripts can also include control statements, such as if statements and loops. Writing shell scripts is discussed in Chapter 19.

Applications

Applications are programs. Most of the applications you use for your work are large, complex applications like word processors, spreadsheets, or databases. Many applications are installed when your system is installed. You can install a new application when you need it. Installing applications is discussed later in this chapter.

Different Linux distributions include different software, hundreds or thousands of applications. The distribution defines a default set of software to install. You can modify the set during installation, installing more, fewer, or different applications.

Most distributions install a set of common applications. The Linux commands are installed. Utilities for administering your system are installed. A desktop is usually installed. Certain types of applications are installed, although different distributions may select different specific applications. For instance, all applications will install a text editor, but might install different text editors. Most distributions include a word processor, usually OpenOffice, and a graphics application, usually Gimp.

An application is a program, or group of programs, so it's started by typing a program name. When you click a menu item or an icon to start an application, the program name is sent to Linux. For instance, when you click OpenOffice Writer on the menu, oowriter, the name of the program, is sent to Linux.

You can add or remove applications on the main menu. Right-click the main menu icon and select Menu Editor. The window on the right displays, with the current menu in the left pane.

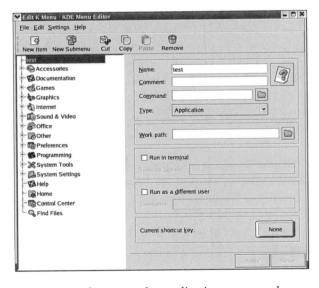

To add an application, highlight the location where you want the new item and click New Item. In the Command field, type the path/program name or browse to the program that is to run when this menu item is selected. You can select an icon by clicking the ? button on the right. If you want a desktop icon that starts the application, you can drag the newly added menu item onto the desktop.

Managing Application Software

At some point in your Linux use, you are likely to need to add to or update the application software on your system. You may not have installed all the software needed during installation. Or a new version of your current software may be released with new features that you really need. Or you want to perform a task that your current software can't seem to handle and you have located, by googling and/or consulting with peers, a package that you believe can handle the new task.

Application software is available in packages that provide the application program and any files and programs that are needed to install it. Applications can be installed from source code or from package files created specifically for Linux installation.

- **RPM files:** Files created to use with the RPM (Red Hat Package Manager) utility that installs, updates, and removes software. If it's possible to install from an RPM, it's preferable to do so. It's much easier than installing from source.

- **Source code:** Text files containing source code. You compile and install the software yourself. Sometimes it's necessary to install from source, either because no RPM exists for the software you're installing or because you need to install the software with a different configuration than the RPM provides.

NOTE
Debian developed DEB files, similar in function to RPM files. If you are using Debian, look into DEB files and the apt software that installs them.

You can install software from:

- **Installation CD:** Most distributions provide a utility that shows what's available on the CDs and installs a requested package. Only install from very recent CDs because packages are updated often. CDs may not contain current versions.

- **Distribution Web site:** The Web site for your Linux distribution provides many packages. Most distributions include utilities that check the Web site for available packages and download and install the packages.

- **Internet:** Some more specialized or unusual software may not be available on the distribution Web site. Or the version may not be the most recent. In this case, you may need to find the software on the Internet, download it, and install it. You may find it on a Web site that archives RPMs or on the Web site for the specific software, such as its project Web site.

Many software packages access and use other software; the package depends on the other packages being present. The packages needed are called "dependencies." The RPM utility and the desktop utilities inform you of any unmet dependencies when you are installing software, sometimes installing the needed software automatically.

Installing from the Distribution CDs

Most distributions include several CDs, containing many packages that can be installed. A default set of packages is installed during installation. You can modify the list of packages to install during installation. However, this process is not restrictive. You can install packages from the distribution CDs later if needed.

Most distributions include a GUI application for installing software from the CDs. In Fedora, open the main menu and select System->Install/Remove Packages to see the window in Figure 10-1.

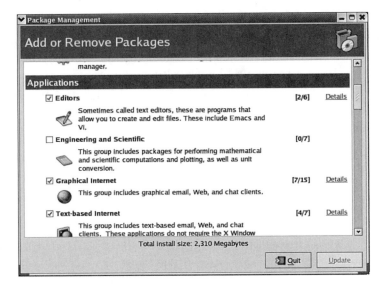

FIGURE 10-1   Package manager.

The screen in Figure 10-1 lists groups of packages that you can check to install. When a group is checked, the Details link provides a list of individual packages that can be checked for installation. Uncheck any currently checked packages to remove them.

When the package(s) you want to install are checked, click Update. A window will tell you how many packages are to be installed or removed and the disk space required. Click Continue. A progress bar monitors the update. You are prompted to insert CDs when needed.

Mandrake and SuSE have similar utilities. In Mandrake, access the Mandrake Control Center from main menu->System->Configuration->Configure your computer. Click the Software Management icon. In SuSE, use YaST to install software from the CDs.

Installing from the Distribution Web Site

Distribution specific RPMs are provided on most distribution Web sites. Most distributions provide utilities you can use to install software from the Web site. Fedora includes YUM, a command-line utility used to connect to the Red Hat Web site and to download and install packages. Fedora also includes Up2date, a utility that provides a graphical interface to YUM. Up2date is installed during Fedora installation and requires you to be registered with the Red Hat Web site.

Up2date requires a connection to the Internet. It provides an icon on your desktop panel, shown on the right, that notifies you of your update status. The blue icon with the check on it means that all the packages on your system are up-to-date. If the icon is red, with an exclamation point, there are updates available for your system. A tool tip with status information displays when you move the mouse pointer over the icon.

To use up2date, right-click the status icon. Select Launch Up2date. An information screen displays. When you click Forward, a screen displays that shows the channels you can update. One channel should be Fedora Core. Be sure that at least one channel is checked. Click Forward. A screen for selecting software that you don't want to update displays. By default, it exempts the kernel. You can add any other software you don't want to update.

Up2date connects to the Red Hat Web site and displays a list of available packages—packages that are not installed or that are newer than your currently installed packages. Check one or more that you want to install. Or you can check "Select All" to update all your packages. Up2date checks the dependencies for the packages you check to install and installs any needed packages. Up2date displays a message when it is finished installing packages.

SuSE installs and updates packages using YaST, the same YaST that is used to install packages from the distribution CDs. Open Main Menu. Select System->YaST. Click Online Update. YaST selects the closest Web site for packages for your update. You can select Configure Fully Automatic Update to have YaST find and install any updates automatically, daily, without your intervention.

Mandrake also provides updates from a Web site. Access the Mandrake Control Center from main menu->System->Configuration->Configure your computer. Click the Software Management icon. Click Updates. A screen displays the list of software available for installation, with descriptions.

Finding Packages on the Internet

You want to perform a task, but your current software doesn't seem to do it. After googling the Web and consulting with peers, you have the name of a package that you believe will do the job. It may be a new package or an updated version of your current software. First, determine that the package is not on your system. RPM gives you a list of all packages installed when you type:

```
rpm -qa | more
```

The list displays one page at a time. If the package is not installed, is not on your distribution CDs, and is not at the distribution Web site, you need to look for the package on the Internet. Most software has a home Web site where you can get information about the package and its dependencies and download the latest version.

Often, using the software name in a URL will find the package home site. For instance, the superuseful package may be found at www.superuseful.com or www.superuseful.org. If not, you can google to find the Web site.

The download format varies. For instance, the home Web site for MySQL, an open source database, provides download files in the following formats:

- **Binaries:** Compiled, ready-to-run files that just need to be copied to the correct location on your system. Often the binary distribution consists of more than one file, but the files are compressed into one file, called a tarball because it's created using the tar command.

- **RPMs:** RPMs for specific distributions may be available, particularly for popular distributions such as Fedora. Or, a generic RPM for Linux may be available. RPMs are installed using the RPM command-line tool, described later in this chapter. An RPM package has a filename that ends with .rpm.

- **Source code:** Source files that you download and compile on your system. Instructions for installing software from source code are provided later in this chapter. Source code consists of several files compressed into a single file, called a tarball.

Many packages are available in RPM repositories maintained on the Web. You can search for packages, check their dependencies, and download all the software needed in one stop. However, packages in repositories are generally a version or two behind the packages available on the home Web site. Some repositories are:

```
www.rpmfind.net
freshrpms.net
dries.studentenweb.org/apt/
```

Installing Packages Using RPM

RPM is a command-line utility that is included with almost all distributions. RPM maintains a database that keeps track of the packages and versions installed. If a package is not available on your distribution Web site, you can find and download it, described earlier in this chapter. After it's downloaded, you can use the rpm commands to install the software.

RPM filenames include the package name, the version, and the type of machine. For instance, a MySQL database server rpm could be named MySQL-server-4.1.7-0.i386.rpm. It's packaged for i386 machines, meaning almost any Intel or AMD computer. Download the package to the directory where RPMs are stored on your system. On Fedora, the directory is /RPMS.

To install an RPM, change to the directory where the RPM file is stored and type:

```
rpm -Uvh rpmfilename
```

For instance:

```
rpm -Uvh MySQL-server-4.1.7-0.i386.rpm
```

RPM will tell you if the package is already installed. It will check the dependencies before it installs and display an error message for any missing dependencies, such as:

```
Error: Failed dependencies:
dependencypackagename >= 5.3 needed by packagename
```

The message means the package (*packagename*) is dependent on *dependencypackagename*, version 5.3 or newer, being installed. You need to download and install the missing package before you install your new package.

Using the -U options installs or updates, whichever is appropriate. You can use an -i option for install only. The -v options results in informative output. The -h option results in a status report, a line of ###.

You can display information about packages by typing:

```
rpm -qi packagename          (for installed packages)
rpm -qip packagename         (for packages not installed)
```

You need to have root permissions to install packages.

Installing Packages from Source Code

Sometimes it's necessary to install a package from source code. Perhaps the package you need is only available in source code. Perhaps you need the package installed with a configuration that's not available as an RPM. You can download the source code, compile it on your own computer, and install it.

Instructions for installing are available on the package home Web site and included in the package. In general, the procedure for installing from source code is:

1. **Download the source code file.** Filenames are *packagename.version*.tar.gz. For example, the source code file for PHP could be named php-5.0.2.tar.gz. The directory /src or /local/src is often used to store source code.

2. **Unpack the tarball.**

   ```
   cd /local/src
   gunzip -c packagename.tar.gz | tar -xf -
   ```

   A new directory called *packagename* is created with several subdirectories. Change to the new directory (e.g., `cd packagename`).

3. **Read any installation notes.** Often you see files such as INSTALL.TXT.

4. **Set up the configuration files needed to compile.** Type:

   ```
   ./configure
   ```

   Often you use options with the configure command, as follows:

   ```
   ./configure -option -option
   ```

   The installation instructions will explain the available options. Lines are output as the configure procedure runs. This step may take several minutes. If there's a problem, an information error message displays.

5. **Compile the software.** Type:

   ```
   make
   ```

   You will see many lines of output. This step may take a few minutes. The executable files are created in this step.

6. **Install the software.** Type:

   ```
   make install
   ```

   This step copies the files into the proper locations.

Some packages require additional or unique steps. Be sure to read the available documentation.

Summary

Programs and applications on Linux are organized into files. Programs are files that contain instructions that Linux follows to perform tasks. Applications are one or more programs that perform work. A program can be quite simple or quite complicated, but the principle is the same. The program contains instructions that Linux follows.

You can write programs yourself or use programs and applications developed by others. Different Linux distributions include different software, hundreds or thousands of applications. The distribution defines a default set of software to install. You can modify the set during installation, installing more, fewer, or different applications. Or, you can download and install applications after Linux is installed to add new software or to update the software you're using.

This chapter explains:

- What programs are and how to run them

- How to use and add Linux commands

- The formats in which applications are available

- How to install applications from CDs and from the application Web site

- How to find application packages on the Internet

- How to use RPM

- How to install applications from source code

The next chapter discusses the most used application—word processing. OpenOffice, an office suite similar to Microsoft Office, is introduced. Instructions for creating and editing documents and using advanced word processing features are provided.

## CHAPTER 11

Word Processing

I think I can safely assume that you are acquainted with word processing. It's the most widely used application among computer users. Word processing is used to create documents as simple as a letter or as complex as a corporate report, a newsletter, or a legal document. The leading word processors are Microsoft Word and WordPerfect.

OpenOffice is an office suite, similar to Microsoft Office or WordPerfect Office. OpenOffice Writer is the word processor in OpenOffice. It has functionality equal to either of the leading word processors. It includes all the advanced features, such as spell checking, mail merge, storing graphics in the document, drawing in the document, and others.

Word processing applications store both the content of the document and the information needed for formatting the text. A word processing document file includes information about margins, text size, indents, font style and type, and many other things. Different word processing documents store the formatting information differently. Consequently, one word processing application can't open documents from another word processing program. However, most word processors provide features that allow the exchange of documents with major word processors. For instance, Word can convert WordPerfect files, and vice versa.

OpenOffice Writer can read Word files. In fact, it converts Word files more successfully than any other application. Word can't read OpenOffice Writer files in Writer format, but OpenOffice Writer can save documents in Word format, so that Word can open them. Writer also reads and writes documents in formats, such as HTML and RTF, that are general formats, allowing document exchange with other word processing applications. Read more about document formats in the section "Document File Formats."

Creating a Document

When you start OpenOffice Writer, the window shown in Figure 11-1 opens.

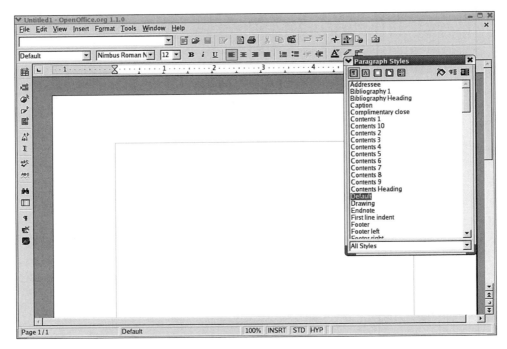

FIGURE 11-1   OpenOffice Writer.

It opens with a blank document, ready for you to enter content.

All documents are based on a template. The document in the figure opens with a blank template, installed with OpenOffice Writer. The blank template is used because no default template has been defined. Templates are discussed later in this chapter.

You can create a new document by clicking File and selecting New->Text document. The file will open with the default template you have created, or with the blank template if you have not yet created a default template.

If you want to open the document with a template you have created, other than the default template, click File and select New->Documents and Templates.

The box on the right of the window is called the Stylist. It's used to apply character, paragraph, page, and other types of styles. Styles are discussed later in this chapter.

Menus and Toolbars

The menu and toolbars at the top of the OpenOffice Writer window look very much like the Word menu and toolbars. The menu, however, does not include a Table item. Tables are inserted using the Insert menu item and formatted using the Format item.

Like Word, the top toolbar, called the function bar, provides actions, such as open, save, print, copy, and undo. Also like Word, the second toolbar, called the object bar, contains icons useful for the object currently selected. The default object toolbar contains icons for formatting text, such as font size, italics, bold, and color. If you select a table or a graphic, the object toolbar changes to provide more useful icons. The field on the left shows the URL to the document you are editing. You can type a URL directly into this box to open a file.

Unlike Word, another toolbar, called the main toolbar, displays down the left side of the window. It provides quick access to features such as insert, spell check, or finding files.

Writer provides fly-out toolbars. An arrow pointing down or right indicates a fly-out toolbar is available. To access the toolbar, long-click the icon (press the mouse button and hold it down). The top icon on the left tool  bar is the Insert button. Notice the arrow pointing to the right. Long-clicking the button opens the fly-out toolbar shown on the right. To select an item on a fly-out toolbar, slide the mouse pointer to the desired icon and release the button. You can tear-off the toolbar and move it elsewhere on the screen.

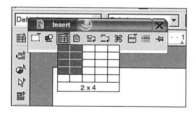 Notice that some of the icons on the fly-out toolbar have arrows, indicating that they too have fly-out toolbars. If you long-click the Table icon, the fly-out toolbar on the left opens that allows you to set the number of rows and columns in the table you are inserting.

Tool tips, on by default, display information about each button. You can get more information about each button by clicking Help and selecting Extended Tips.

All menus and toolbars are configurable. You can select toolbars to display and add, remove, or reorder buttons and menu items. You can create totally new toolbars.

Formatting

OpenOffice Writer has the same formatting options as Word:

- **Manual formatting:** Formatting by highlighting text or selecting paragraphs and clicking toolbar buttons. You also can format manually from the Format menu. You can format characters (font, size, color, etc.), paragraphs (indents, spacing, borders, etc.), or pages (margins, background, headers/footers, etc.). From the Format menu, you can also change columns and numbering. Manual formatting is useful for occasional formatting of small amounts of text. However, most formatting is better done using styles.

- **Styles:** Styles are collections of formatting that you can apply to a document component. In OpenOffice Writer, you can create page, paragraph, character, graphics, and numbered/bulleted list styles. Writer comes with many built-in styles that you can use as is or modify and use. For instance, Writer includes First Page, Left Page, and Right Page styles. Styles also can be shared with co-workers for company-wide standard documents. Creating and applying styles is discussed later in this chapter.

- **Templates:** Templates can be viewed as blueprints for documents. Templates store the styles for a specific type of document. For instance, you may want a memo to look very different than the annual report to the stockholders. You use templates to format the components of the document. Templates can be shared with co-workers. Creating and using templates is discussed later in this chapter.

Using styles and templates to format your documents requires some planning. However, the time saved by using styles more than equals the time spent developing and creating the styles. Styles and templates allow you to make a formatting change to an entire document easily. For instance, if you use a body paragraph style that specifies one font, you can change the font in the entire document just by changing the font for the body style. In addition, company-wide documents are very difficult to standardize. The use of shared templates and styles can make standardization much easier to attain.

If you need to change some manual formatting throughout a document, you can use Search and replace in the Edit menu to do so. To change format only, leave the text box empty, click Format, and select the format from the list. For instance, you can change underlined characters to italicized characters by selecting underline for the search text box and italics for the replace text box. However, if the text had been formatted with a character style, changing the format would be much simpler. You would just need to change underlined to italics in the style to change all instances in the document. You can also enter text and select a format in the search field, such as bold, and change them to different words, keeping the bold format.

Styles

OpenOffice Writer is installed with many built-in styles. To apply styles, use the Stylist—the list box shown in Figure 11-1—that provides the available styles, listed by type. The icons across the top of the Stylist select the type of style listed—paragraph, character, frame, page, and numbering. To apply a style from the Stylist, select the object to be formatted (e.g., click on a paragraph or page or highlight some characters), click the appropriate icon on the top of the Stylist, and double-click the desired style in the list. You can also apply styles using the drop-down list on the object toolbar, as you can in Word. The drop-down list contains the styles that currently are in use in the document.

To create or modify a style, click Format on the menu bar and select Style Catalog. The window in Figure 11-2 opens.

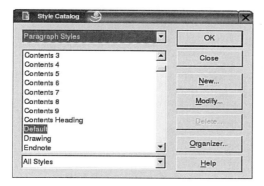

FIGURE 11-2   Styles window.

Because Default is currently selected, the settings for the default style are shown in the screen that opens when you press New or Modify. Different windows open, depending on the type of style you are modifying or creating. Modify makes changes to the selected style. New creates a new style with the settings of the current style. After you make the modifications you need, you give the new style a new name. After using modify, you have the same style with different settings. After using new, you have the same style with the old settings plus the new style with the new settings.

Clicking Organizer allows you to copy styles from one template to another. Templates are discussed later in this chapter.

Using Templates

A template is a blueprint for a document. A template contains the styles to be used in the document and text, graphics, and any other content you desire. For instance, a memo template can contain the spacing desired, the styles, and the memo headers so that the user only needs to fill in the specific information for the headers, such as the date and subject. In fact, a field can be included that automatically fills in the current date for the user. A monthly report template might include a table with titles so that only the table cells need to be filled in.

To create a document from a template, click File and select New->Templates and Documents. The window in Figure 11-3 opens.

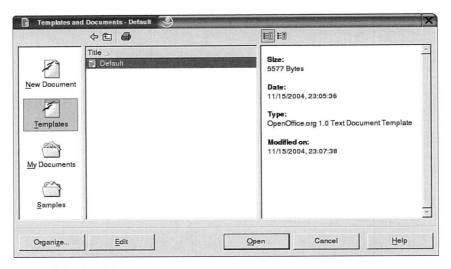

FIGURE 11-3 Template window.

Notice that the Templates icon is selected in the left pane. When the window first opens, a list of categories (folders) is shown in the middle pane. Double-click a category to see the templates. The figure shows the templates in the Default category. Highlight a template to see its properties or a preview in the right pane. The two buttons above the right pane switch between preview and properties. The figure shows the properties of the template named Default.

Double-click the template name to open a document based on the template. The default template is used to create a text document when you select New->Text Document. You can designate any template to be the default template, shown later in this chapter.

Creating Templates

To create a template, you just create a document with all the content you want, such as memo headers, footers, titles, company logo, etc., and all the styles you need. Then save the document as a template by clicking `File` and selecting `Templates->Save`. Every document that you create using the template is associated with the template; the template name is shown in the properties window (`File->Properties->General`) for the document. If you change a template style and then open a document that was created using the unchanged template, a dialog box informs you that the styles have changed, asking whether you want to change the document to match the current styles.

NOTE

If you save the template using `File->Save As->Template`, the documents created from the template aren't associated with it and aren't automatically updated when the template is changed.

To change a template, click `File` and select `Templates->Edit`.

Templates must be located in the template folders. To see where the templates are located, click `Tools` and select `Options`. Click the `Paths` tab to see a list of paths where files are located. Find the path to Templates. The path might look like the following:

`/opt/OpenOffice.org/share/templates/English;/home/janet/OpenOffice.org1.1/user/templates`

The template location above specifies two directories, separated by a semicolon. You can edit this path to store templates in a different or an additional location.

You can create a new folder by clicking `File` and selecting `Templates->Organize` to open the organizer. Highlight any folder in the left pane. Click `Commands` and select `New`. The new folder is named untitled. Type a new name and press `<Enter>`.

The default template is used when you create a new text document. You can edit the template file named Default or select a different template to be the default. To specify a template as the default, open the organizer and highlight the template that you want to be the default. (It must be located in the default template folder.) Click `Commands`. Select `Set as Default Template`.

A printer setting is included in a template. To define a printer, open the organizer, highlight the template, click `Commands`, and then click `Printer Settings`.

You can copy styles from one template to another. In the organizer, set both panes to Templates, using the drop-down menus below the panes. Double-click the template, and then click the `Styles` icon to see the styles. To move a style, drag a style from one template to a template in the other pane. Hold the `<Ctrl>` key while dragging to copy the style.

Editing Document Contents

The process of adding and editing document content is familiar to word processing users. Type text; delete text with <Backspace> or <Del>; replace text by highlighting it and typing new text over it; insert graphics, tables, symbols, files, and other objects using the Insert menu items. The Edit menu contains familiar items, such as copy, cut, paste, and find and replace.

OpenOffice Writer provides the Navigator, a tool useful for editing documents. To open the Navigator, click Edit. Select Navigator. The window on the right opens. A list of document components displays, with a plus sign (+) by those in the current document. Click + to see the elements in the document, such as the list of headings shown in the figure. Double-click an element in the list to jump to that location in your document. Or drag an element from the Navigator into your document to insert a copy of the element at the new location.

The top row of icons provides navigation. The second icon provides a fly-out toolbar where you can select the type of document object to find. Click and hold down the mouse button to see the toolbar shown on the left. The

Table icon is highlighted. The next two icons in the Navigator represent next and previous, referring to tables. The number box allows you to select which table to jump to. The remaining icons allow you to set characteristics of the Navigator, such as opening and closing the list box.

Navigator also serves as an outline of your document. When you have the Headings list open, you can move sections of your document around. The top two icons on the right of the toolbars move a highlighted section, such as Poodle, up one section or down one section. The bottom two icons change the outline level of a section either up or down (e.g., heading 3 up to heading 2).

You can undo a series of actions, as in Word. By default, you can undo 20 steps. You can change the number of steps allowed by clicking Tools and selecting Options. Click Memory. Change the number of steps. The more steps, the more memory used.

Autocorrection

As you enter or edit content, OpenOffice Writer assists you by changing text that it identifies as incorrect. You may find some or all of its actions annoying. You can change the settings to stop or modify the objectionable help. Click Tools and select Autocorrect. A window opens with the following tabs:

- **Options:** A list of corrections you can check and uncheck, such as "Capitalize the first letter of every sentence."

- **Replace:** A table of character strings and words or symbols that replace them when they occur. For instance, if you type hte, Writer changes it to the. You can add your favorite errors to the table. Just type the error and its correction in the top text boxes and click New. You can remove a correction by highlighting it and clicking Delete.

- **Exceptions:** Lists of exceptions for two of Writer's autocorrection features. The two features sometimes correct unfortunate errors, but other times create errors. You can turn the corrections completely off in the Options tab. Or, you can modify the corrections using the Exceptions tab.

  - **Uppercase first letter of sentence:** The end of the sentence is identified by the period. However, this can result in the first letter after an abbreviation being changed to uppercase, not what you want. Writer maintains a list of abbreviations. Letters after the abbreviations are not changed to uppercase. You can add abbreviations to this list. And remove them.

  - **Lowercase second letter.** When Writer sees the first two characters of a word in uppercase, it changes the second letter to lowercase, assuming that it's an error. Sometimes, the two uppercase letters are intended. Writer maintains a list of words that begin with two uppercase letters, such as CDs and PCs. The second letters are not changed to lowercase for these words. You can add words to this list. And remove them.

- **Word Completion:** A list of frequently used words. When you type three letters that match one of these words, Writer completes the word for you. You can disable the feature in the Word Completion tab. Or, you can add words to the list. Or remove words.

Spell Checking

OpenOffice Writer provides a spell checker and thesaurus, similar to Word. Both are found on the Tools menu. When the spellchecker finds an incorrect word, the window in Figure 11-4 opens.

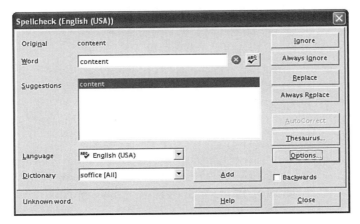

FIGURE 11-4   Spellcheck window.

You can replace the word or ignore it. You can look for a word in the thesaurus. You can add the word to the dictionary by clicking Add.

To change the settings for the spell checker, click Options. A list of options, such as "Check words with numbers" and "Check uppercase words," that you can check and uncheck displays.

Several dictionaries are installed with Writer, depending on the settings chosen during installation. You can add dictionaries for other languages. To add a dictionary, click File and select Autopilot. Choose Install new dictionaries. A list of available dictionaries displays. Select the language you want to display installation instructions. You can also create and use custom dictionaries.

OpenOffice provides custom dictionaries that you can edit. You can also create new custom dictionaries of your own. A custom dictionary is useful for project specific words that you don't want to add to your main dictionary. To edit or create dictionaries, click Tools and select Options. Click the + by Language Settings and select Writing Aids. The window in Figure 11-5 opens.

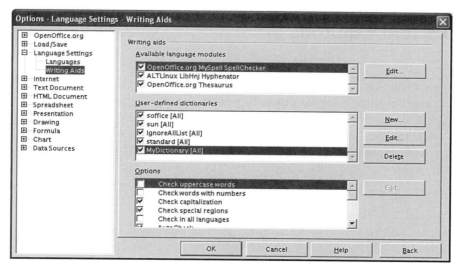

FIGURE 11-5 Edit dictionaries window.

The second list box contains the user-defined dictionaries. To create a new dictionary, click New. Type a name for the new dictionary when prompted. Put a check in the box by the new dictionary so that it's used in a spell check. At this point, it's empty.

To add words to a dictionary, highlight it and click Edit. A window opens with a list box showing the words currently in the dictionary. Type a word into the text box labeled Word and click New to add the word to the dictionary. You can delete words from the dictionary by highlighting a word and clicking Delete.

A spell checker doesn't find words that are used incorrectly, as long as they are spelled correctly. You may want to manually check certain words in your document that often get used incorrectly, such as you/your or to/two/too. You can cre-

ate an exception dictionary containing words that you want the spell checker to mark incorrect, even if they are spelled correctly. To do so, create a new dictionary as described previously. When the window above prompts for the dictionary name, check the "Exception" box. Any words added to this dictionary will be marked incorrect by the spell checker.

Tables and Columns

OpenOffice Writer does not have a separate menu item for tables. Tables are inserted from the Insert menu or from the Insert button (the top button) on the main toolbar (on the left side). When you select Table from the insert menu, a window opens where you can select the number of rows and columns and the borders. A default table style is applied. You can change the default table style by clicking Tools and selecting Options. Click Text document. Click Table. Change the settings and click OK.

Writer stores formats, collections of shading, colors, and borders that you can apply to a table. Click the Autoformat button to see a list of predefined table formats that you can select. You can add formats to your autoformat choices. With your cursor in the format-ted table, click Format and select Autoformat. Click Add. Type a name for the format when prompted.

You can convert text into a table. Highlight the text. Click Tools. Select Text->Table. You can convert a table to text, as well.

When your cursor is in a table, the Format menu includes items for formatting tables. If you select Tables, a window opens where you can set spacing and alignment, text flow, column widths, borders, and background colors. The menu also includes items for for-matting numbers, cells, columns, and rows.

Tables can be used to control page layout when paragraph styles prove insufficient. For instance, a sidehead layout, such as a resumé, can be formatted into table cells with the borders turned off. Tables can also be useful to position graphics on a page.

You can set up multiple column layouts on a page. The column layout is part of the page style. To set up the column layout, click Format and select Column. In the window that opens, you can set the number of columns, widths, separators, and space between columns. The settings apply to the entire page and to all pages with the same page style. If you want different pages with different column layouts, you need to define different page styles.

To have different column layouts on the same page, you must use sections. Insert a sec-tion from the Insert menu. A window allows you to format the section in columns. You can also format the section spacing, background, and footnotes.

Frames

Frames are boxes into which you can type text or insert graphics or sound files. Frames can be moved and formatted. A frame can be anchored to a page, a paragraph, or a character. When the page/paragraph/character moves, the anchored frame moves with it, with the same orientation, bringing its contents along. A frame can also be treated like a character. Frames are useful for laying out your document pages.

To insert a frame, click Insert and select Frames. The window in Figure 11-6 opens.

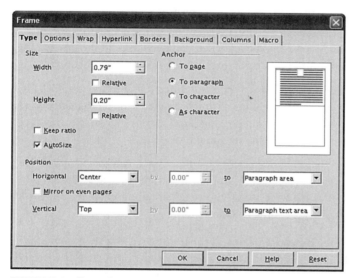

FIGURE 11-6   Frame formatting window.

The window in Figure 11-6 shows many options for formatting the frame. In the Type tab, set the width and height. By default, it's anchored to a paragraph. The horizontal and vertical positions are set relative to the anchor object, e.g., paragraph.

You can change the formatting at any time. Select the frame by clicking its border, displaying the frame handles. Drag the frame around to move it or drag the handles in or out to resize it. The Frame toolbar contains icons to arrange and align the frame. Or, click Format and select Frames to see the window in Figure 11-6.

You can link text frames together so that the content of one frame flows into another frame. With the first frame selected, click the link icon on the toolbar, and then click the second frame. A line appears, showing the flow from one frame to the next.

Graphics in Documents

OpenOffice Writer provides two methods for adding graphics to your document. As in Word, you can add graphics by:

- **Inserting:** Inserting a graphic contained in another file.

- **Drawing:** Using Writer's built-in tools to draw directly in the document.

You can insert graphics from a file using two methods:

- **Embed:** Inserting the graphic into the document. When you embed the graphic, it's always part of the document. You don't need to be concerned with a separate graphics file. Embedding is often preferred when you need to send the document to others. When you copy and paste a graphic, it is automatically embedded.

- **Link:** The graphic is not included inside the file. Rather, a link to the graphics file is included in the document. The document is much smaller without the embedded graphic. In addition, when the graphic file is updated, the graphic in the document is also updated. No need to reinsert the new graphic.

You can insert a graphic directly into a document or into a frame. A frame is useful for keeping the graphic and its caption together. A graphic or a frame can be anchored to a page location, a paragraph, or a character. When the page/paragraph/character moves, the graphic/frame moves with it, with the same orientation.

If you want to put your graphic into a frame, insert the frame first, and then insert the graphic inside the frame. To insert a graphic into a document or frame, click Insert and select Graphics->From File. A window opens where you can browse to the graphic file. To link the graphic, rather than embed it, check the Link box at the bottom of the window. A Preview box is also available to be checked.

To add a caption to a graphic, select the graphic, click Insert, and select Caption. The screen to the right appears. Select a Category or type a new one (e.g., Figure). Type the caption text. A caption preview appears at the top. The number is added automatically. The graphic is put into a frame when a caption is added, which keeps the caption and graphic together when they move.

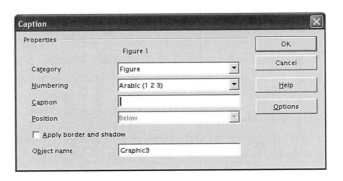

You can change the graphic in several ways. When it's selected, drag it around to move it or drag its handles in or out to resize it. Right-click to see options for changing the alignment, to put the graphic behind text, to change its anchor, or to allow text to wrap around it. Or select Graphics from the right-click menu to see a window with many options, similar to the window in Figure 11-6.

You can create a drawing directly on a page or in a frame. The drawing tools are provided on a fly-out toolbar, shown on the right, opened by long-clicking the main menu draw icon, shown on the left. Click the shape you want to draw. The cursor changes shape. Click a location in the document and drag the mouse to draw the shape. Each shape is an individual figure, but several figures can be grouped to create a fairly complicated drawing. You can also add text to the drawing with the text tool on the Draw toolbar.

When a drawing is selected, the object toolbar provides icons for drawing features, as shown in Figure 11-7.

FIGURE 11-7 Drawing object toolbar.

You can change the style (arrowheads, dashes, etc.), the width, and the color of the lines. You can set a color that will fill in the shapes, such as circles. You can change the anchor for the drawing, such as page, paragraph, or character.

Shapes have one handle larger than the others. When the mouse pointer is moved over the large handle, it changes into a hand. When the hand drags the handle, the corners of a rectangle are rounded.

You can select more than one figure at once. Select one drawing. Then, Shift-click one or more additional drawings. The handles will change to bracket all the selected figures.

You can align figures vertically or horizontally. Select all the figures to be aligned. Click the icon on the far right on the object toolbar. A menu of alignment options displays. You can align the top, bottom, or middle of the figures.

You can group figures together, so they move together. Select the drawings to be grouped. Right-click the selected drawings and select Group->Group. If you select a group of figures and right-click, you can select Ungroup, which breaks the group back into individual figures, or Edit, which allows you to change an individual figure in the group without breaking the group apart.

The Gallery

OpenOffice Writer provides a gallery to organize your graphic and sound files. Writer includes several objects in the gallery and you can add files to it. To access the gallery, Click Tools and select Gallery. The gallery opens at the top of your document, between the toolbars, as shown in Figure 11-8.

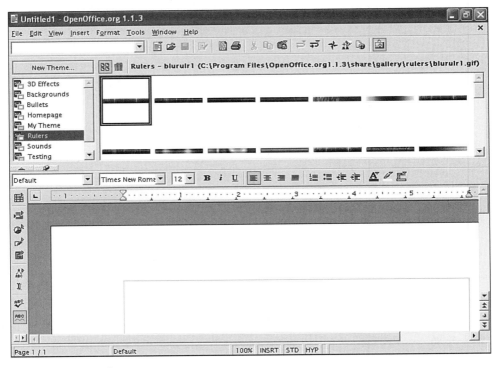

FIGURE 11-8 The gallery.

When you select a theme, the graphics are shown in the right pane. You can select any object and drag it into your document.

Graphic files can be added to the gallery without being moved into the Gallery directory. To add graphics to the gallery, click New Theme or highlight a listed theme, right-click, and select Properties. Click Find Files to locate the directory that contains the graphic you want to add. When you select a directory, all the graphic files in the directory are shown in the list box. Highlight the filename and click Add. Or, click Add All.

Two buttons at the top of the gallery, to the right of the New Theme button, allow you to switch the gallery display between icons, as shown, or a listing that includes the path to the file of the gallery object.

Document File Formats

OpenOffice Writer uses XML to store its documents. XML is a widely used, standard format for storing information in an application-independent format. An OpenOffice Writer document is stored in a file with an .sxw extension. The file, however, is not a single file; it is a zip archive containing several files required for managing an XML document. An .sxw file cannot be opened in another word processor.

You can save your document as other types of files:

- **Microsoft Word:** All versions of Word back to Word 6.0, with a .doc extension.

- **RTF:** A format that most word processing applications understand, used for transferring programs between applications. If you are unsure what application might need to open the document, you can use RTF. The file is saved with an .rtf extension.

- **StarOffice:** Word processing application published by Sun. OpenOffice evolved from StarOffice. File is saved with an .sdw extension.

- **Text:** File that contains only the content, without any formatting. File is given a .txt extension.

- **HTML:** Document is saved as a file containing HTML code, with a .html extension.

If you routinely exchange documents with Word users, you can set Writer to save documents in Word format by default. Click Tools. Select Options. Click the plus sign (+) by Load/Save. Click General. In the Always save as drop-down list, select the file format you prefer.

Writer can read files formatted as Word documents. When you open the file, Writer recognizes it as a Word document and opens it correctly. Although Writer can open the document, some advanced or complex elements may not be converted correctly. The simpler a document is, the more likely it is to convert without problem. Some elements that may be converted incorrectly and require manual correction are AutoShapes, revision marks, OLE objects, form fields, indexes, tables, frames, multicolumn formatting, hyperlinks, bookmarks, Microsoft WordArt graphics, and animated characters/text.

You can save your documents in PDF format. Click File. Select Export as PDF.

Tracking Changes

If one or more people are working with you to produce a document, you can mark all the changes you make in the document so your collaborator(s) can see what you have done. You can also add notes and comments to the document.

To mark changes, click Edit and select Changes->Record. Record starts marking changes, but whether you see the revision marks depends on whether Show is checked. Click Edit and select Changes->Show to toggle show on or off.

You can change the way revisions are marked. Click Tools. Select Options. Click the plus sign (+) beside Text Documents. Click Changes. The window in Figure 11-9 opens.

FIGURE 11-9   Changes options.

You can change the way insertions or deletions are marked. Notice that Color is By author. This means that each author's revisions are marked in a different color.

You can add notes and/or comments. A comment is associated with a specific revision; a note is added anywhere in the document. To add a comment, click on a revision mark, click Edit, and select Changes->Comment. A window opens where you can type a comment. Click OK. The comment displays in a tool tip when the mouse pointer moves over the revision mark.

To add a note, click in any text in the document. Click Insert. Select Note. Type the note. Click Author if desired. Click OK. The location of the note is marked in yellow. If you move the mouse pointer over the yellow marker, the note appears in a tool tip.

Changes can be accepted or rejected. When a change is accepted, the revision mark is removed from the document, and the change history can no longer be recovered. When a change is rejected, it's removed from the document. That is, inserted text is removed or removed text is put back in. Click Edit. Select Changes->Accept or Reject. The window in Figure 11-10 opens.

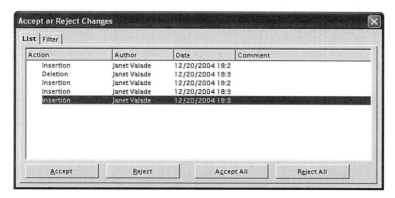

FIGURE 11-10   Accept or Reject Changes window.

You can accept or reject a single change or all changes at once. Click the Filters tab to display only specific changes, such as changes by an author or changes by date.

To stop recording changes, toggle record by selecting Edit->Changes->Record again.

You can merge two documents into one document, with the changes from both documents marked in the merged document. Click Edit and select Changes->Merge Document. Select the document to merge. The changes in the selected document are merged into the current open document. You can merge additional documents if needed. Select Changes->Merge Document and select a document as many times as necessary, until all documents, with their changes, are merged into the current document.

If you have two documents that are two versions of the same content saved without tracking the changes, you can compare the documents to find the changes between the documents. Click Edit and select Compare Document. Select a document to compare to the current document. The window in Figure 11-10 opens, showing all inserts and deletions. In addition, the revision marks are added to the current document, showing insertions and deletions. The open document now looks as if it were edited with track changes on to produce the document it was compared to. The changes can now be accepted or rejected individually or all at once.

Summary

OpenOffice is an office suite, similar to Microsoft Office or WordPerfect Office. The word processing application in the suite is called Writer. It's possible to exchange documents between Writer and Microsoft Word. Writer can read Word files. Word can't read Writer files, but Writer can write files in Word format. The exchange is not necessarily perfect. Sometimes information is not interpreted correctly. But most file content is converted successfully. The simpler the document, the more likely it is to convert successfully.

Writer is very similar to Word. People familiar with Word will feel at home in Writer. However, not everything is exactly the same. Writer has almost all the functionality of Word, but the features are not always found at the same location or activated in exactly the same manner. This chapter explains how to use the following features in Writer:

- Styles
- Templates
- Autocorrection
- Spell checking
- Tables
- Columns
- Frames
- Graphics
- Tracking changes

Another popular application in the OpenOffice Suite is the spreadsheet application. OpenOffice Calc is described in Chapter 12.

Spreadsheets

Spreadsheet applications are widely used. Spreadsheets organize data into rows and columns. You can enter numbers into the spreadsheet and perform mathematical operations on them, simple operations or very complication operations. Spreadsheets facilitate analysis and "what if" questions. You can also enter text data—column or row labels, comments, notes, etc. Spreadsheets can be simple or extremely complex.

Calc is the spreadsheet application in OpenOffice. It has functionality equal to Microsoft Excel, the leading spreadsheet application. It includes all the advanced features, such as functions, charts, storing graphics in the document, drawing in the document, and others.

Spreadsheet applications store both the content of the spreadsheet and the information needed for formatting it. A spreadsheet file includes information about margins, text size, indents, font style and type, colors, and many other things. Different spreadsheet files store the formatting information differently. Consequently, one spreadsheet application can't open files from another spreadsheet application. However, most spreadsheet applications provide features that allow the exchange of spreadsheets with major applications. For instance, Excel can convert Lotus, QuatroPro, and dBASE files.

OpenOffice Calc can read Excel files. Excel can't read OpenOffice Calc files in Calc format, but OpenOffice Calc can save documents in Excel format, so that Excel can open them. Calc also reads and writes documents in formats, such as HTML and SYLK, that are general formats, allowing the exchange of spreadsheets among applications. Read more about document formats in the section "Saving and Printing."

Creating a Spreadsheet

When you start OpenOffice Calc from the main menu (Office->OpenOffice Calc), the window shown in Figure 12-1 opens.

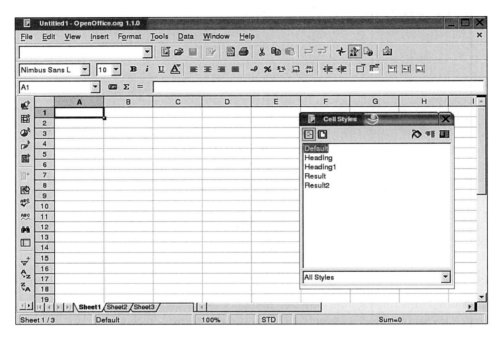

FIGURE 12-1   OpenOffice Calc.

It opens with a blank spreadsheet, ready for you to enter content.

You can create a new spreadsheet at any point in OpenOffice, when you are in Calc or when you are in Writer, by clicking File and selecting New->Spreadsheet.

Each spreadsheet is created with three pages, or sheets, named Sheet1, Sheet2, and Sheet3 by default. You can change the name of a sheet by right-clicking the tab for the sheet, at the bottom of the screen, and selecting Rename Sheet. You can add more sheets if three aren't enough. Click Insert and select Sheet.

The box on the right of the window is called the Stylist. It's used to apply cell and page styles. Styles are discussed later in this chapter.

Menus and Toolbars

The menu and toolbars at the top of the OpenOffice Calc window look very much like the Excel menu and toolbars. The menu bar offers the same choices as Excel.

Like Excel, the top toolbar, called the function bar, provides actions, such as open, save, print, copy, and undo. The field on the left shows the URL to the spreadsheet currently open. You can type a URL directly into this box to open a file.

Also like Excel, the second toolbar, called the object bar, contains icons useful for the object currently selected. The default object toolbar contains icons for formatting cells, such as font size, color, and number formats. If you select a different object, such as a graphic, the object toolbar changes to provide more useful icons. The third toolbar provides a place to enter formulas, also similar to Excel.

Unlike Excel, another toolbar, called the main toolbar, displays down the left side of the window. It provides quick access to features such as insert, spell check, or sorting.

Calc provides fly-out toolbars. An arrow pointing down or right on an icon indicates a fly-out toolbar is available. To access the toolbar, long-click the icon (press the mouse button and hold it down). The second icon on the main toolbar is the Insert Cell button. Notice the arrow pointing to the right. Long-clicking the button opens the fly-out toolbar shown on the right. To select an item on a fly-out toolbar, slide the mouse to the desired icon and release the button. You can tear-off the toolbar and move it anywhere on the screen.

Tool tips, on by default, display information about each button. You can get more information about each button by clicking Help and selecting Extended Tips.

All menus and toolbars are configurable. You can select toolbars to display in the View menu. Select Toolbars and click a toolbar name to display or remove a toolbar. You can add, remove, or reorganize items on the toolbars. Click View and select Toolbars-> Customize.

Formatting Cells

OpenOffice Calc has two formatting options:

- **Manual formatting:** Formatting by highlighting cells, columns, or rows and clicking toolbar buttons. You also can format manually from the Format menu. You can format cells (font, size, color, number format) or pages (margins, background, headers/footers, etc.).

- **Styles:** Styles are collections of formatting that you can apply to one or more component of your spreadsheet. In Calc, you can create cell or page styles. Calc comes with built-in styles that you can use as is or modify and use. Creating and applying styles is discussed later in this chapter.

Styles allow you to make a formatting change to an entire spreadsheet easily. For instance, if you use a default cell style that specifies one font, you can change the font in the entire spreadsheet just by changing the font for the default style. Styles also can be shared with co-workers for company-wide standard spreadsheets.

First, select the cells to be formatted. You can select a single cell by clicking it, a row or a column by clicking the letter or number, or any rectangular section of cells by dragging the mouse across the cells.

To format from the Format menu, select Cells to see the window in Figure 12-2, which allows you to set many formatting options—number format, alignment, borders, etc.

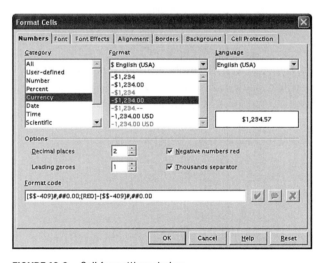

FIGURE 12-2   Cell formatting window.

You can format the height of rows and width of columns with the mouse. Move the mouse pointer over the line between two letters or two numbers. The pointer turns into a line. Drag the line to make the row or column larger or smaller. You can also format width and height from the Format menu. Select Column to set the column width or Row to select the row height.

Quick manual formatting is available from the object toolbar. You can set the font and size with the drop-down lists. You can click icons for bold, italics, and underline, set colors for text and background, align the contents of the cell vertically and horizontally, and turn borders on and off. You can format numbers as currency or percentages and change the number of decimal places by clicking the icon repeatedly.

OpenOffice Calc is installed with some built-in styles. To apply styles, use the Stylist—the list box shown in Figure 12-1—that provides the available styles, listed by type. The two icons above the list box switch the list between cell and page styles. To apply a style from the Stylist, double-click the desired cell style in the list.

To create or modify a style, click Format on the menu bar and select Style Catalog. The Style Catalog window opens (shown in Figure 11-2), in which you can create or modify styles. When you press New or Modify, the window shown in Figure 12-2 opens, displaying the values for the currently selected style. Modify makes changes to the selected style. New creates a new style with the settings of the current style. After you make the modifications you need, you save the style with the changes, providing a new name if it's a new style. After using modify, you have the same style with different settings. After using new, you have the same style with the old settings plus the new style with the new settings.

You can apply conditional formatting to cells. Click Format and select Conditional Formatting. You can apply styles to cells based on the values in the cell. For instance, you can direct Calc to apply style "large" to cells when the value is higher than 100.

Stored formats—collections of shading, colors, and borders—are available for you to apply to the highlighted section of your spreadsheet. You can highlight the complete spreadsheet. Click the Autoformat button to see a list of predefined formats that you can select. You can add formats to your Autoformat choices, but you must add them using OpenOffice Writer. See the Tables and Columns section of Chapter 11.

You can combine two or more cells into one cell. Select the cells you want to combine. Click Format. Select Merge Cells->Define.

Formatting Pages

You can format a spreadsheet page from the Format menu. Select Page to see the window in Figure 12-3.

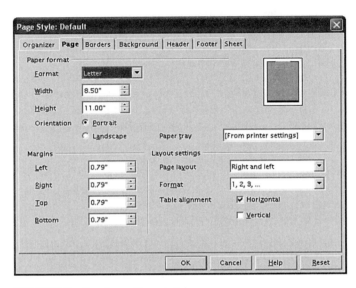

FIGURE 12-3 Page formatting window.

From this window, you can set page size, orientation, margins, background, borders, and more. To set a header, click the Header tab. A window allows you to turn the header on and set margins and spacing. The More button allows you to set borders and background for the header. Click the Edit button to add the content to the header. Type the content and/or use buttons to add the filename, page numbers, date, and time.

You can create and use page styles in the same way you create and use cell styles, described in the previous section. You can apply the page format using the Stylist. You can create or modify a page style from the Format menu, selecting Style Catalog, selecting Page styles from the drop-down list above the list box, and clicking New or Modify.

Editing the Spreadsheet Content

The process of adding and editing spreadsheet content are familiar. Type numbers, text, or formulas into cells; delete cell contents with <Backspace> or <Del>; replace text by highlighting it and typing new text over it. The Edit menu contains familiar items, such as copy, cut, paste, and find and replace. You can insert a row or a column by right-clicking a number or letter. You can insert cells by right-clicking a cell.

Calc provides an automatic fill feature. When you select a cell, the lower-right corner shows a small box. If you drag the box over some cells, the contents of the cell are inserted into all the cells highlighted. If the box contains a number or a month, the value is incremented in each cell.

You can split your window, either vertically or horizontally, so you can edit two parts of the spreadsheet at once. Highlight any cell (except A1) in row 1 to split vertically or in column A to split horizontally. Click View. Select Split Window. The window splits at the selected cell. You can drag the window separator to resize the windows. To return to a single window, select View->Split Window again.

You can make any section of rows or columns non-scrolling to keep the labels on the screen. Select a cell below the row that you don't want to scroll and to the right of the column you don't want to scroll. Click Window. Select Freeze. For instance, if you select cell B2, both row 1 and column A will stay on the screen when you scroll. If you select cell A2, only row 1 will stay on the screen.

OpenOffice provides the Navigator, a tool useful for moving around in the spreadsheet and moving elements of the spreadsheet to different locations. Use of the Navigator is described in Chapter 11, in the section "Editing Document Contents."

You can add graphics to a spreadsheet, just as you can to a document. Graphics can be inserted from another file or drawn directly into the spreadsheet using the OpenOffice drawing tools. Graphics in spreadsheets are handled the same as graphics in word processing documents, as described in Chapter 11.

You can create and edit charts in your spreadsheet. Highlight the cells you want to include in the chart. Click Insert. Select Chart. A wizard opens that allows you to select the type of chart (bar chart, pie chart, etc.), labels, and other features and creates the chart. When you select a chart in your spreadsheet, the main toolbar (on the left) changes to provide several buttons that change the appearance of the chart. For more changes, you can double-click any element in the chart to see an element-specific window that allows you to change the borders, colors, fonts, labels, transparency, etc.

Formulas and Functions

As in any other spreadsheet, Calc lets you enter formulas. Formulas can add (+), subtract (-), multiply (*), divide (/), or raise to a power (^n). They can also include greater than (>), less than (<), greater than or equal to (>=), less than or equal to (<=), or not equal to (<>).

To enter a formula, select a cell and type =. All formulas must begin with an equal sign. Type the formula following the =.

Many functions are available that assist in entering formulas. Functions accept a range of cells indicated by a colon (:), such as B2:B5, and a series of cells indicated by a semicolon (;), such as B2;B4;B8. For instance, you can add the cells B3, B4, and B5:

`=SUM(B3:B5)`

Sum is such a popular function that it has a button on the formula toolbar—the middle icon shown on the right. Select the cell where the sum should go and click the Sum icon. Calc will guess the range of cells to sum, selecting them with a blue box. You can change the range by dragging the corner handle of the blue box.

You can find the function you need by clicking the first icon shown on the toolbar above, before the Sum icon. The window in Figure 12-4 opens.

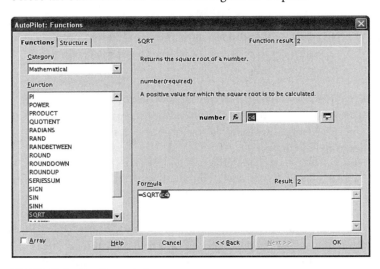

FIGURE 12-4 Functions window.

The functions are shown in the list box, by category. When you double-click a function, fields are available to enter the numbers or cell names needed.

Saving and Printing

OpenOffice Calc uses XML to store its documents. XML is a widely used, standard format for storing information in an application-independent format. An OpenOffice Calc spreadsheet is stored in a file with an .sxc extension. The file, however, is not a single file; it is a zip archive containing several files required for managing an XML document. An .sxc file cannot be opened in another Office application.

You can save your document as other types of files:

- **Microsoft Excel:** All versions of Excel back to Excel 5.0. All sheets are saved. (.xls extension)

- **StarCalc:** Spreadsheet application published by Sun. OpenOffice evolved from StarOffice. (.sdc extension)

- **dBASE:** Spreadsheet data is formatted as a dBASE file. (.dbf extension)

- **Data Interchange Format:** A format for exchanging files between spreadsheet applications. (.dif extension)

- **SYLK:** A text file format commonly used to exchange tabular, spreadsheet type data between spreadsheet applications. (.slk extension)

- **Text:** File that contains only the content, without any formatting. (.txt extension)

- **HTML:** File that contains HTML code (.html extension)

Calc can read Excel spreadsheets. Although Calc can open the document, some advanced or complex elements may not be converted correctly. The simpler a document is, the more likely it is to convert without problem.

You can turn on a view that shows where your pages break. Click View. Select Page Break Preview. The page breaks will start new pages when printed. You can insert manual page breaks from the Insert menu.

You can print part of your spreadsheet. Select the cells to print, click Format, and select Page Ranges->Define. You can print a row or column of labels on each page. Highlight the row or column to be repeated. Click Insert and select Names->Define. Type a name for the highlighted area and click Add. Select the name you just added to the list box, click More, and check "Repeat Column" or "Repeat Row."

You can prevent the printing of cells. Highlight the cells. Right-click a highlighted cell and select Format Cells. Click the Cell Protection tab. Check "Hide when printing."

You can save your documents in PDF format. Click File. Select Export as PDF.

Summary

Spreadsheet applications are widely used. Calc is the spreadsheet application in OpenOffice. It has functionality equal to Microsoft Excel, the leading spreadsheet application.

OpenOffice Calc uses XML to store its documents. XML is a widely used, standard format for storing information in an application-independent format. OpenOffice Calc can read Excel files. Excel can't read OpenOffice Calc files in Calc XML format, but OpenOffice Calc can save documents in Excel format, so that Excel can open them. Calc also reads and writes documents in formats, such as HTML and SYLK, that are general formats, allowing the exchange of spreadsheets among applications.

This chapter describes how to:

- Create a spreadsheet
- Format cells and pages
- Edit a spreadsheet
- Use formulas and functions
- Save and print spreadsheets

The next chapter discusses the use of graphics on Linux, including drawing, presentation graphics, and pictures. Drawing and presentation graphics are created using the OpenOffice applications Impress and Draw.

 CHAPTER 13

Graphics

L inux has graphics tools for the most common graphics needs:

- **Pictures:** Applications can create and edit graphic files containing digital images—pictures. You can create the pictures in the graphic application or you can edit a picture contained in another file. For instance, you can edit a picture taken with a digital camera or scanned by a scanner. On Linux, the most powerful, full-featured application for creating or editing pictures is the GIMP (GNU Image Manipulation Program). The GIMP offers similar functionality to Photoshop.

- **Diagrams:** Drawings comprised of shapes and lines connecting the shapes. Organizational charts and network diagrams are composed of shapes and lines. Dia is a diagramming program, similar to Visio.

- **Drawings:** Drawings are line art, usually just black and white. Cartoons and logos are commonly made with a drawing application. OpenOffice provides an application called Draw that allows you to create and edit drawings. You can draw directly in OpenOffice documents, as described in Chapter 11. Or, you can export drawings made using Draw in general graphics formats that can be used by other graphics applications.

- **Presentation Graphics:** Creating slides that accompany talks and presentations is a common use of graphics. OpenOffice provides the Impress application for creating slides, comparable to using PowerPoint in MS Office.

The source of your graphics can be original art or drawings that you create. It can also be photographs that you take yourself. If you are using art or photographs originated by someone else, you need to be sure you can legally use the picture. Pictures are copyrighted by default and can't be used without permission.

Archives of pictures are available on the Web. Some pictures need to be purchased; some are free. You need to read the information accompanying any pictures you wish to use. If explicit permission is not provided for public use, you need to get specific permission from the copyright owner.

Graphics File Formats

Graphics files contain information that describes images. An application must be able to interpret graphic formats in order to read or display a graphics file. A text editor or a word processing program can't correctly open a graphics file to produce a picture, although you can insert a graphics file into OpenOffice documents.

The information stored in a graphics file can be in one of several formats, with different purposes. Usually the file has an extension that identifies the type of format. Graphics applications save files with the appropriate extension. However, because Linux recognizes file types by information inside the file, rather than by the extension, when using a Linux application, you might see a message stating that the file extension does not match the file format. Some common formats are shown in Table 13-1.

TABLE 13-1   Graphics File Formats

Ext	Name	Used for	Advantages/Disadvantages
.bmp	MS Windows bitmap format	MS Windows graphics files	Recognized by most Windows applications.
.gif	**G**raphics **I**nterchange **F**ormat	Web page images: line drawings, cartoons	Better quality than .jpg for images with 256 or fewer colors. Used for animated graphics.
.jpg	**J**oint **P**hotographic Experts **G**roup	Most used type for Web page images: photographs, art	Better quality for photographs than .gif. Smaller file size than .png.
.png	**P**ortable **N**etwork **G**raphics	General graphic images; recognized by browsers	Newer format designed to replace .gif. A universal format with no patent restrictions. Smaller file size than .gif. Better transparency support. No animation support.
.tif	**T**agged-**I**mage **F**ile **F**ormat	Popular for graphics exchanged between operating systems	Early type that was designed to be hardware and OS independent. The newer .png format is better suited to exchange in many environments.

You can convert files from one format to another. You can read a file into an application and use Save as to save the file in a different format. If you want to convert quickly, without editing, use the convert command at the command line. For example, to convert an existing .gif file to a .jpg file, use:

```
convert rose.gif rose.jpg
```

Viewing Graphics Files

Images can only be displayed by applications that can interpret the information in a graphics file. The application must understand the specific format the graphic file is stored in. An application may understand .jpg files, but not .bmp files.

Konqueror can display most graphics formats. Konqueror can display thumbnails of the graphics files when it displays the files in a directory. Thumbnails are small versions of the image. To configure Konqueror to display thumbnails, click View and select Preview to see the submenu shown on the right. Select Show Previews. Check or uncheck the types of previews you want to see. For graphics thumbnails, check Pictures and Images.

With previews on, thumbnails of most graphics files display, but not all. For instance, thumbnails of .bmp files and .tif files are not shown. However, this doesn't mean that Konqueror can't render the graphics format. If you double-click the icon for a .bmp or .tif file, the image displays in the Konqueror window.

Graphics file extensions are associated with applications, as described in Chapter 9. To see which application is associated with a particular file type, highlight a file with the extension, right-click, and select Edit File Type. You can see, and change, the application that opens the file with the given extension.

Konqueror can interpret most graphics file types, but not all. For instance, Konqueror can't interpret .svg files, a graphics file type that uses XML. If you double-click an .svg file icon, it opens in the application associated with the .svg file type, usually sodipodi.

Scanning Documents

If you have a scanner, you can scan documents in Linux. You can scan two types of documents:

- **Images:** A document is scanned and stored in a graphics file format. The image must be viewed with software that can display graphics. The image is a picture of the document.

- **Text:** A document that contains text can be converted into a text document. Using a process called optical character recognition (OCR), the characters that are scanned are read as letters and stored in a text file. OCR doesn't get the characters 100% correct. Its accuracy depends on the quality of the document being scanned. However, if you need to edit a document, it's often faster to scan it and edit the OCR errors than to type the document from scratch.

Scanning on Linux is provided via Kooka, an open source raster image scan program that is an official part of the KDE Graphics Package. Kooka uses the SANE (Scanner Access Now Easy) library. Kooka provides OCR, as well as scanning documents in image format.

The SANE Web site allows you to search a database of scanners. You can enter a manufacturer and model to determine whether the scanner is supported (www.sane-project. org/cgi-bin/driver.pl). If possible, check for scanner support before purchasing a scanner.

If you want to use OCR on your scanned image, additional software is required. You may need to install it. Check your distribution software for a package called gocr. If you can't find it on your system or your installation CDs, you can install a package from jocr.sourceforge.net. See Chapter 10 for information on installing packages.

Start Kooka from the main menu, in the graphics or multimedia submenu, or select Run and type kooka. When Kooka starts, it scans your system for scanners and provides a list of scanners found. Select the scanner you want to use.

When Kooka is open, look at the bottom-left section for your scanner settings. What settings you can change depend on the scanner you are using. You can usually set color and resolution and often brightness and other options. You may have to experiment with settings to obtain the best scan. Higher resolution can improve the image, but can result in huge image files. The default is often 72 for a screen display, appropriate for Web images. However, if the document is text that you want to transcribe using OCR, choose a higher resolution.

Preview the picture first. Click Preview Scan when the document is in the scanner. When it's been scanned, click the Preview tab. In the image preview section, you can select a section of the picture to scan, rather than the whole picture. Select the section to scan with the mouse. Click ImageCanvas and select Create from selection. When you are satisfied with the preview, click Final Scan.

When the final scan is complete, a window (shown on the right) opens where you can select the graphics format for the image. A description of a format displays when you highlight a format from the list box.

If you check the "Don't ask again" box below the list box, Kooka will save all future images in the selected format. To change the format in the future, click Settings and select Configure Kooka->Save Image->Always show memory assistant.

Click OK when you have selected the desired format.

The final image displays in the right section of the Kooka window. Right-click the image to see some View options, such as Scale to width, Zoom, or Rotate Image.

You can click the Gallery tab to see a list of the images you have scanned. When you are ready to save a scanned image, right-click its name in the gallery and select Save Image.

If the image you scanned is a document that you want to transcribe using OCR, click ImageCanvas and select OCR image. A window that allows you to change some settings displays. Again, you may need to experiment to achieve the best results. You can start with the defaults. Click Start OCR. The process may take a little time. When it's finished, a window opens showing the output from the OCR process, with an editing window below. You can try different settings for more accurate results.

When you are satisfied with the OCR output, click Open in Kate. Kate is a KDE text editor, described in Chapter 18. Kate can be used to edit the file if necessary, including checking the file with the spell checker, useful for finding the OCR errors in the file. You can save the file from Kate as a text file. You can then open it in any text editor or word processor for further use or editing.

Presentation Graphics

You can use OpenOffice Impress to create presentation graphics, similar to PowerPoint in MS Office. Start Impress from the main menu with Office->Presentation or from Writer with File->New->Presentation. When you start Impress, an OpenOffice AutoPilot runs that asks questions. First, select whether you want to open an "Empty Presentation," open "from Template," or "Open Existing Presentation." If you check Empty Presentation for a new presentation and click Next, you are asked to select a background and an output medium. Select Original to use your own background.

Next, you are asked to select a slide transition from a drop-down list and a presentation type. Default means the presentation requires a key click to move from one slide to the next. Automatic means the presentation moves from one slide to the next automatically.

When you click Create, the screen in Figure 13-1 opens.

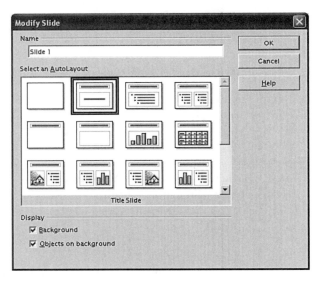

FIGURE 13-1   Impress layout screen.

The window provides layouts for the slide. If you want to create your own layout, select the first layout—the blank page. The layouts provide sections for slide components. For instance, the layout in the lower-left corner has a title across the top, a graphic section on the left and a bulleted list on the right. Select a layout. Click OK.

Figure 13-2 shows the Impress window. It's open with the lower-left layout selected from Figure 13-1.

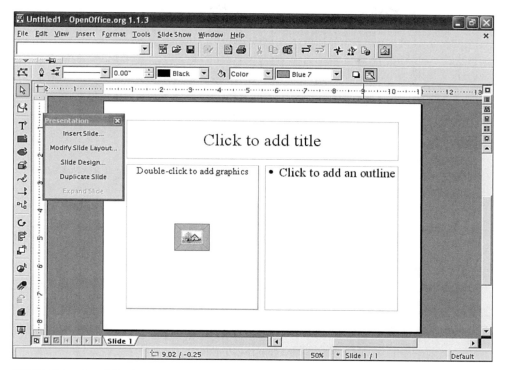

FIGURE 13-2 OpenOffice Impress.

The layout provides instructions for adding your contents—click to add text and double-click to add a graphic. Notice the small menu window. You can use this window to insert the next slide, to follow the current slide. Notice the tabs at the bottom showing which slide is open. A tab displays for each slide in the presentation.

If you selected the blank page layout, you can add your own content, placing it according to your own layout. The main toolbar (left) and the object toolbar provide drawing tools (described in the section "Drawing with OpenOffice Draw"). For instance, long-click the T icon (text) to see three choices for adding text—a horizontal text box, a vertical text box, and callouts. The Insert menu also provides objects you can add to your slide, such as spreadsheets, charts, and special fields (date, author, filename).

You can save your presentation as an Impress presentation, which has an .sxi extension, or as a PowerPoint format. You can also export your presentation to PDF, HTML code, Flash, or one of many graphics formats, such as .gif or .jpg.

Digital Cameras

Konqueror is the simplest way to move pictures from your camera to your computer. Konqueror uses a package called gphoto2, which is usually installed on your Linux system, to read pictures from your camera.

Linux provides support for many digital cameras. To see whether your camera is supported, open a terminal window and type:

```
gphoto2 --list-cameras
```

A long list of cameras displays (currently more than 400). If you don't find your camera listed, check the Web site (gphoto.sourceforge.net) for the most recent version. If a newer version is available, install it. Installing packages is discussed in Chapter 10.

To move your pictures, connect your USB digital camera to your computer. Instructions should be provided with your camera. On many Linux distributions, a camera icon appears on your desktop when you connect your camera. If you double-click the icon, you see your camera directories and can copy files to your hard disk.

If the camera icon doesn't appear, you can navigate to the pictures using Konqueror. Open Konqueror with the navigation panel open. If the navigation panel is not displayed, click Window and select Show Navigation Panel.

Type the following into the Location field:

```
camera:/
```

An icon for your digital camera appears in the main window. Click the icon to see the folders related to your camera. Navigate to your photo directories. Copy the picture files or drag and drop them into a folder in your navigation window on the left.

Screen Shots

You can use software to take a picture of the screen and store it in a graphics file. You can use Ksnapshot for this. From KDE, open Ksnapshot from the main menu in Graphics or Utilities. Ksnapshot may be on the GNOME main menu. If not, you can select Run from the main menu and type Ksnapshot. Ksnapshot opens with the window shown in Figure 13-3.

FIGURE 13-3   Ksnapshot window.

When Ksnapshot opens, it takes a picture of the screen, displaying the snapshot in the Current Snapshot section. The current snapshot in the figure shows a Linux desktop. You can print or save the snapshot. The snapshots are saved in .png format.

You can change the settings and take another snapshot. You can set a delay, so you have time to display some software on the screen that you want in the shot. You can set it to grab only the window containing the pointer, rather than the complete screen. When you have the settings changed, click New Snapshot. Ksnapshot closes its window. Click the window you want to take a picture of. Ksnapshot reopens with the new snapshot previewed.

If you're going to edit the screenshot, you can take a screenshot directly in GIMP. When GIMP is running, click File and select Acquire->Screen Shot. Check "Single Window" or "Whole Screen." Click OK. The screen image opens in GIMP, where you can edit and/or save it.

Diagramming with Dia

Dia is designed for diagramming, such as organizational charts or network diagrams. Dia creates graphic images with shapes and lines, similar to Visio. You insert shapes and connect them with lines.

Dia may be available on the main menu. In Fedora, it's available in the graphics submenu. If it's not on your system, you can download it from www.gnome.org/projects/dia. Installing packages is discussed in Chapter 10.

Start Dia from the main menu. A window in Figure 13-4 opens.

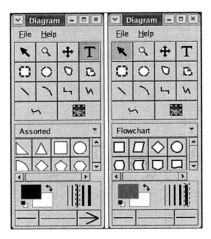

FIGURE 13-4   Dia toolbox window.

Figure 13-4 shows two different versions of Dia's open window. The top section of the windows is the same. The bottom section differs. The top section contains a basic set of tools for creating drawings. The second row contains basic shapes, such as rectangle and circle. The third row contains several styles of lines—straight, curved, jagged. The large T in the top row is a tool for inserting text. To its left is the move tool, used to move shapes around the drawing.

To create a drawing, click File and select New. The window in Figure 13-5 opens.

Insert shapes into your drawing. Click a shape from the window shown in Figure 13-4 and click this window. Drag the shape to move or resize it. Insert as many shapes as you need.

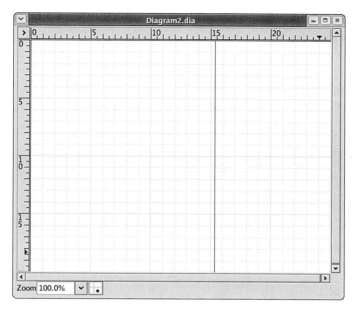

FIGURE 13-5   Dia Diagram window.

Connect the shapes with lines. Click a line in the Dia toolbox. Click one shape and then another shape to connect the shapes with the lines. If the line ends aren't connected to the shapes, drag a line end to a handle on the shape. The line end turns red when it locks into the shape handle.

Dia can align the shapes for you. Select the shapes to be aligned with shift-click. Right-click and select Object->the appropriate alignment (vertical or horizontal) choice.

The bottom section of the Dia toolbox allows you to select color and line styles. For instance, the left window in Figure 13-4 shows an arrowhead added to the line on the bottom-right button. Click any of the buttons or line displays to select a different style.

Above the color and line settings section, the shapes libraries display. The Assorted library is shown in the window on the left (Figure 13-4). Triangles, pentagons, and other shapes are available. In the window on the right, the Flowchart library is open. Shapes available for creating flow charts are shown. The drop-down list allows you to select one of several libraries. In addition, you can create and add your own library of shapes.

Save the diagram in Dia format. Only documents in Dia format can be edited at a later time. Dia format is XML. If you need the diagram in a general graphics format, for instance to use in a Web page, you can export the diagram. Click File and select Export. If you don't know what format you need, .png is a flexible choice.

Drawing with OpenOffice Draw

Start OpenOffice Draw from the main menu in the Office submenu. Or you can open a drawing from Writer by clicking File and selecting New->Drawing. An open drawing window is shown in Figure 13-6.

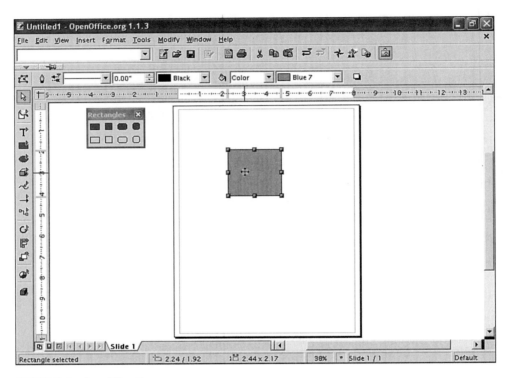

FIGURE 13-6 OpenOffice Draw.

When you create a new drawing, the page is blank. The object toolbar and the main toolbar (left) offer selections related to drawing. The object toolbar specifies black lines with blue filler, which can be changed by selecting from the drop-down list.

In the figure, a rectangle has been added to the drawing. The rectangle shape tool opens by long-clicking the fourth icon down on the main toolbar. The fly-out menu is torn off in the figure and moved closer to the drawing. The rectangle is selected, showing its handles. Drag the handles with the mouse to resize the rectangle. The cursor is inside the rectangle, but is a crosshair, rather than a pointer. The crosshair allows you to drag the rectangle anywhere on the drawing page. The left and the top of the window are numbered rulers. Markers move on the rulers to identify the location of the cursor. Currently, the markers show the cursor at 3,3.

The two shape buttons below the rectangle button allow you to add ovals and circles and 3D shapes. The large T icon adds a text box where you can insert text.

Below these buttons are buttons that allow you to add lines to the drawing. Long-clicking the first line button opens a fly-out menu with some line styles you can select, as shown on the right. More line choices are available on the object toolbar. Drop-down lists allow you to set the width and style of the lines, such as continuous, dashed, dotted, etc. You can select a style of arrowhead to add to either end of the line. Click the arrowhead button to the left of the line style drop-down list to see a fly-out menu, shown on the left.

When you have more than one shape on the drawing page, you can align them. Select all the shapes you want to align using shift-click. Long-click the align button on the main toolbar and select an alignment method from the fly-out toolbar shown to the right.

You can group shapes together, so that they move together when you drag them. Select all the shapes to group using shift-click. Right-click the shapes and select Group. The shapes are now a single group, moving as one. You can still edit a single shape in the group. Right-click the group and select Enter Group. You can now select one shape and change it, without ungrouping the shapes.

You can flip and rotate a shape or group of shapes. Right-click the shape to be rotated and select Flip. Select Vertically or Horizontally. To rotate, right-click the shape and select Position and Size. Click the Rotation tab to see the window to the right. You can select the axis around which to rotate. (The center is the default.)

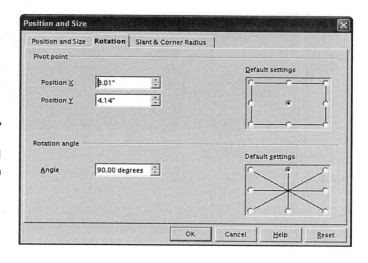

Then, select the degree of rotation, such as 90 degrees. Remember, you can undo any changes, so feel free to experiment.

You can save your drawing in one of several graphics formats. Click File and select Export to save as HTML, PDF, Flash, .bmp, .jpg, .png, and other formats.

Creating and Opening Images in the GIMP

You can start the GIMP from the main menu. When the GIMP starts, it opens the GIMP toolbox, discussed later in this chapter. No window for images opens until an image is created or opened, which opens a separate window. When you click File and select New or Open, an editing window opens. Figure 13-7 shows an open image.

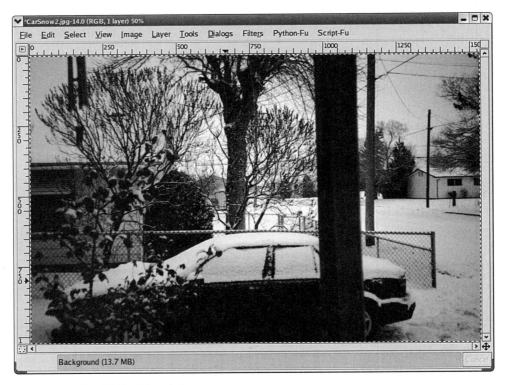

FIGURE 13-7 The GIMP editing window.

If you select New, the window opens with a blank page in the window. If you open another image, it opens in a new window, without closing the current window.

In the editing window, you can create or edit an image using the toolbox, which is still open in a separate window. The toolbox contains tools for the most common editing functions. You can also use the menu items in the editing window. You can perform many operations on the image, such as modify all or part of it, change its color, remove parts of the image, add figures to the image. You can also create many special effects, such as change it to sepia tones like an old photo, add fog, clothify the image, whirl it, and many other effects. It's wise to create a copy of an existing image before experimenting on it, although you can undo a series of steps to return the image to its original condition.

The GIMP Toolbox

When you start the GIMP, it opens the toolbox, shown on the right. The top section of the toolbox contains a set of tools, activated by clicking an icon. There are tools you can use to select a section of the image and tools that change the image. For instance, the first tool selects a rectangular section of the image. Other tools include a paintbrush, a pencil, an eraser, a tool that adds text to the image, tools that change colors, and more. In this image, the paintbrush is selected. When you click an icon, the mouse pointer changes into an associated shape. You then use the mouse to edit the image in the image window.

The left section below the tool icons is used to select colors you can use, in this case gray (foreground) and white (background). To change a color, double-click one of the colored squares.

The right section allows you to open a section for setting brush options, a section for setting patterns, or a section for selecting a gradient.

The bottom section of the toolbox displays options related to the tool chosen. In the figure, the paintbrush is chosen. The options in the lower box apply to the paintbrush, such as Opacity and Brush size. If you click the space by Brush, you can select different brush sizes. If the text tool were chosen, the bottom section would offer text options, such as font type and size.

The first button of the four bottom buttons sets the selected options to be the default. The second button restores the most recently saved defaults. The button on the right restores the defaults to the values set by the software developers.

Changing Image Size in GIMP

You can change image size in one of three ways:

- **Crop:** Keep part of an image and discard the rest.
- **Scale:** Change the size of an image, keeping all the content of the image. For instance, if you scale the image smaller, all parts of the image shrink to fit the new image size.
- **Resize:** Change the size of the window, while keeping the image the same size. This is generally used to make the window larger, thereby making room to add new elements to the image.

To crop an image, you select the section you want to keep and throw away the rest. Use a select tool from the toolbox to select the part of the image to keep. For instance, click the first tool to use the tool that selects a rectangular section of the image. Then, move your mouse to the image window. The mouse pointer now shows a rectangle beside the pointer, so you know which tool is active. Click and drag the mouse to enclose the image section that you want to keep. To remove the selection and select again, right-click and select Selection->None.

Click Image on the image window menu bar and select Crop to Selection. The image outside of your selection disappears. You can undo a crop to return the cropped part of the image.

To scale an image, click Image and select Scale Image. A dialog window opens that allows you to specify the width and height wanted for the new size. Or, in the ratio fields, you can specify the percentage to scale by, such as .60 (60%) or 1.5 (150%). By default, the ratio of width to height remains the same. If you want to change the shape of the image, click the link icon to the right of the ratio fields. It separates into two links. Then you can set the height and width independently.

To resize an image, click Image and select Canvas Size. A dialog window opens, similar to the scale image dialog window. You can set the width and height of the window. If you resize the window smaller, you can only see part of the image in the window. If you resize the window larger, extra space is added to the window where you can add elements to the image.

Removing Elements from an Image in GIMP

The simplest way to remove an element from the image is to use the eraser tool. However, erasing part of the image leaves an empty space where the element was removed. A better way to remove an element from an image may be to cover it up. You can select a section of the image and cover it with a plain color or a pattern using the bucket fill tool—the tipping paint can in the toolbox. The section is filled with a color from the foreground/background colors, whichever you select.

However, covering the element to be removed with a solid color is seldom the solution. In most cases, the element is on grass, water, snow, or other backgrounds. The element being removed needs to be covered by its background. For instance, in Figure 13-7, there's a telephone pole in the background, between the camera and a distant house with snow, a house, and the sky as its background. You can remove the telephone pole by covering the bottom section with the color of the snow, the middle section with the color of the house behind it, and the top part with the color of the sky.

The clone tool from the GIMP toolbox is useful for covering elements with their background. The clone tool copies a section of a picture from one place and adds it in a different place. Thus, you can copy a section of the background and place it over the element to be removed.

The clone tool icon in the toolbox looks like a rubber stamp. It's in the bottom row of the tool icons shown in the section, "The GIMP Toolbox," earlier in this chapter. When you click the clone tool button, the clone options display in the bottom section of the toolbox. The brush size determines the size of the section that is copied. Click Brush to select a different brush size.

To move a section of the image from one location to another, follow these steps:

1. Ctrl-click the section to serve as the source. A section matching the brush size is selected.

2. Move the mouse pointer to the element you want to cover up.

3. Click the new location. The source section replaces the target section. If you hold the click down and drag the mouse around, a corresponding section from the source area is copied to the target area.

With practice, any figure in an image can be removed by covering it up with the background behind it so that the replacement looks natural.

Adding Elements to an Image in the GIMP

Elements can be added directly into your image, using tools from the toolbox and items from the menu. However, it's usually a better idea to add a layer to your image and add elements on the new layer. Adding a layer is like adding a page to the image. The new layer doesn't affect the existing image; it just places a new layer on top of the existing image. You can then add elements on the new layer.

The new layer can be the size of the current image, smaller, or larger. Smaller layers are useful when you add small elements. For instance, you can add a bird to the sky by adding a bird size layer with the bird figure on it. You can drag the new layer around the image to position it. You can scale the image to match the size scale of the image. And, at any time, you can delete the new layer, deleting only the new elements, returning the image to its original condition.

To add a layer, click Layer and select New, which opens the window shown on the right. You can give the layer a meaningful name. Two fields allow you to enter the layer width and height. The default displays, which is the image size. You can type a width and/or height for the layer. The bottom section selects the fill for the new layer. It can be transparent, which means you can see the contents of the layer beneath it. Or, you can make the layer a solid color, either white or the foreground or background color shown in the GIMP toolbox. You can then add content to the new layer.

You can paste a figure from another image into the image. In the image being copied, click Edit and select Copy to copy the entire image or, if a section of the image is selected, to copy the selection. Move the mouse pointer to the image where you wish to add the figure and click Edit and select Paste. The copied section is added to the image as a floating selection, which can be moved. You can position the pasted figure and anchor it as part of the active layer. Or you can convert the floating image to a new layer. Click Layers and select either Anchor Layer or New Layer. Nothing else can be worked on until you set the floating selection.

When you save your image, save it as a GIMP file (.xcf extension) to save the layer information. If you save it in a different format, you may lose part of the file information. If you need a different format, save a copy. Before you save as a .gif or .jpg, you need to merge the layers. Click Layers and select Flatten Image to merge all layers into one. Be sure to save the image first in GIMP format, in case you need to change the image later. The .gif or .jpg image does not contain the layers information.

Working with Layers in the GIMP

Many images consist of a stack of two or more layers. An image is generally easier to manipulate when its elements are on different layers, allowing an individual element to be worked on without disturbing the other elements. A layer has four basic attributes:

- **Active/inactive:** You can only change the active layer.

- **Opacity:** An image is a stack of layers. Opacity is the degree to which you can see through a layer to the layer beneath it.

- **Visible:** A layer can be visible or invisible. You can't see an invisible layer at all. However, it's still there.

- **Position:** The location of the layer in the stack of layers—top, bottom, or somewhere in between.

To see layer information, click Dialogs and select Layers, which opens the window on the right. The dialog shows three layers in the image, with thumbnail images. Use this window to manipulate the attributes.

Highlight a layer to make it active (in this figure, the first layer). This does not mean you can see the layer. Other layers may be covering it up. However, in this figure, the active layer can be seen because it is on top.

The eye on the left means the layer is visible. If a layer is covering up the active layer, the toolbar tools affect the active layer, but you can't see what is happening. Click the eye to make the layer invisible, so you can see the active layer.

The box between the eye and the thumbnail is a link. When this box is clicked for two layers, they move together when moved with the move tool.

The background layer is the bottom image. It can't be moved. However, the two upper layers can. If you click the down arrow, the highlighted layer moves down one position. The up arrow moves it up one position.

The active layer can be acted upon by any of the toolbox tools. It can be moved using the move tool in the toolbox. It can be deleted. Any effects in the menus can be applied to it. Images can be pasted into it. It can be duplicated using the middle button on the bottom of the layers dialog.

Summary

Graphic images are stored in files in one of several graphic formats. The most common formats are .bmp (mainly used for Windows files), .gif, .jpg, .png (3 formats for Web images), and .tif (used for exchanging graphics files between operating systems). To view a graphic image on the screen, you must use an application that understands the specific graphics format. Konqueror can understand and display most graphic file formats.

Images are obtained from several sources. This chapter discusses how to obtain images from the following sources:

- **Scanner:** Describes scanning using the Kooka application

- **Digital camera:** Describes moving pictures from the camera to the computer using Konqueror

- **Screen shots:** Shows how to take screen shots using Ksnapshot or the GIMP

- **Create using an application:** You can create your own images. Or you may need to edit existing images. This chapter describes how to create and edit three types of graphics using applications that are installed on almost all Linux distributions:

  - **Drawings:** Describes how to create and edit drawings using OpenOffice Draw

  - **Presentation Graphics:** Describes how to create and edit slide shows using OpenOffice Impress

  - **Pictures:** Describes how to create and edit images using the GIMP

CHAPTER 14

Printing

Printing on Linux, as on Windows, requires a printer driver that is specific to the printer connected to your computer. The printer driver sends the information from the computer to the printer in the format that particular printer understands. Therefore, Linux needs to know the manufacturer and model of the printer, so that the correct printer drivers are used.

A printer can be connected directly to your computer. If your computer is connected to a LAN (local area network), you can send files to a printer that is connected to another computer on the LAN or connected directly to the LAN. You specify the type of connection when you install the printer.

Files sent to the printer are sent to a queue that is associated with the printer. The print job waits in the queue until its turn to print. You can create more than one queue to a printer, although you are unlikely to need to. If a printer is a network printer, print jobs from more than one computer on the network can be sent to the same queue.

The software that handles printing for most Linux systems is called CUPS (Common UNIX Printing System). CUPS handles all the details from clicking the Print button on the application to passing the data to the printer in an understandable format. LPRng is another printing system available on most Linux systems, but it's rare that you would choose to use it rather than CUPS.

Installing Your Printer on Fedora

On Linux, files to be printed are first sent to a queue, where they await their turn to print on a specific printer. Before you can use your printer, you need to set up at least one queue for the printer. Most Linux distributions provide a utility with a GUI interface that makes it easy to set up your printer.

Before you start installing your printer, be sure it's connected to the computer and turned on, so that Linux can recognize it. You must use the root account.

On the Fedora main menu, select System Settings->Printing. The window in Figure 14-1 displays.

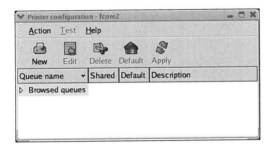

FIGURE 14-1   Printer configuration window.

When the configuration window opens, it displays any printers currently configured. In this figure, no printers are currently shown. Click New to start printer installation. In the print queue windows, you can click Forward to move to the next window or Back to return to a previous window.

1. An Add Print Queue window opens.

2. A window requests the name and description for the printer. Type a short name that you can remember. Add a description with more information if you have more than one print queue, so you can identify which is which.

3. A Queue Type window opens. Select the appropriate item from the "Select a queue type" drop-down list at the top. If your printer is connected to your computer, select Locally-connected. Other choices might be Networked Windows (the printer is connected to a Windows computer on the same network as your computer) or Networked CUPS (the printer is connected directly to the network, rather than to a specific computer).

   The list box shows the printer connections found of the type selected. For instance, if Locally-connected is chosen, you might see /dev/lp0.

4. The next windows allow you to select your printer manufacturer and model. Generic is selected by default. Click Generic to see a drop-down list of manufacturers. Select your manufacturer and a list of models is provided, as shown in Figure 14-2. Find and select your model.

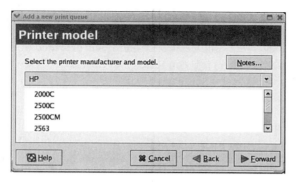

FIGURE 14-2   Printer model window.

5. In the next window, click Finish to create the new print queue.

6. You are asked whether you want to print a test page. It's best to click Yes. You are then asked whether the test page printed correctly. Wait until the page prints and click Yes or No. If you answer no, you are given information to help you determine and correct the problem, usually an incorrect manufacturer or model. If you answer yes, your new printer is added, as shown in Figure 14-3.

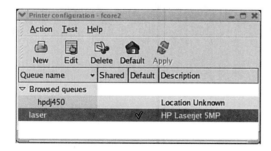

FIGURE 14-3   Installed printers.

Figure 14-3 shows two print queues available. The names and descriptions shown are the information typed in Step 2. Hpdj450 is a printer connected to a different computer on the same network. The printer was installed on the other computer. Laser is the default printer, meaning files are sent to this queue unless you specify the other queue. To set the default, highlight a print queue and click Default.

Installing Your Printer on Other Distributions

Most distributions have a utility, similar to the Fedora utility, that allows you to install a printer. You must use the root account to install a printer.

Mandrake provides a printer management utility called Printerdrake, provided in the Mandrake Control Center. Be sure your printer is connected and turned on. Open the main menu. Select `Configure your computer->Hardware->Printer`.

When the printer utility starts, it scans the hardware to detect any connected printers. If a printer is detected that hasn't been installed yet, it asks whether you want to install it now. If you say yes, the installation procedure runs. Mandrake may need to install software. For instance, it may need to update the CUPS software. You may be requested to insert a CD from the installation CDs.

When the utility window opens, it lists all the installed printers, as shown in Figure 14-4.

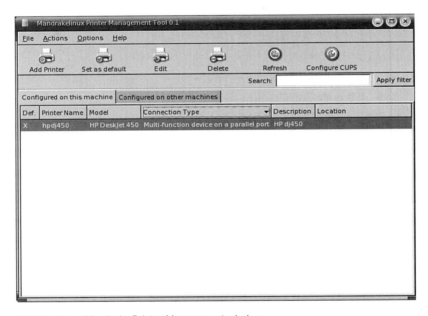

FIGURE 14-4 Mandrake Printer Management window.

From this window, you can add, edit, or delete a printer. Or set a printer as the default.

Printers on SuSE are installed using YaST. Click `Hardware`. Click `Printer`. The utility will autodetect a list of printers found. Select the printer to install and click `Configure`. If your printer was not detected, select `Other` and click `Configure` to start a manual configuration procedure for installing and testing the printer.

Printing

Most printing is done using the application that created the file. The Print button in the application sends the file to the default printer. When you press the Print button, you see a window that looks very much like the print window on Windows, where you can select a printer, pages to print, number of copies, and other options.

The KDE desktop provides kprinter, an application that prints files to printers or to PDF files. If you can't find it on the main menu, select Run and type kprinter. In the window that opens, click Expand to see the window in Figure 14-5.

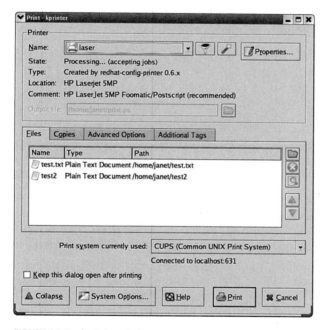

FIGURE 14-5   kprinter window.

In Name, you can select the printer. You can also select Print to File (PDF). The folder to the right of the list box allows you to browse for the files to print. Click tabs to select pages to print, number of copies, and schedule a time for the job to print.

You can send a file to a printer from the command line with the following command:

```
lpr -Pname filename
```

name is the name of the print queue, such as Laser. If you leave the -P option out, the file is sent to the default print queue.

Managing Print Jobs

Print jobs sit in the queue until it's their turn to print. They remain in the queue until the entire file is sent to the printer. Even a complete reboot may not remove a print job from the queue. You can look at the print queues and manage the jobs in the queue from the KDE Control Center. Open the Control Center from the main menu. Click `Peripherals`. Click `Printers`. Or, if you are unable to locate the print manager in the main menu, click Run and type `kjobviewer`. The window in Figure 14-6 opens.

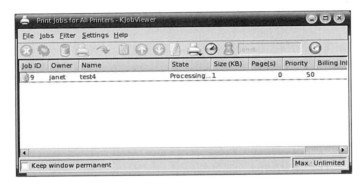

FIGURE 14-6   Print job manager.

The print job in the figure shows a status of Processing, meaning it's printing. In most cases, the job prints. Nothing else is needed. However, occasionally a print job may show a status of Error. A job can encounter problems and be unable to print. Or, sometimes a job prints garbled output to the printer, often using huge amounts of paper. The print manager allows you to remove print jobs from the queue. You can also hold and resume jobs, send a job to the printer, restart a job, raise or lower the priority of a job, and other management tasks.

You can check print queues from the command line with the command:

```
lpq
Laser is ready
no entries
```

lpq shows no jobs are in the print queue. You can use an -l option to get additional information. You can remove a print job with:

```
lprm jobid
```

You can also find out information about the queues with lpstat (see Appendix B).

Summary

Files sent to the printer are sent to a queue that is associated with the printer. The print job waits in the queue until its turn to print. You can create more than one queue to a printer, although you are unlikely to need to. If a printer is a network printer, print jobs from more than one computer on the network can be sent to the same queue.

The software that handles printing for most Linux systems is called CUPS (Common UNIX Printing System). CUPS handles all the details from clicking the `Print` button on the application to passing the data to the printer in an understandable format.

This chapter describes how to:

- Install a printer in Fedora, Mandrake, and SuSE
- Send files to the printer from the desktop and from the command line
- Manage print jobs in the queue

Chapter 15 describes how to connect to the Internet and how to access resources on the World Wide Web.

CHAPTER 15

The Internet

An Internet connection is standard for most computers today. I believe I can assume that you have experience using the Internet, probably with Microsoft Internet Explorer. Your Linux system can access the Internet. The process is basically the same:

1. Set up a connection to the Internet. You may have set up your connection during installation. If not, you can set it up now.

2. Access the Internet using a browser.

If you are using a computer at work, you are probably connected to your company network. The first step above is handled by your company. However, you can connect to the Internet from your home computer. In the past, connecting from Linux was difficult. More recently, many Linux distributions have designed utilities that make connection as simple as it is for Windows.

Accessing the Internet

To connect to the Internet, you need networking hardware and access to the Internet. Access is provided in one of the following ways:

- **Office LAN:** A work computer is connected to a company LAN. You may need to configure your connection in Linux, or this may be automatic. Your system administrator will provide you with the information you need. Or, your IT department may configure the connection. Connecting the LAN to the Internet is handled by the company.

- **Home broadband:** A home computer is connected via broadband—cable modem, DSL, or wireless services, provided by a cable or phone company or an independent Internet service provider (ISP). Your broadband connection needs to be configured with your connection information. You may have done this during installation. If not, you can do it now. The information is provided by your ISP.

  Some service providers install software on your computer that you run to connect to the Internet. If so, the service provider may or may not support Linux. Discuss Linux support with the service provider. However, many broadband connections are now "always on" connections. The connection opens when your computer boots and you can use it any time. It doesn't matter if the connection is made from Linux or another operating system.

- **Home dial-up:** A home computer is connected via phone line and a modem. The connection to the Internet is provided by an ISP, via a phone number provided by the ISP. Many ISPs provide software that you install and use to dial the ISP number. Not all ISPs support Linux. For instance, if the software they provide doesn't run on Linux, you may not be able to connect from Linux using the specific ISP. You need to discuss this with the ISP before signing on to their service. Or, if you are already using an ISP, you may need to find a new one.

Broadband connections are more expensive, generally, than dial-up connections. However, with more and more graphic and multimedia content on the Web, the gain in speed is more than worth the cost. Usually broadband costs a modest amount more than dial-up. Broadband can be up to 50 times the speed of dial-up connections. Waiting for large graphics to download over dial-up connections can be painful.

Hardware for Accessing the Internet

Connecting to the Internet requires that either a modem (dial-up) or an Ethernet port is installed in your computer. In addition, a broadband connection requires additional hardware.

- **Modem:** All computers sold in the last few years include a 56K modem. Most hardware modems are detected by Linux. You can check the Web site for your distribution to be sure your modem is supported.

  Software modems, also called Winmodems, require Linux drivers to work. Winmodems are becoming more and more popular with computer manufacturers because they cost less. Newer laptops usually come with Winmodems. More and more modem vendors are providing Linux drivers. Also, projects developing Linux drivers are making progress. As time moves along, Winmodems will become less of a problem. At the present time, your life will be simpler if you don't have a Winmodem. Information on using Winmodems with Linux is available at linmodems.org and at walbran.org/sean/linux/linmodem-howto.html.

- **Ethernet port:** Your computer may or may not include an Ethernet port, either on a separate card (network interface card [NIC]) or built in to the motherboard. To use a broadband connection, you need an Ethernet port. Many broadband service providers, such as cable companies, install a NIC if it's needed as part of the broadband setup. Linux can detect the port. Check the Web site for your Linux distribution to be sure your NIC is supported.

- **Broadband hardware:** Broadband connections require hardware between your computer and the broadband source. Each type requires a different setup.

  - **Cable modem:** The cable modem signal is transported on the cable that brings in your cable TV signal. A cable modem, not a phone modem, is connected to your Ethernet port and to the cable to translate the signal.

  - **DSL:** A DSL modem, provided by your DSL provider, is connected to your Ethernet port and to your phone line. It is not a phone modem.

  - **Wireless:** Wireless service requires a hardware unit that includes the electronics and antenna for receiving and transmitting the wireless signals, usually installed outside. A cable runs from the unit to your Ethernet port.

After you have the required hardware, you need to set up your network connection, providing some information. For instance, for a dial-up connection, you provide the phone number. The information needed is provided by your service provider. Most Linux distributions include a GUI utility for setting up network connections.

Checking Your Network Connections

Your connection may have been set up during installation. The quickest way to test a connection is to try it. If you have a broadband connection, try your browser. Or, dial your ISP using your dial-up connection. Or, you can check your network connections using utilities provided with your Linux distribution.

To see your network connection setup on Fedora, open the main menu and select System Settings->Network. Figure 15-1 shows the Network Configuration window.

 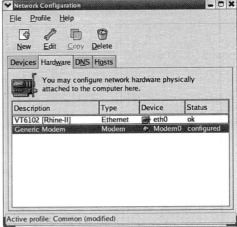

FIGURE 15-1 Network Configuration on Fedora.

The window on the left in Figure 15-1 shows the network devices that are set up. In this case, it shows one active network connection on device eth0. This is an Ethernet connection through a NIC. This computer is set up for a broadband connection. If you double-click the entry, a window opens showing the device configuration.

If you click the Hardware tab, the window on the right in the figure opens. It shows the network hardware detected by Linux. In this case, Linux found one NIC and one modem. If you double-click an entry, you can see the configuration of the hardware.

The Linux system represented by Figure 15-1 detects a modem, but no network device is configured to use the modem. You can configure a connection for the modem. In this figure, a network device is configured to use the NIC. If the NIC and your broadband were connected during Linux installation, your system is probably configured to use the NIC. You can add a connection device at any time. Adding a device is discussed in the next section.

Adding a Dial-Up Network Connection

If your modem is installed and Linux recognizes it, but you can't reach the Internet, you can configure a network connection using the window opened in Figure 15-1. Click New. Select Modem to see the window shown in Figure 15-2.

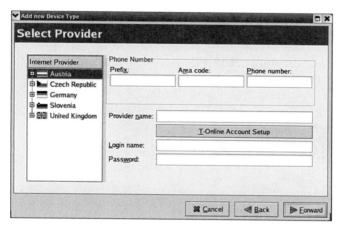

FIGURE 15-2   Modem configuration on Fedora.

Don't select a country. Enter the information you received from your ISP or system administrator. The "Provider name" is a label of your choice for this connection.

When you click Forward, a window opens with two choices: "Automatically obtain IP Address Settings" or "Statically set IP address." This information is also provided by your ISP. After this screen, your modem connection is configured. The Network Configuration window (Figure 15-1) will show a new line for the modem. The status is shown as Inactive. Click Activate to change the status to active.

You can add an icon to your panel to start your connection. In the main menu, select System Settings. Right-click Network and select Add This Launcher to Panel.

If you have a problem, your modem setup may be inaccurate. In the hardware window (Figure 15-1, right side), highlight the modem and click Edit. You can change modem configuration there. The modem is probably shown as /dev/modem. This might be incorrect. If you are also running Windows and can use the modem there, see where the modem is installed. If it's COM1, try /dev/ttyS0 on Linux; COM2, /dev/ttyS1, etc.

More information on setting up your modem can be found in the Modem How To, found at www.tldp.org.

Adding a Broadband Network Connection

If your NIC and broadband modem (cable or DSL) were connected when you installed Linux, your connection is probably already working. If you add the connection hardware to a working system, Linux detects it during the next reboot and configures it. The configuration process asks you whether to "Automatically obtain IP address settings from DHCP" or "Statically set IP address." The information needed to choose between these options is provided by your ISP.

If you need to configure a connection, you can add one in the Network Configuration window shown in Figure 15-1. Click New. Select xDSL to see the window shown in Figure 15-3.

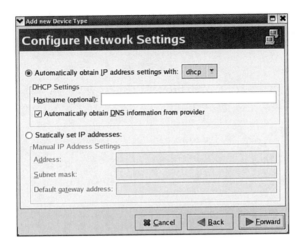

FIGURE 15-3   Broadband configuration on Fedora.

Your ISP provides you with the information needed for this configuration window.

After this screen, your cable or DSL connection is configured. The Network Configuration window (Figure 15-1) will show a new line for the connection, similar to the line shown in the current figure. The status is shown as Inactive. Click Activate to change the status to active.

Most broadband connections are "always on" connections. The connection is always available and open when your computer is running. You don't need to "start" it, as you do with a dial-up connection. Just open your browser and connect.

Web Browsers

Web browsers get Web pages from Web sites on the World Wide Web (WWW) and display the Web pages on your screen. For dynamic Web sites, information is often sent from the browser to the Web site as well, such as user ID/passwords, information provided in forms, and product orders. The major Web browsers for Linux are:

- **Konqueror/Nautilus:** The Web browsers provided with the major Linux desktops. Konqueror (KDE) and Nautilus (GNOME) are fully functional, but Mozilla has many more powerful features. Konqueror is discussed in other chapters.

- **Mozilla:** The major open source browser, based on the Netscape source code that was made open source in 1998. Netscape provides some support for the Mozilla project. Mozilla is a suite of products, including a Web browser, email software, a news reader, and an HTML editor. Email is discussed in Chapter 17. Mozilla is included in most major Linux distributions. Mozilla runs on Windows, as well as Linux.

- **Mozilla Firefox:** The next generation Mozilla Web browser. Firefox is a browser only, not a suite. It's faster, more efficient, and better than Mozilla. Firefox 1.0 was released in October 2004, and its use is growing rapidly. Firefox runs on Windows, as well as Linux. Currently, Firefox is not included in most distributions, so you must download and install it yourself. Installing software is discussed in Chapter 10. (www.mozilla.org)

- **Netscape:** Netscape is very similar to Mozilla, but it isn't an open source project. Netscape uses Mozilla as its base, but adds more documentation and user friendly interface features. Netscape runs on Windows and Mac, as well as Linux. Netscape is not included with Linux, so you must download and install it yourself. Installing software is discussed in Chapter 10. (www.netscape.com)

- **Lynx:** A character based browser for use at the command line. It doesn't display graphics or play multimedia files. It's used most often for system administration tasks. Lynx is probably installed on your Linux system. Open it in a terminal window.

This chapter discusses the Mozilla browser. Most of the information applies to Firefox, as well. Firefox has most of the same features, but they may be found in a different location. For instance, Mozilla settings are found in `Edit->Preferences`; Firefox settings are found in `Tools->Options`. Most of the information applies to Netscape, as well.

Browsing with Mozilla

A Mozilla browser window open to fedora.redhat.com is shown in Figure 15-4.

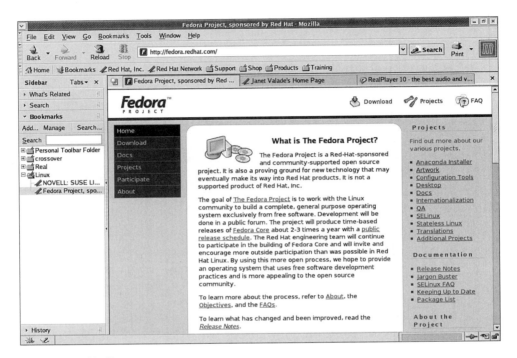

FIGURE 15-4 Mozilla.

To go to a Web page, type its URL into the location bar. To overwrite the current address, click the icon at the beginning of the location bar first; then type the URL.

You can search using the location bar. Type in search terms and click Search to run a Google search. The results display in the sidebar.

You can change the settings for Mozilla. Click Edit and select Preferences. Click Appearance to change fonts and colors. Click Navigator to change Mozilla behavior. In the Navigator windows, you can set your home page, set Mozilla to be your default browser, select which buttons are on the toolbars, change the search engine used, and set many other options.

You can copy or save all or part of a Web page using the Edit menu. You can print the page from the Print button.

Mozilla Menus and Toolbars

The menu is similar to the IE menu bar, except Mozilla says Bookmarks rather than Favorites. The Mozilla Windows menu is where you can open the other applications in the suite, such as email or address book. The Go menu is similar to History in IE.

There are two toolbars. The usual buttons for back, forward, stop, search, home, etc. are on the toolbars. You can select the items you want on your toolbars by clicking Edit and selecting Preferences. Click Navigation. In the bottom section of the page, check the items you want on your toolbars—Home, Search, Print, Bookmarks, and Go.

The second toolbar is the personal toolbar, a place for you to store frequently used Web pages. The bookmarks on the personal toolbar are Red Hat Web pages, added by the Fedora developers. If you download and install Mozilla yourself, links to mozilla.org and mozillaZine appear on the personal toolbar.

You can customize the personal toolbar completely. You can add a bookmark to your personal toolbar. Copy a bookmark or a folder of bookmarks from your bookmark drop-down list and paste it onto the personal toolbar. You can also add a bookmark to the personal toolbar from any open Web page. Drag the icon at the beginning of the location bar to the personal toolbar.

You can delete any bookmark from the personal toolbar. Right-click the bookmark and select Delete.

You can hide any toolbar by clicking the small triangle on the left side of the toolbar. Click the triangle again to redisplay the toolbar. You can totally remove a toolbar, including the triangle section, by clicking View and selecting Show/Hide.

The status bar appears at the bottom of the browser. The left section of the status bar is the component bar. Buttons for switching to other applications in the Mozilla suite, such as email or the address book, are found on the component bar. The component bar is not found on Firefox because Firefox is not a suite.

The Mozilla Sidebar

The Mozilla sidebar is an area where you can keep the items you use often. Each item is accessed using a tab. If the sidebar is not available, click View and select Show/Hide-> Sidebar. You can add or remove items from the sidebar.

By default, the sidebar contains default items: Search, Bookmarks, and History. If you click a tab, the features for the item open in the sidebar. For instance, if you click the Search tab, the features of the search function open as shown in the window on the right. You see a field where you enter search terms (PHP is entered). You can select a search engine in the drop-down list (Google is currently selected). Click Search. The search results display in the sidebar. Click a result to open the Web page in the browser window. The sidebar retains the search results for your use.

If you click the Bookmarks tab, all your bookmarks are available in the sidebar (shown in Figure 15-4). You can open a bookmarked page by clicking it. The History tab is similar, listing pages you have previously visited.

You can add items to your sidebar—news, weather, address book, stock quotes, FedEx, many others. Or you can remove items. Click Tabs in the upper corner of the sidebar. Select Customize Sidebar. The window below opens.

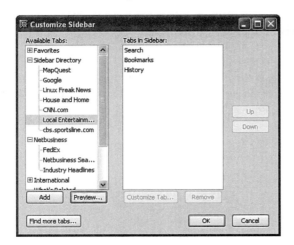

The left pane shows available tabs. The right pane shows the current sidebar tabs. To add a tab to the sidebar, click the tab in the left pane and click Add. You can click Preview, before you click Add.

To remove a tab from the sidebar, click the tab in the right pane and click Remove.

Notice the dotted area on the middle right border of the sidebar—the sidebar handle. Click this area and the sidebar will close. Click it again and the sidebar opens.

Tabbed Browsing in Mozilla

Tabbed browsing in Mozilla allows you to keep more than one Web page open in a single browser window. You use its tab to bring a Web page forward.

Tabbed browsing is shown in Figure 15-4. Figure 15-5 shows the tabbed browsing section of Figure 15-4.

FIGURE 15-5   Mozilla tabs.

The Fedora project page is open in Figure 5-4. Figure 15-5 shows the top of the Fedora Web page. Notice the top row of this figure. There are three tabs. The tabs display the title for the Web page, the title that appears in the Web page title bar, as much of the title as space allows.

The first tab is currently the Fedora Project tab. The second tab shows Janet Valade's Home Page. If you click this tab, you see the home page. The third tab shows RealPlayer 10. If you click this tab, the RealPlayer Web page displays.

To see another Web page, you can replace one of the current tabs in the Web page or open a new tab. When a tab is selected and the Web page in the tab is visible, you can type a URL to open a new Web page in the selected tab. For instance, with the Fedora Web page open, you can type a URL into the location box and the new Web page will replace the Fedora Web page, still in the current tab.

To open a new tab, right-click a blank space on the bar on which the tabs display. Select New Tab. A new tab opens in the current browser window. The new tab will be blank, labeled (Untitled). You can also open a new tab by clicking the New Tab button, shown at the beginning of the tab bar, to the left of the first tab.

If you have only one Web page in the browser window, with no tabs currently open, you can begin tabbed browsing by clicking File and selecting New->New tab. The current Web page remains and is given a tab and a new blank tab opens in the browser window.

Controlling Pop-Ups with Mozilla

Some people do not want pop-up and pop-under windows. However, some sites provide some of their functionality in pop-up windows. For instance, a site might provide their login page in a pop-up window or allow printing through a pop-up window. Mozilla allows you to block pop-up windows. It also allows you to set up a list of sites that are exceptions to the pop-up blocking.

To configure pop-up settings, click Edit and select Preferences. Expand Privacy and Security (click +). Click Popup Windows. The window in Figure 15-6 opens.

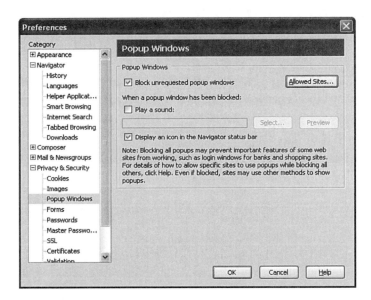

FIGURE 15-6   Mozilla pop-ups.

Check "Block unrequested popup windows." You can have a sound play when a pop-up is blocked. The Allowed Sites button opens a window where you can enter sites that are exceptions, sites whose pop-ups you want to accept. In the Sites window, type a URL and click Add.

You can check "Display an icon in the Navigator status bar." The icon displays when a pop-up is blocked. If you click the icon, the Sites window opens, with the site URL already filled in; you only need to click Add to add the site to the exceptions list.

Downloads, Forms, Passwords, and Cookies

Mozilla provides managers for several features:

- **Download Manager:** When a download starts, the download manager opens a list of recent downloads, adding the new one to the list. The time required for the download is shown. A status bar keeps track of the download progress. If a download takes hours, you can do something else on your computer, leaving the download to the download manager. Just don't close the download manager until the file is completely downloaded.

- **Password Manager:** When you log in to a Web site, Mozilla ask whether you want to save the password for future use. If you save it, Mozilla will automatically enter it whenever you return to the login page for this site. In addition, Mozilla can display your passwords. Click Tools. Select Password manager->Manage Stored Passwords. A window opens that lists the Web sites and login names saved. To see passwords, click Show Passwords. You can remove any login information from the list.

- **Form Manager:** When you fill in a form, Mozilla asks whether you want to save the information. If you save it for a few sites, Mozilla can fill in forms for you, saving a great deal of typing. At a blank form, you can double-click a field. Or, at a blank form, click Edit. Select Fill in Form. A window opens showing the data Mozilla is about to enter. You can check or uncheck any information you don't want entered. None of the data filled in by Mozilla is sent until you actually submit the form by clicking Submit or a similar button.

- **Cookie Manager:** Mozilla keeps track of cookies stored on your computer. You can open the cookie manager at Tools->Cookie Manager to see a list of cookies, with information about each cookie. You can remove individual cookies or all cookies.

The password and form managers are saving potentially sensitive information. If other people can access your computer, you can encrypt this information so they can't see it. This is less convenient because you must set and remember a master password for the encryption. To use encryption, click Edit and select Preferences. Expand Privacy & Security. Click Master Password to set a password. Click Passwords to turn on encryption.

Firefox has similar features, but they are accessed in different places. For instance, to access the Download Manager, click Tools->Downloads. To access passwords, forms, and cookies, click Tools->Options->Privacy.

Plug-Ins

Plug-ins are small programs that expand the functionality of Mozilla. Plug-ins can be installed when Mozilla is installed. You can install additional plug-ins later as well.

Plug-ins typically are opened within Mozilla. For instance, the RealPlayer plug-in gives Mozilla the ability to play video clips inside the browser, not needing to open a separate application to play the clips. Other popular plug-ins are Macromedia Flash Player and Java.

Mozilla was probably installed when your Linux was installed. Some plug-ins are usually installed with it. You may have installed additional plug-ins since. For instance, if you encounter a media file on the Internet that requires an application to play, you may be prompted to download the plug-in.

Some popular plug-ins can be downloaded from addons.update.mozilla.org/plugins/. The available plug-ins are:

- **Acrobat Reader:** Opens Acrobat PDF files in your Mozilla browser.
- **Flash Player:** Plays Flash files.
- **Java:** Allows your computer to run applications and applets that use Java technology.
- **RealPlayer:** Displays video files in RealVideo format inside your Mozilla browser. Installing and using RealPlayer is discussed in detail in Chapter 16.

Plug-ins are installed, by default, in the plug-ins subdirectory in the directory where Mozilla is installed.

To see which plug-ins are currently installed, go to this Netscape Web page that also works for Mozilla at channels.netscape.com/ns/browsers/plugins.jsp. You can look in the plug-ins directory to see which plug-in files are there.

NOTE
In Firefox, you can see which plug-ins are installed by clicking Tools. Select Options. Click Downloads. Click the Plug-Ins button.

Summary

Your Linux system can access the Internet. The process is basically the same process used to access the Internet from Windows:

1. Set up a connection to the Internet. You may have set up your connection during installation. If not, you can set it up now.

   This chapter describes:

   - What types of Internet access are available

   - What hardware is needed

   - How to configure a network connection

2. Access the Internet using a browser.

   This chapter describes:

   - What browsers are available

   - How to browse the Internet with Mozilla

   - How to use Mozilla menus, toolbars, sidebar, and tabs

   - How to control pop-up windows with Mozilla

   - How to manage downloads, cookies, passwords, and forms with Mozilla

   - How to add plug-ins

## CHAPTER 16

Multimedia

M ultimedia refers to digital sound and video. The possible uses for sound and video on computers is boundless—from playing CDs and DVDs to communicating over distances with sound and video to providing virtual tours to software that speaks and understands human languages. This is an application area that is growing and changing rapidly. Yesterday something was impossible; today it's feasible.

Sound and video are everywhere. Web excursions frequently encounter sound or video that you want to explore. Although working with multimedia files is much easier than it used to be, both for Windows and Linux, it can still be problematic on occasion. You are more likely to encounter problems in this area than any other.

This chapter describes more common uses of multimedia files. Most of the applications discussed in this chapter work easily out of the box. Some are included with Linux and some need to be installed. Software for more advanced multimedia applications, useful for musicians and moviemakers, is available, such as sound recorders, sound and video editors, and so forth. Advanced applications are not discussed in this chapter. See linux-sound.org for more information.

One music problem unique to open source software is the legal status of MP3. MP3 encoding (writing music into an MP3 file) is a patented procedure. Software that can encode in MP3 format must pay license fees, a requirement not compatible with open source licensing. Therefore, Linux distributions can't include MP3 encoders without paying license fees. Some Linux distributions include applications that can encode several types of files, including MP3 files, with the MP3 encoding disabled. Or don't include any MP3 encoders at all. For instance, Fedora includes the X Multimedia System without MP3 capabilities. Using MP3 encoding software for personal use, if you don't sell any MP3s, is believed by most to be perfectly legal. Licensing is applied to the developers of the encoders, not the users. You can see more at http://www.mp3licensing.com/.

However, an open source sound file format, Ogg Vorbis, is available with better sound quality for a given compression than MP3. If you're saving sound files for use on your Linux system, Ogg Vorbis is a better choice than MP3.

Configuring Your Sound Card

In most cases, your sound card was detected and configured during installation. It may have been tested, as well, during installation. If you are unsure whether your sound card was properly detected and configured, you can test it using the configuration procedures for your distribution, usually found on the main menu.

- **Fedora:** select System Settings->Soundcard Detection. Fedora probes for your sound card and displays a screen showing which sound card it detected. The window includes a Play test sound button.

- **Mandrake:** select Configure your computer->Hardware->Hardware. The HardDrake application probes for hardware and opens a window showing all the detected hardware in the left pane. The sound card detected is listed under Sound card. Click the entry for a sound card to see details in the right pane.

- **SuSE:** select System->YaST. Click Hardware in the left pane and Sound in the right pane to detect and configure the sound card. Mandrake probes for a sound card, then opens a window listing the detected sound card. Buttons are available to add a sound card and to configure options.

If your sound card is not listed, you may need to locate and install a driver for your sound card. Or your sound card may not be supported. Check the Web site for your Linux distribution to see whether the sound card is supported. Perhaps you just need to download a driver. Also check the manufacturer's Web site for information.

Most distributions provide a mixer application that allows you to configure the sound. In Fedora, open the main menu and select Sound & Video->Volume Control. The window in Figure 16-1 opens.

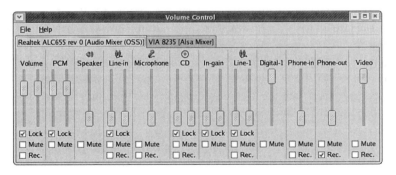

FIGURE 16-1 Fedora volume control.

In Mandrake, open the main menu and select Multimedia->Sound->Kmix. In SuSE, in the open sound window, click Volume.

Playing Audio CDs

Most Linux distributions install with a CD player. The player starts automatically when a CD is put into the drive. Or, often an icon for a CD player is in your system tray on the desktop panel. Or start a CD player from the main menu.

Two common CD players are:

- **CD Player:** A simple CD player, often the default CD player in GNOME. It opens in the following window.

    The player includes the usual play/pause, stop, rewind, fast forward, previous track, next track, and eject buttons. When a CD is playing, the name of the CD that's playing is usually displayed.

- **KsCD:** The KDE simple CD Player is usually the default CD player on KDE desktops. It opens in the following window.

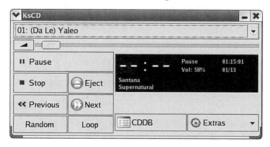

In addition to the volume slider and the stop, play/pause and other usual buttons, the Random button tells KsCD to play the tracks on the CD in random order. The Loop button creates a loop that plays the CD repeatedly.

The Extras button lets you select Configure KsCD. A window opens where you can select colors. You can check "Show icon in the system tray." You can specify "Autoplay when CD inserted," "Eject CD when finished playing," and/or "Stop playing CD on Exit." The latter is important because the CD keeps playing until "Stopped," even if the CD player window is closed.

Downloading Music

Many legal music files are available on the Web. There are sites that offer free downloads and sites that charge for downloading, either by the song or a monthly fee. Many performers offer music downloads for free on their Web sites.

Most music files available from the Web are in MP3 format. MP3 is one of the most popular sound formats for music because it combines good compression (small files) with high quality. MP3 files generally compress file size to approximately a megabyte per minute. MP3 files are actually MPEG (Moving Pictures Experts Group) files in a format that encodes sound.

Many Linux distributions don't provide an application that plays MP3 files, so you need to install one yourself. Two multimedia sound applications that play MP3 format, as well as other formats, such as WAV files, are:

- **Xmms:** Xmms (X Multimedia System) is installed by default on many Linux distributions. However, in some distributions, such as Fedora Core, MP3 support is disabled. You can install a version with MP3 support to make xmms more useful for playing music from your hard disk. You can download and install xmms from www.xmms.org. Installing software is discussed in Chapter 10.

- **Rhythmbox:** The default music player for GNOME on Fedora. Rhythmbox stores a play list that you can set up to play in order or randomly. In addition, Rhythmbox stores Internet radio stations that you can start with a click. However, on Fedora, Rhythmbox doesn't include support for MP3. You can add MP3 support from www.rhythmbox.org. Installing software is discussed in Chapter 10.

Xmms

Xmms is a popular audio player, installed on many Linux distributions and available on the main menu. For instance, on the Fedora main menu, you can start xmms by selecting Sound & Video->Audio Player. If you don't find it on your distribution, you can install it from www.xmms.org, as discussed in Chapter 10.

NOTE

On Fedora, xmms is installed but doesn't include MP3 support. You can download and install xmms from the project Web site with MP3 support.

When you start xmms, it opens the window shown on the right, with all the expected buttons, such as play/pause, stop, next track, etc. When a sound file is playing, its name, length, and other information displays. The left slider under the window is the volume

control. The right slider controls the balance between speakers. Xmms has other functions that are not displayed until needed. If you click EQ, an equalizer, as shown on the left, opens under the xmms main window, allowing you to adjust the sound as needed.

The PL button opens the play list editor window shown on the right. You can add and remove songs located anywhere on your hard disk. You can create and save different play lists and use whichever play list you want. In the main xmms window, you can check SHUFF to play tunes randomly from the play list or select REP to have the play list repeat endlessly.

Much of the xmms functionality is provided by plug-ins. A few are installed by default. Many more are available. You can add plug-ins for your needs. For instance, each type of sound file format has its own plug-in. The plug-in for MP3 is not included by Fedora. One input plug-in plays music from a CD. There are output plug-ins that change the sound, such as an echo plug-in.

If you right-click on the xmms window, you can open a window that allows you to configure many settings, such as which information displays when xmms is playing and the format of the information displayed.

Rhythmbox

Rhythmbox is a music player for GNOME. For instance, Fedora provides Rhythmbox as the default music player on GNOME.

Rythmbox opens the window shown in Figure 16-2.

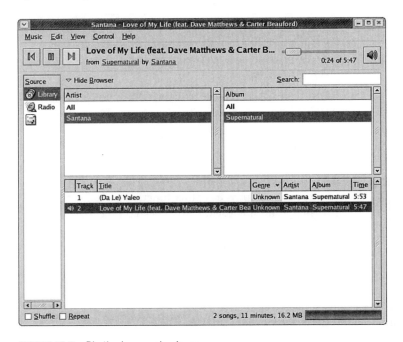

FIGURE 16-2 Rhythmbox music player.

The sidebar on the left lets you choose between Library (music on your hard disk), Radio (stations you set up), and a play list (if you have created one).

The figure shows Library selected. Music is playing, showing the artist, the album (a folder), and two tracks. The second track is playing, 24 seconds into 5:47 total length. To add music to the Rhythmbox library, click Music. You can select Folder or URL. You can also select Import from CD, which opens Sound Juicer, an application that copies music from an audio CD, discussed later in this chapter.

If you click Radio in the sidebar, the radio stations set up in Rhythmbox display in the main pane. You just click a station and it begins playing.

Video Players

Video players can play sound, as well as video. However, they are intended for video. Two useful video players are:

- **RealPlayer:** RealPlayer is a favorite application on Windows. RealPlayer 10 for Linux (10.0 first released in August 2004) is greatly improved over previous Linux RealPlayer versions. It's based on the open source player, Helix. The Helix player supports many open source formats, such as Ogg Vorbis. RealPlayer is built on top of the Helix player and supports several non-open source formats, such as RealAudio, RealVideo, and MP3.

  RealPlayer is not installed in most Linux distributions, but it's quite easy to install from the Real Web site (www.real.com). Installing RealPlayer is described later in this chapter. In addition, a RealPlayer plug-in for Mozilla allows you to play video clips in your browser, rather than opening a separate RealPlayer window.

- **MPlayer:** The Movie Player is a good, popular video player that you can use on your Linux system. MPlayer supports the most common video formats, such as MPEG, AVI, WMA/WMV, MOV, and others, including REALMEDIA (.rm) files that RealPlayer uses. MPlayer is not installed with most Linux systems, so you need to download and install it yourself. Installing MPlayer is discussed later in this chapter.

RealPlayer

RealPlayer is an application that plays sound and video in several formats. If you have experience with Windows, you may have used RealPlayer in that environment. RealPlayer 10 for Linux is much improved over previous Linux versions. It's particularly useful for playing .mp3 and .mpeg files.

At the current time, many distributions do not include RealPlayer, so you may need to install it yourself. In the future, it may be included so check the main menu before installing.

RealPlayer provides an installer for Linux. The installation procedure is somewhat unusual for Linux, different from the package installation procedures described in Chapter 10. To install RealPlayer 10:

1. Open Mozilla and go to www.real.com. You should see the following Web page.

FIGURE 16-3 RealPlayer Web site.

NOTE

If you go to the RealPlayer Web site from Windows, you see a different Web page, appropriate for RealPlayer for Windows.

---

2. Click the yellow button to download RealPlayer.

3. A file named RealPlayer10GOLD.bin is downloaded. Save the file to disk.

4. After the file is downloaded, open a terminal window. If necessary, change to the directory where the downloaded file is saved.

5. Execute the file, using the root account. Be sure you have execute permission for the file. For instance, type the following commands:

```
chmod a+x RealPlayer10GOLD.bin        (notice the uppercase characters)
./RealPlayer10GOLD.bin
```

6. When you see the prompt:

```
Configure System-wide symbolic links? [Y/n]
```

Type: Y<Enter>

7. When prompted for a path to use for installing RealPlayer10, type a path that is included in your system path, such as /usr/local/bin. Remember the path you select, because you occasionally need to enter this path in response to prompts.

8. When the installation completes, start the newly installed RealPlayer. You can start it by executing the file realplay in the directory you designated during the installation procedure (e.g., /usr/local/bin/realplay). In addition, a menu item has been added for RealPlayer in Main Menu->Sound & Video.

When you start RealPlayer the first time, a configuration procedure runs. Answer the questions asked. When the window displays the following two questions, uncheck the first check box and check the second. (Because you just downloaded the software, no update check is needed.)

```
Check for updates
Configure mozilla helpers
```

When RealPlayer starts from the menu, the RealPlayer window shown on the right opens. The video plays in the window. You can change to a full screen video in the View menu.

If you open an audio file, the video screen in the window disappears, as shown below. The player now looks similar to an audio player, with play, stop, etc. buttons,

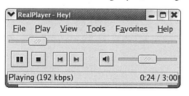

a volume slider, and information about the sound file that is playing.

In addition, a Mozilla plug-in is installed when RealPlayer 10 is installed so that you can run files directly in Mozilla. For instance, if you encounter a .mpeg file on the Web, Mozilla can play it in the browser window. Test the plug-in by running a video file. For instance, go to www.imdb.com and run some movie trailers.

MPlayer

MPlayer (the Movie Player) is an application best suited for playing video. It's the most popular application for video on Linux. At this time, you probably need to install MPlayer yourself, although in the future it may be included in some distributions. Check your system to see whether MPlayer is installed before installing it.

MPlayer is installed using the procedures described in Chapter 10. It's best installed from source. However, you need to include additional files with MPlayer when you download and install it. The following is a brief summary of the installation procedure.

Download MPlayer from www.mplayerhq.hu. When you click the Download link, the download page offers several different files. The first table provides the MPlayer software itself. The remaining three tables provide software that is needed by MPlayer, so you need to download additional files. Download and save to disk (e.g., /usr/src):

- The MPlayer source.

- A font package, such as Arial-Western.

- A skin. A skin is required for the GUI version of MPlayer. A skin refers to software files that provide the look and feel of an application. Many Linux applications allow you to change the appearance of an application using skins. For MPlayer, many skins are provided. You can pick one to download or you can download several and change them.

After downloading, unpack the bz files, using the following command on each download:

```
bunzip2 -c filename | tar -xf -
```

To install:

1. Compile and install the source. Change to the directory where you unpacked the source. When installing, use a configuration option that creates a GUI version. The simple install commands, accepting the defaults, are:

   ```
   ./configure --enable-gui
   make
   make install
   ```

   Remember that the first two steps can take a while to complete. More information on installing software is provided in Chapter 10.

2. Select one of the subdirectories in the font directory you unpacked and copy it into /usr/local/share/mplayer/font.

3. Copy an entire skin directory that you unpacked into /usr/local/share/mplayer/ Skin/default. In other words, if you unpacked a skin and it created a directory called Blue, copy the entire Blue directory, with subdirectories, into /usr/local/ share/mplayer/Skin and rename it to default. There must be at least one default skin. You can also copy other skin directories into Skin, but at least one must be named default.

After MPlayer is installed, to start the GUI version, open the main menu, select Run, and type gmplayer. Two windows open: one that is the video window where the video plays and one that is a control window, where you load, start, stop, change skins, etc. What the windows look like depends on the skin you use. The control window shown above is using a simple skin called Carnelian. Other skins can look very different.

Whatever skin you use, you can right-click MPlayer to see the features provided, as shown on the right.

You can open a file on your hard disk or a URL. Or, you can play from a VCD (Video CD) or DVD.

The usual play options are available from the menu and also shown on the MPlayer window.

You can change the size of the window playing the video to double the opening size or to full screen.

MPlayer offers an equalizer, accessed from the menu selection or the EQ button in the MPlayer window above.

You can select Skin browser in the menu or the S button to change skins on-the-fly. The Skin directory will open, showing the subdirectories you have stored there. You can select any directory (e.g., Blue), and the look and feel will change immediately.

You can create a play list from video files on your hard disk.

If you play an unusual format, you may get an error message about the format, possibly referring to a missing codec. If so, download the needed codecs from the Web site, unpack them, and copy them to /usr/local/lib/codecs.

You can also use MPlayer from the command line, without the GUI. See the man pages or the MPlayer manual to see how.

Listening to Radio

Many people enjoy music while they work. Or other sounds. You can play CDs, as described earlier in this chapter. Or you can listen to the radio on your computer, via Internet Radio. Thousands of Internet radio stations are available. Some require Windows Media Player, but not all. Many broadcasts are in MP3 format that can be played by your audio player that has MP3 support or a multimedia player, discussed earlier in this chapter in the section "Downloading Music."

Many broadcasts originate from radio stations that make their programs available live on the Internet. If you have a favorite station, check their Web site to see whether they are available on the Internet. A radio-locator Web site is available (www.radio-locator.com) where you can search for radio stations. Then, check their Web sites to see whether they offer Internet radio. In addition, many radio broadcasts are initiated by Internet broadcasters. The broadcast is available only on the Internet, with no "real" radio station.

You can listen to radio stations through the browser, as long as the browser can play the sound file format. Or you can use an audio or multimedia player to access radio stations. Some players allow you to set up radio station URLs so you can play them through the player, rather than the browser. For instance, Rhythmbox, RealPlayer, and Windows Media Player allow you to set up radio stations.

Some Web sites provide access to many radio stations. For instance, Shoutcast (www.shoutcast.com) offers thousands of Internet radio broadcasts. You can search the stations by name, song, artist, or genre. When you find a station you want to listen to, click the Tune In button. Shoutcast also allows you to set preferences for which media player to use. Another site is www.live-radio.net, which provides only real radio stations from many countries. You can listen to an African radio station live if you so desire. However, you must put up with a lot of ads. There's no shortage of radio stations. Googling for Internet radio results in millions of hits.

When playing radio stations through the Mozilla browser, it may recognize the format and play without a problem, perhaps using plug-ins you installed. In some cases, Mozilla doesn't recognize the file format and displays the window in Figure 16-4.

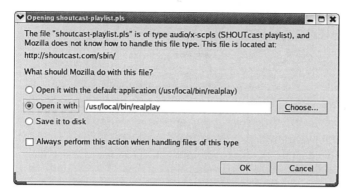

FIGURE 16-4 Mozilla file type prompt window.

You can select either the first or second options. The first option shows realplay as the default application, so you could choose that option. The second choice allows you to specify which application to use with the file. You can browse to find the application, if necessary. In this case, the default application is specified, so the first option should be chosen instead. You could probably have typed /usr/bin/xmms as the application to Open With.

Notice the check box at the bottom of the screen. When you check this option, Mozilla will remember how to handle audio/x-scpls type files and handle them in the future without displaying this window.

Copying Music Files from CD to Hard Disk

You can copy music tracks from a CD to your hard disk. It's useful for listening to music without needing to find and insert the CD. Copying the music and distributing it to other people is illegal. Copying the music to your computer and returning the CD for a refund is plain theft. The process of transferring the digital file for a piece of music from an audio CD to hard disk is called ripping. An application that transfers music tracks is called a CD Ripper.

Transferring music from a music CD to the computer's hard drive includes converting the file into a different format. The most popular format is MP3. However, you can store music in the open source format Ogg Vorbis, a format with better compression. If a piece of music is stored in MP3 and Ogg Vorbis in the same size file, the Ogg Vorbis file sounds better.

The Sound Juicer CD Ripper is available in the main menu of most Linux distributions. The Sound Juicer window is shown in Figure 16-5.

FIGURE 16-5   Sound Juicer CD Ripper.

Sound Juicer reads the CD in the CD drive and lists the tracks. When you click Extract, the tracks that are checked are copied to hard disk. You can select the format to save the files in.

Summary

Multimedia refers to digital sound and video, an application area that is growing and changing rapidly. Although working with multimedia files is much easier than it used to be, both for Windows and Linux, it can still be problematic on occasion. You are more likely to encounter problems in this area than any other.

This chapter describes the more common uses of multimedia files. It explains how to:

- Configure your sound card
- Listen to audio CDs
- Listen to downloaded music files
- Listen to Internet Radio
- Copy CD tracks to your hard disk
- Play video files

Advanced multimedia applications are also available for Linux, but not discussed in this book. For more information, see www.linux-sound.org.

The next chapter discusses email applications—how to select one and how to use it.

▌▌ CHAPTER 17 ▌▐▌

Email, Messaging, and News

The Internet makes worldwide communication possible. Three of the most popular forms of communication are:

- **Email:** One of the first applications on the Internet, predating even the WWW. I expect that all of you have experience with email, perhaps using Outlook or Outlook Express on Windows. Email is modeled after the postal service, sending messages to addresses, putting the messages into mailboxes. However, it's much faster. An email message gets to the recipient often in seconds. Recipients don't need to be on-line to receive email; they can read and answer messages at their own convenience.

- **Instant messaging:** While email is modeled on postal service, instant messaging is modeled on telephone service. Instant messaging sessions resemble conversations, where the participants need to be online simultaneously. Text messages are sent and responses received instantly. A window on the participants' screens displays the instant messages in the order they are sent, showing the ongoing conversation. Instant messaging is free and available for all computer users who are connected to the Internet.

- **Newsgroups:** Usenet newsgroups are also an early application (1978) on the Internet, bringing people with similar interests together. Each newsgroup is like a public bulletin board devoted to a specific subject. Anyone can post a message and read existing messages. The cumulative expertise available in a newsgroup is extensive. Most questions on a subject are answered immediately. Tens of thousands of newsgroups are available, covering every imaginable subject.

This chapter provides instruction for communicating using all three methods.

Email Accounts

To send and receive email, you need an email account. That is, an email address. An email account is established for you by a system administrator. This may be your system administrator at your place of employment. Or it may be a system administrator at your ISP or Web hosting company. Some ISPs provide you with more than one email account. Or you may have more than one email address from different sources, such as one from your ISP and one from your Web hosting company. Each email account includes a mailbox where incoming email messages are stored.

Email is sent to the mailbox by a software application called the SMTP server. It receives all the email addressed to a particular domain and sends it to the individual mailbox. The SMTP server also handles the outgoing email, sending it across the Internet to the intended destination. In addition, if your email messages are received and stored on a remote server, such as your ISP's computer, the messages must be downloaded to your computer. An additional software application handles the downloading—either a POP3 server or an IMAP server.

Mail software on your account allows you to read, send, and otherwise manage the messages in your mailbox. Several email software applications are available. Some major email software is described in the next section.

You need to set up your email software for each email account you use. The email software needs to communicate with the SMTP server. If you need to download email from an ISP, the email software needs to communicate with the server that handles the downloading. You provide the email software with the server addresses when you set up the email account. Your ISP or system administrator provides you with the needed information.

Email Software

Some email software available on Linux is:

- **Evolution:** An open source email package. Evolution is very similar to Outlook. Those with experience with Outlook or Outlook Express will feel at home in Evolution. Evolution has an integrated calendar and address book. Like Outlook, icons in the sidebar provide access to Inbox, Calendar, Tasks, and Contacts. Evolution, available from Novell, is usually installed by default. For more information, see www.novell.com/products/desktop/features/evolution.html.

- **KMail:** An email application that is part of the KDE desktop installation. KMail is only available as part of KDE, not in a separate package.

- **Mozilla:** Mozilla is a suite of applications, including a full-featured email application. Mozilla is included by default on many Linux distributions. However, not all Mozilla installations include the email application. For instance, Fedora installs Mozilla by default without the email application. You can add it later from the installation CD, as discussed in Chapter 10.

- **Thunderbird:** The next generation Mozilla email software. Thunderbird is email software only, not a suite. It's faster and easier than Mozilla. Thunderbird runs on Windows, as well as Linux. Currently, Thunderbird is not included in most distributions, so you must download and install it yourself. Installing software is discussed in Chapter 10. (www.mozilla.org)

- **Netscape:** Based on the Mozilla mail client. Similar functionality and interface.

This chapter discusses Mozilla email. Most of the information applies to Thunderbird, as well. Thunderbird has basically the same features, plus some additional features, but they may be found in a different location. For instance, Mozilla settings are found in `Edit->Preferences`; Thunderbird settings are found in `Tools->Options`. Most of the information applies to Netscape, as well.

It's not necessary to use email software on Linux. If you prefer to use Webmail, you can. Webmail refers to an email account that you access through your browser, such as a Yahoo! or Hotmail email account. The email software and messages reside on a computer on the Internet. From your browser, you log in to read email, send email, get addresses from your address book, etc. Webmail is unrelated to your operating system. You can use a Webmail account equally easily from Linux or Windows.

Setting Up an Email Account

Before you can use your email software, you must provide it with information, provided by your system administrator or ISP, to set up your email account. When you start Mozilla email the first time, you see the screen shown in Figure 17-1.

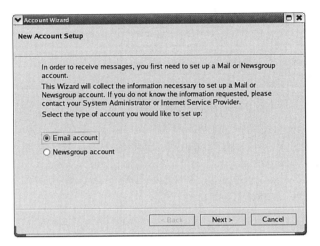

FIGURE 17-1 Mozilla email setup start screen.

Check Email account. Newsgroups are discussed later in this chapter.

The next screen asks you for your name and email address. The name you enter will be displayed to the recipient whenever you send an email. Your email address is supplied by your ISP, such as janet@ispname.com.

The information requested by the next screen is shown in Figure 17-2.

```
Select the type of incoming server you are using.
    ⦿ POP   ○ IMAP

Enter the name of your incoming server (for example, "mail.example.net").
    Incoming Server:  [                            ]

Enter the name of your outgoing server (SMTP) (for example,
"smtp.example.net").
    Outgoing Server:  [                            ]
```

FIGURE 17-2 Mozilla email setup mail servers.

Enter the server information provided by your ISP or system administrator.

The information shown in Figure 17-3 is requested.

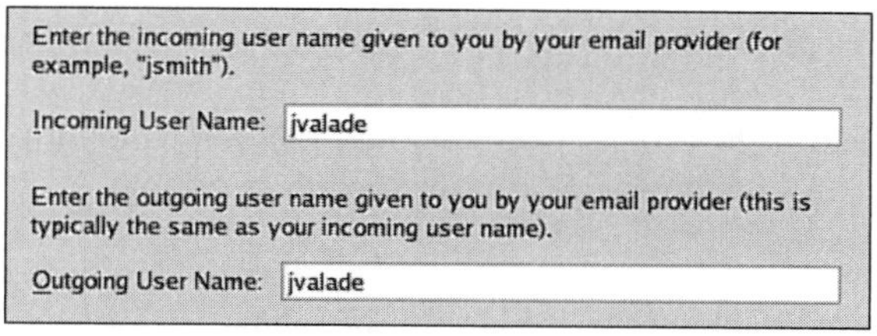

Enter the incoming user name given to you by your email provider (for example, "jsmith").

Incoming User Name: jvalade

Enter the outgoing user name given to you by your email provider (this is typically the same as your incoming user name).

Outgoing User Name: jvalade

FIGURE 17-3   Mozilla email setup usernames.

Enter the information provided by your ISP. The information shown in Figure 17-4 is requested.

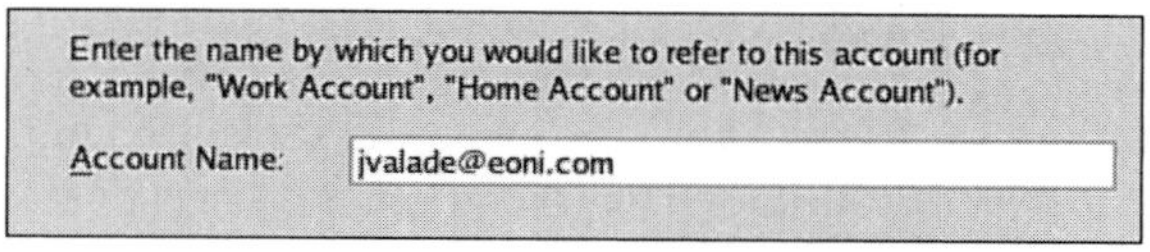

Enter the name by which you would like to refer to this account (for example, "Work Account", "Home Account" or "News Account").

Account Name: jvalade@eoni.com

FIGURE 17-4   Mozilla email setup mail servers.

Enter a name that is meaningful to you.

When you have finished entering information, a window headed Congratulations! displays, showing all the information you entered. Check it for accuracy. Click Finish to set up your account.

Other email software needs the same information and provides similar procedures for entering the information. Most software automatically runs the procedure to set up an account when you start the email software the first time. If you need to set up another account, you can start the procedure manually from the menu. For instance, in Mozilla, click File. Select New->Account.

Configuring Mozilla Email

Many email actions can be configured. Mozilla provides two different types of configuration. One group of settings is for the software in general. Another group of settings is specific to the email account you are using.

To change settings for a specific account, highlight the account in the sidebar. Click Edit. Select Mail & Newsgroup Account Settings. Some settings you can change are:

- **Signature:** Content that is added to every outgoing message. Create a text file containing the signature for every message. Highlight an account. Check "Attach this signature." Type the path to the signature file or click Choose to browse to the file.

- **Server Names:** Change the name of the incoming server. Click Server Settings.

- **Downloads:** Set how often messages are fetched from the incoming server. Default is when you open the software and every 10 minutes. Click Server Settings.

- **Return Receipts:** You can customize return receipts for this account. Specify whether to request them and what to do with receipt requests the account receives. Click Return Receipts.

To change settings for the email software—for all accounts, click Edit and select Preferences. Double-click Mail & Newsgroups to expand the category. Some settings you can change are:

- **Window Layout:** Choose between two layouts, as follows:

- **Spell Check:** Check spelling of outgoing mail when you click Send. Opens a window when an error is detected that allows you to correct the spelling.

- **Address Autocompletion:** When typing addresses, Mozilla matches your typing to entries in your address book and completes the address when it finds a match. Click Addressing.

- **Return Receipts:** Specify whether to request them and what to do with receipt requests the account receives. Click Return Receipts.

Reading Email in Mozilla

Open Mozilla email by clicking the email icon on the status bar of the Mozilla browser. Or select it from the main menu, probably located in the Internet submenu. The window in Figure 17-5 opens.

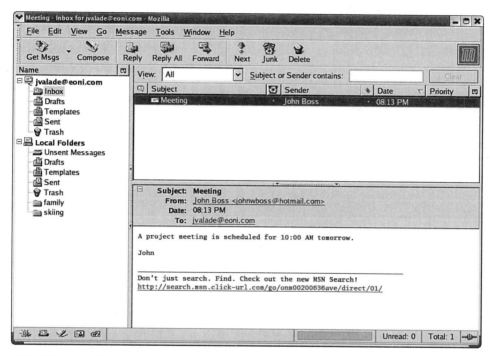

FIGURE 17-5 Mozilla mail window.

The sidebar shows the accounts that are currently set up. In the figure, two accounts display: jvalade@eoni.com and Local Folders. Local Folders is a special account, specifically for storing email messages on your hard disk.

You can expand an account (click +) to see the folders stored for the account. You can create new folders. In the figure, the last two local folders (family, skiing) were created by the user. The other folders are all created by default by Mozilla mail. To create a folder, click File. Select New->Folder. Supply a name and location.

In the figure, the inbox is open. One message is in the inbox. To read a message, click it in the top pane; the contents display in the bottom box. In the figure, the inbox message is highlighted, so the message is open in the bottom pane.

You can drag any message from the open top pane to a folder in the sidebar.

Sending Email in Mozilla

To send an email, click Compose. The window in Figure 17-6 opens.

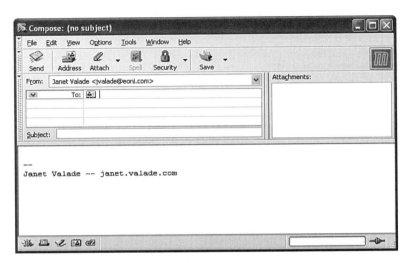

FIGURE 17-6 Mozilla mail compose window.

As you type an email address into the To line, Mozilla will fill in the address with matches from your address book. You can add another address by clicking the next line in the address window to open another To line. If you click the blue down arrow, a drop-down list opens with email headers you can use, such as cc and bcc.

You can also send a message, using the same window, by clicking Reply, Reply All, or Forward when a message in the top pane is highlighted. When you reply to a message, the content of the message is included in your reply by default. You can change this setting in File->Mail & Newsgroup Account Settings->Composition & Addressing.

You can send your message immediately by clicking Send. Or, you can send your message later. Click File in the compose window and select Send Later. The message is stored in the Unsent folder. At any time, you can click File and select Send Unsent Messages.

When any message is sent, a copy is stored in your Sent folder.

If you want to send any attachments, click Attach. A window opens where you can browse to the file you want to attach.

Mozilla Message Filters

You can set up a set of rules that direct incoming email into folders, rather than into your inbox. If you receive a lot of email, organizing your email is very helpful. Click Tools. Select Message Filters. The window in Figure 17-7 opens.

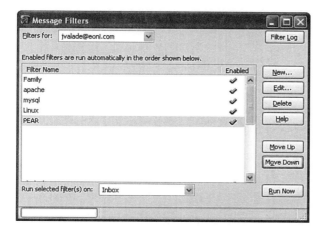

FIGURE 17-7   Mozilla message filters window.

The window shows a list of the current filters—sets of rules.

You can create a new filter, delete a filter, or edit an existing filter. You can also change the order of the filters in the list using the Move Up and Move Down buttons.

Each filter has one or more rules in it. Rules test whether incoming email meets specific criteria. If the message matches, it's handled as defined by the rule. For instance, a rule might look for messages coming from mom@home.com and send any messages from that address into the "Family" folder.

You can log the action of your filters. Click Filter Log. Check "Enable the Filter Log."

Click Run Now to apply the filters to the folder selected in the drop-down list at the bottom of the window. Any messages found that match an existing filter are handled immediately.

Creating a message filter is discussed in the next section.

Creating a Message Filter in Mozilla

When you click New in the window shown in Figure 17-7, the window in 17-8 opens.

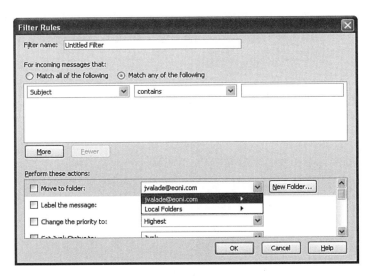

FIGURE 17-8   Mozilla mail window.

The conditions to match are set up in the top pane. The first field specifies what to match, such as subject, sender, body, date. The second field specifies a type of match, such as contains, doesn't contain, begins with, ends with. In the third field, type the characters for the match. For instance, a match might be Body contains big raise. To add another match condition, click More. If you have more than one match condition, check "Match all of the following" or "Match any of the following."

The bottom panel specifies what to do when a match is found. A common choice is to move the message into a folder. Check "Move to folder" and indicate which folder. The drop-down list allows you to select any existing folder. Or you can click New Folder to create a folder for messages that match this filter. Other actions for handling messages that match are to flag the message, mark the message, or change its priority.

Enter a name for the filter in the Filter Name field at the top. Enter any name that's meaningful to you.

You can also create a filter from a message. Right-click the From line of the open message and select Create Filter from Message.

Spam

Spam, called junk mail by Mozilla, is unsolicited mail that shows up in your mailbox. Most people prefer not to receive spam. However, most people prefer receiving spam to not receiving legitimate mail. Consequently, spam filters must balance between letting too much mail through, thereby missing some spam, and not letting enough mail through, thereby identifying some "real" mail as spam (false positives).

Mozilla includes a Bayesian spam filter. This type of spam control looks at a sample of real mail and a sample of junk mail and uses statistical analysis of the contents of the messages to identify spam. Consequently, the more messages of junk/non-junk status it has to analyze, the better it gets at recognizing spam.

The Mozilla junk mail controls must be "trained" before use. You should identify as large a sample of mail as possible. To mark the messages, highlight them. Click `Message`. Select `Mark->as junk` or `Mark->as not junk`. Junk mail is marked with a blue trash can. You can also mark mail as junk by clicking the round icon in the Junk column, something that can happen accidentally when you click a message to read it. The junk mail handler requires both junk and nonjunk messages to analyze.

Junk mail controls, shown on the right, are opened by highlighting an account, clicking `Tools` and selecting `Junk Mail Controls`. Check or uncheck the box to enable junk mail handling.

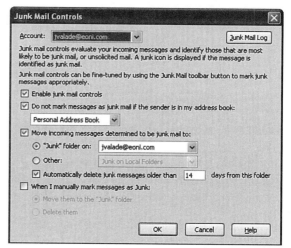

Check whether you want to mark mail as junk when it comes from a sender in your address book. Although junk mail may not come from a familiar address, a virus very well might mail itself from a familiar address.

You can log your junk mail activity. Click `Junk Mail Log` and check the `Enable` box.

Check your Junk folder frequently for false positives. Mark them as not junk. The more classified messages in the junk mail database, the better Mozilla becomes at correctly identifying junk without false positives.

Mozilla Address Book

Mozilla provides a full featured address book where you can store email addresses and other information, such as addresses, phone numbers, titles, etc., for contacts. You can have more than one address book for different categories of contacts. By default, two address books are set up for you: Personal Address Book and Collected Addresses.

To access the address book, click the address book icon in the lower right section of Mozilla. The window in Figure 17-9 opens.

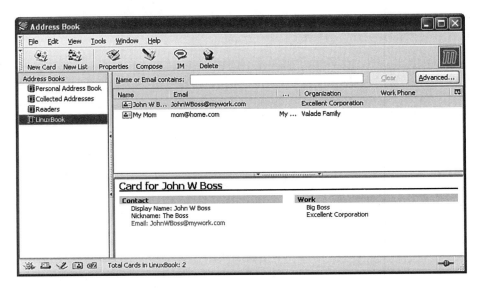

FIGURE 17-9 Mozilla address book.

In the address book, each contact has a card. In the figure, four address books appear in the sidebar. Two are default Mozilla address books. The last two are address books created by the user. To create one, click File and select New->Address Book.

In the figure, the LinuxBook address book is open. It contains two cards. The first card is open, showing information for John W Boss. To sort the address book, click View. Select View->Sort by.

You can search your address book. Click Tools and select Search Addresses. A window similar to Figure 17-8 opens, where you can define search queries. The first field provides a drop-down list that defines what to search, such as Any Name, Email, Work Phone, etc. The second field specifies a type of match, such as contains, doesn't contain, begins with, etc. You type the search terms into the third field. So, you might define a search like: Any Name contains Smith.

Adding and Editing Address Cards

When you open an address card, the window shown on the right opens to display the information. If you are creating a new address card, the fields are blank.

To create a new address card, click New Card in your address book. From the drop-down list at the top, select the address book where the card should be stored.

The window has three tabs where much information is collected. You can also define fields if additional information is needed.

In addition, you can add a new address from a message you receive. Click the To, cc, or bcc line in an open email message and select Add to Address Book. The window opens with the Email address already filled in.

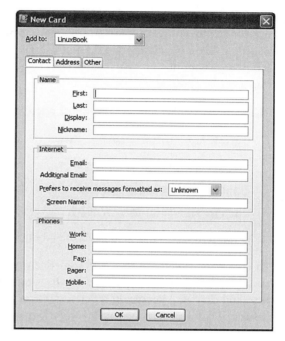

If you double-click an address line in your address book, this window opens, displaying the stored information for the address you clicked, so that you can edit the address card.

Mozilla automatically stores any address to which you send email. To change the setting for an address book, select an address book. Click Edit and select Preferences. Double-click Mail & Newsgroups. Click Addressing. Check or uncheck "Add Email Addresses." Select the address book where you want to store the addresses from the drop-down list. Collected Addresses is an address book that is set up by default for automatic email collection.

Mozilla can import address books from other mail software. Click Tools and select Import to start a wizard for importing address books.

You can create a mailing list. Click New List. Add the addresses for the list. You can drag the address cards from the address book to the mailing list.

Instant Messaging

Instant messaging (IM) is a service that allows you to communicate with other people in real time. If two of you are online at the same time, you can communicate by sending messages that immediately pop up on the other person's screen. Both sides of the conversation display in the message window, labeled with the sender's name, so you can see the ongoing dialogue.

There are several IM services. The most popular are:

- **AIM:** AOL Instant Messenger (www.aim.com)
- **MSN:** MSN Messenger (messenger.msn.com)
- **Yahoo:** Yahoo! Messenger (messenger.yahoo.com)
- **ICQ:** I Seek You (www.icq.com)
- **Jabber:** An open source, XML-based instant messaging service (www.jabber.org)

You can only instant message with someone who is logged in to the same IM service that you are logged in to. However, you can be logged in to more than one service at the same time and chat with people on different services at the same time. This chapter provides instructions for using AIM and MSN, the two most popular services.

Two steps are required for instant messaging:

1. **Sign up with the service you want to use.** You do this at the IM service Web site.

2. **Sign on to the service and send/receive messages.** This step requires IM client software. Most services provide proprietary software, specific to their service, for Windows. Only Jabber provides Linux software. If you used IM on Windows, you probably used the IM service client software.

   On Linux, you can use open source IM client software called Gaim that provides the basic IM services, without the unrelated features and ads that come along with the IM service proprietary software. Gaim can sign you on to any of the IM services listed above, several at once if you want to.

Signing Up for AIM

You need to sign up for an AOL Screen Name to use the AIM service. To create a Screen Name, go to the Web page my.screenname.aol.com. On the right side of the page, click the link "Need an Account? Create one free." A Web page with the form shown on the right opens.

When you fill in the form and submit it, you may see the message "Screen name not available," meaning someone else is using this name. Enter another name.

When you have entered a name that no one is using, you see a screen with the message "Congratulations! Your Screen Name is: **name.**"

You need to use the screen name and password you entered here to use AIM.

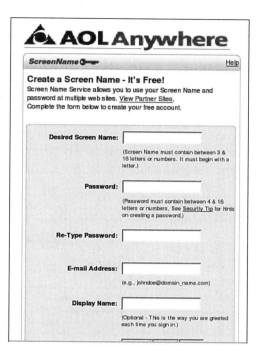

Signing Up for MSN Messenger

You need to sign up for a .NET Passport to use the MSN Messenger service. You can use a hotmail email account. Or you can sign up using your own email address.

To sign up and create a new hotmail account, go to registernet.passport.net. A Web page with the form shown on the right opens. The form requests information, such as name, zip code, and birth date. You enter an email account name for a new hotmail account.

The agreements are listed at the end of the form. You enter your name and click I Agree to submit your form for a Passport. A Web page displays saying "Registration is Complete." It shows your email address that serves as your Passport.

To sign up using your own email address, go to the Web page register.passport.net. A Web page with a shorter form opens. You need only fill in your email address and a password you choose for your Passport.

You need to use the email address and password you entered here to use MSN Messenger.

Signing On with Gaim

Gaim is IM client software. Many Linux distributions include Gaim. If necessary, you can download Gaim from gaim.sourceforge.net.

Before you can connect to your IM service, you need to enter your account information into Gaim. Start Gaim from the main menu. For instance, you can find it on the Fedora main menu at Internet->IM. When you start Gaim, the account window opens, as shown in Figure 17-10.

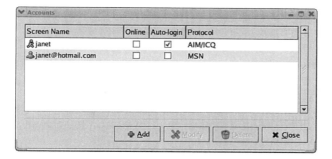

FIGURE 17-10   Gaim account window.

When you first start Gaim, the account window is blank. You need to enter your account. Click Add. The add account screen opens, as shown on the right. Select the protocol—AIM or MSN. Fill in the information for your account.

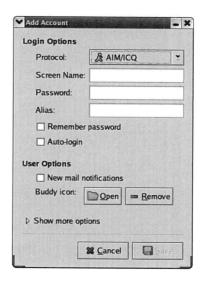

If you check Auto-login, your account will sign on automatically when you start Gaim. If you check Remember password, Gaim can sign your account on without prompting you for your password.

In Figure 17-10, neither account is currently signed on. When you start Gaim, your account signs on automatically if you checked Auto-login when you entered your account. If not, you see a Login window. Select the account from the drop-down list. Type the password. Click Sign on.

 When an account is signed on, an icon for the account is added to the system tray, as shown on the left. You can right-click this icon to send messages and perform other actions.

IM Conversations

When you are signed on, you can instant message to anyone who is also signed on. Right-click the service icon in the Gaim system tray and select New Instant Message. Enter the Screen Name or Passport of the person you want to reach. The window on the right opens, with blank panes.

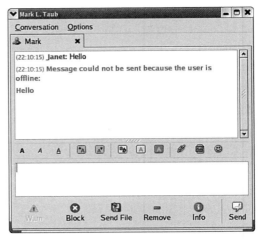

The bottom pane is where you type the messages to send. The icons above the pane set font, color, etc. Click Send.

The upper pane shows all the messages in the order sent, so you can see the entire conversation. In the screen shown above, a message was sent by Janet to Mark saying Hello. The IM service responds that Mark is not online.

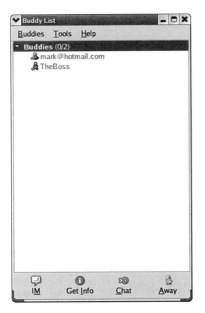

You don't have to guess who is signed on, ready to receive a message. The IM service can keep you informed. You set up a list of contacts. The service tells you whether your contacts are online.

The window on the left opens when you sign on. It lists your contacts and whether they are online. The window shows two buddies in your buddy list, neither of whom is currently online.

To add contacts to your list, click Buddies and select Add Buddy.

You can organize your contacts into groups. The Buddies group is created by default. You can add your own groups. Click Buddies and select Add Group.

Click IM at the bottom to send a message.

Newsgroups

Newsgroups are discussion groups on the Internet provided by Usenet. Each newsgroup is devoted to a specific topic, any topic you can think of and many that would never occur to you. A newsgroup is analogous to a public message board for a specific subject. Anyone can post a message to the newsgroup. Anyone can read all the messages posted. Anyone can respond to any message, posting a response.

Newsgroups are available two ways:

- **Web site:** Many Web sites offer access to newsgroups. Using your browser, you read and post messages at the Web site. Some sites offer a subset of newsgroups. Others let you read, but not post. Some Web sites charge for newsgroup access.

  For example, Google provides access to Usenet Newsgroups. On the Google search page, click Groups. One choice on the resulting page is All Usenet Newsgroups. You can read the public messages. If you want to post to a newsgroup, you need to create a Google account.

- **Newsgroup server:** You can receive newsgroups directly from a newsgroup server. Many ISPs provide a newsgroup server, although some provide only a subset of available newsgroups. Many colleges and universities provide a newsgroup server. Large organizations might provide one. Or, you can independently purchase access to a newsgroup server for a monthly fee from a Usenet news service, such as www.newshosting.com and www.easynews.com.

  To access Usenet newsgroups directly from a server, you need newsreader application software on your computer. Mozilla mail provides a newsreader. It can be quite convenient to receive and post newsgroup messages in the same application that handles email messages. The rest of this section describes using Mozilla to read newsgroup postings.

Using Mozilla mail, newsgroup postings arrive in your mail window looking very similar to email messages. Before you can read and post messages, two steps are required:

1. Create a newsgroup account.

2. Subscribe to newsgroups of interest.

To create a newsgroup account, click File and select New->Account. The screen shown in Figure 17-1 opens. Check Newsgroup. The new account procedure requests the needed information—the name of the newsgroup server you want to use.

To subscribe to newsgroups, highlight the newsgroup account in the Mozilla sidebar. Click File. Click Subscribe. The window in Figure 17-11 opens.

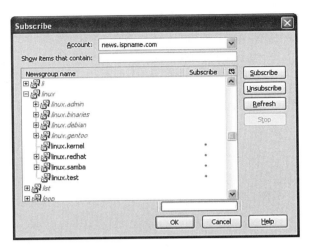

FIGURE 17-11 Newsgroups subscribe window.

When it opens, the list box is blank. The complete list of newsgroup names includes thousands of groups, which takes some time to read in, let alone look at. The search box above the list allows you to search for lists with names of interest. To subscribe to a group, click its name and click Subscribe.

The names of your subscribed groups are listed in the Mozilla sidebar under the newsgroup account. You handle your newsgroup messages basically the same way you handle your email messages, as described earlier in this chapter.

To read the messages in a newsgroup, select the newsgroup and click Get Messages. 500 messages download at one time, unless you change this in Edit->Mail & Newsgroup Account Settings->Server Settings. You post messages by clicking Compose. You respond to messages by clicking Reply.

Summary

The Internet makes worldwide communication possible. Three of the most popular forms of communication are email, instant messaging, and Usenet newsgroups. This chapter provides information on:

- Email accounts
- Email software
- Using Mozilla to read and send messages
- Filtering email messages
- Spam
- Address books
- Newsgroups

The next chapter discusses editing text files. Text files are files that contain only text characters, with no formatting information. HTML files, program source code, and many Linux configuration files are text files.

## CHAPTER 18

Editing Text Files

Text files are files that contain only text characters, with no formatting information. HTML files, program source code, and many Linux configuration files are text files. Although you can edit text files with a word processor, it's generally simpler to use a text editor—an application that has only the features necessary to edit text.

Many text editors have a GUI interface. If you are working on your desktop, a GUI editor is useful. However, sometimes you need a command-based editor to use at the command line. This chapter provides instructions for using a GUI editor and a command-based editor:

- **Kate:** (KDE Advanced Text Editor) A basic text editor with a GUI, similar to Notepad. However, Kate has many more capabilities than Notepad.

- **vi:** A command-based text editor, suitable for use at the command line. vi is installed on every Linux and UNIX system, regardless of what other text editors are installed. Many Linux distributions provide an updated version of vi called vim. Any commands that work in vi also work in vim.

  If you come from a Windows background, the vi text-based environment may be unfamiliar to you. In vi, you press keys to execute editing commands that change the file contents. You may be more familiar with clicking icons or selecting menu items to change the file.

Both editors allow basic editing, such as insert text, delete text, replace text, copy text. Both editors also have major advanced features and features useful for programmers, such as:

- **Multiple document editing:** Can have many documents open at the same time. Can copy from one file to another.

- **Plug-ins:** Can add plug-ins for additional functionality. For instance, Kate has a spell checker plug-in.

- **Syntax highlighting:** Colored highlighting of source code syntax.

Opening a File in Kate

Kate can be started from the KDE main menu (Editors->Kate). Or you can start it by typing Kate at the command line, either using Run or in a terminal window, both in KDE and GNOME. Kate is shown in Figure 18-1.

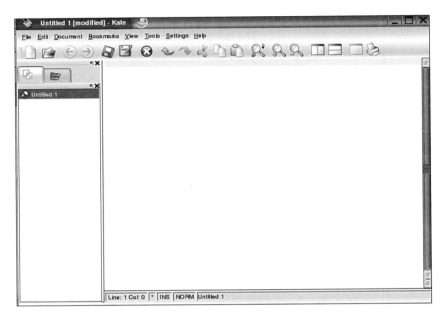

FIGURE 18-1 Kate text editor.

The figure shows Kate empty, with no file opened. By default, Kate opens the last file edited. To stop opening files at startup, click Settings and select Configure Kate. Uncheck "Reopen files at startup." You can open a file from the File menu item or by dragging and dropping a file from the desktop, Konqueror, or other sources into Kate.

In the figure, the Files tab is selected, opening the file list that shows all open files. Currently, only one file is open—Untitled 1. Click the Folders tab, to open the File Selector, where you can locate and open a file.

The editing window can be split, allowing you to edit more than one file at a time or two locations in the same file. Click View and select Horizontal Split or Vertical Split. Select Close Current to close a section of the window. Select New View to open a new editing window.

Editing in Kate

The process of adding and editing document content is familiar to users of text editors (such as Notepad) or word processors (such as Word or WordPerfect). Insert text at the cursor by typing it. Delete text with <Backspace> or <Del>. Replace text by highlighting it and typing new text over it. The Kate Edit menu contains familiar items, such as copy, cut, paste, and find and replace. The undo command can undo up to 256 actions in a row.

Kate allows you to highlight rows, instead of columns. To change to column selection, click Edit and select Toggle Block Selection. Select it again to change back to row selection.

Plug-ins are available for Kate that add to its basic capabilities. For instance, a spell checker plug-in is available. You must activate a plug-in before you can use it. To do so, click Tools and select Configure Kate. Expand Applications (click the plus sign, +) and click Plugins. A list of plug-ins that you can check or uncheck displays. If you check the box by Spell Checker and click OK, a Spelling item is added to the Tools menu.

Kate provides a find command that allows you to find and open a file based on its content. Click Tools and select Find in File to see the window shown on the right. Enter the text you are searching for in the Pattern field. In the Files field, specify the filenames to be searched in. The Directory field specifies where to search. Check recursive to search subdirectories. The files found are shown in the list box. If you double-click a filename, the file opens in Kate.

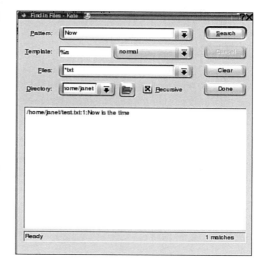

The pattern field in this window allows you to enter a regular expression—a pattern that can be used to match text strings. For instance, you can search for numbers or words beginning with *S*. The Find and Find and Replace commands found on the Edit menu also allow you to search for regular expressions. Using regular expressions is explained in Appendix A.

Kate Features for Programmers

Kate has several features that are useful for writing program code:

- **Line Numbers:** Kate can add temporary line numbers to the beginning of each line in a file. Line numbers are useful for programmers when debugging a program. Click View. Select Show Line Numbers.

- **Syntax Highlighting:** Kate highlights syntax for many programming languages, from C and C++ to HTML and JavaScript. Click Tools. Select Highlight Mode. By default, Normal mode is checked, which means no syntax highlighting. Select a category from Sources, Markup, Games, Scripts, or Other and select the language you are writing code in.

- **Word Wrap:** Word wrap is on by default. You can turn it off by clicking Settings and selecting Configure Kate. Expand Editor (click the +). Click Editing. Uncheck the box by "Enable Word Wrap."

- **Indenting:** You can indent or unindent a highlighted block of text using the Indent and Unindent items from the Tools menu. You can set the number of spaces to indent in Settings->Configure Kate. Expand Editor. Click Editing. Select a number for the "Tab and Indent Width" text box. You can also check "Replace tabs with spaces" if desired. You can set Kate to automatically indent within parentheses and brackets by clicking Indentation and checking "Automatically Indent."

- **Comments:** Kate can add comments to your code, based on the language selected when Highlight mode is turned on. With no text highlighted, you can insert comment marks by clicking Tools and selecting Comment. You can then type the comment text. Or you can highlight some text and select Comment and Kate will comment out the code, using the method appropriate to the selected language. You can also uncomment existing comments by highlighting the comment and selecting Uncomment from the Tools menu.

Opening a File in vi

vi is a command-line editor, for use in a terminal window. To open a file in vi, type:

```
vi testfile
```

testfile is the filename. In Figure 18-2, testfile doesn't exist, so a new file is opened.

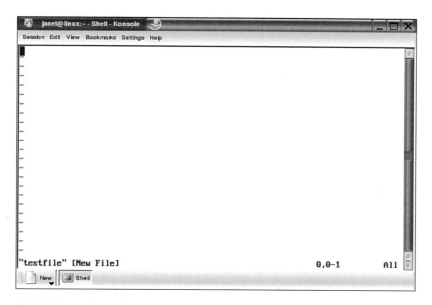

FIGURE 18-2   vi text editor.

The tildes represent lines that don't exist in the file. As you insert text into the file, the tildes disappear. The filename is shown below the open file.

Most Linux distributions provide vim as the major text editor. vim is an advanced version of vi. In most cases, you should use vim. For many distributions, the vi command actually opens vim. If it doesn't, you can type:

```
vim testfile
```

The commands described in this chapter work equally well in vi or vim.

Editing and Saving Files with vi

vi operates in one of two modes. vi behaves differently, depending on which mode it's in:

- **Normal mode:** The characters you type are editing commands that perform operations on your file, such as moving the cursor, deleting a character or a line, etc. There are two types of commands:

  - **Keys sequences:** Pressing keys issues commands to vi. For instance, pressing x deletes the character after the cursor.

  - **Command line:** Pressing a semicolon allows you to type commands with arguments. The cursor moves to the bottom of the screen, waiting for you to type a command.

- **Insert mode:** When you type keys, the characters are inserted into the file. Typing certain commands, such as i (the insert command), puts vi into Insert mode. Pressing the <Esc> key ends Insert mode, returning vi to normal mode.

vi opens a file in Normal mode. vi changes to insert mode when you enter a command that inserts text into a file. For instance, the <i> key is the insert command. It changes vi to insert mode and allows you to type text into the file. vi stays in insert mode until you press <Esc>, which ends Insert mode and returns to Normal mode. Another command that changes vi to insert mode is <a>, the append command, which allows you to insert text after the cursor.

In Normal mode, keys are commands. Most commands are one key, although some require a two key sequence. Almost all the commands allow you to type a number before the command. The command is repeated the number of times specified by the number. For instance, <dd> is the command to delete a line. <3dd> deletes 3 lines. If you enter no number before the command, the number 1 is assumed.

A small set of vi commands is described in this chapter. This set is sufficient for most editing tasks. However, vi has many abilities not presented here. If you often edit at the command line, you will appreciate learning more of vi's capabilities. See the vi (or vim) documentation on your system for complete documentation.

After adding/editing the file content as described in the remainder of this chapter, save the file by pressing <ZZ> (notice that ZZ is uppercase). You can close a file without saving any changes by typing:

:q!

You can save a file without exiting vi with the command :w.

Moving Around a File in vi

Usually, you can use the arrow keys on your keyboard to move around the open file in vi. In some cases, such as a very old or very minimal Linux installation, the arrow keys don't operate.

You can always move around your file using the key commands in Table 18-1.

TABLE 18-1   Commands for Moving Around in a File

Key	What It Does
j	Moves cursor down one line.
k	Moves cursor up one line.
l	Moves cursor one character to the right.
h	Moves cursor one character to the left.
G	Moves cursor to the last line of the file.
L	Moves cursor to the last line on the screen.
Ctrl-d	Moves down one screen.
Ctrl-u	Moves up one screen.
:n	Moves the cursor to line n. For instance, :1 moves to the first line of the file.
$	Moves to the end of the current line.
^	Moves to the first non-space character in the current line.
0 (zero)	Moves to the beginning of the line.
w	Moves to the beginning of the next word.
b	Moves to the beginning of the previous word.
e	Moves to the end of the word.

NOTE

Be sure to use the correct case. vi is case sensitive. It doesn't see a and A as the same command.

In addition to the commands to move the cursor, you can move to specific text characters or strings by searching for them. You can search for a character in a line using the f (find) command. The syntax is fx, where x is the character to find. For instance, fh moves to the next *h*.

To search the entire file, press /. The cursor moves to the bottom of the screen. Type the text to search for. When you press <Enter>, the cursor moves to the next instance of the text. After finding one instance of the text, just press / again to search further for the same text. Use ? to search backward through the file.

vi Editing Commands

vi changes the content of the text file in response to keys that you press. Table 18-2 shows the most useful commands.

TABLE 18-2   vi Editing Commands

Operation	Command	What It Does
Insert	i	Inserts text before the cursor. (Insert mode)
	a	Inserts text after the cursor. (Insert mode)
	o	Inserts a line after the current line. (Insert mode)
	O	Inserts a line before the current line. (Insert mode)
	A	Appends text at the end of the line. (Insert mode)
	I	Inserts text at the start of the current line. (Insert mode)
Delete	x	Deletes the character under the cursor.
	dd	Deletes the current line. Saves line in a buffer.
	dw	Deletes the next word.
	D	Deletes from the cursor to the end of the line.
Replace	rx	Replaces the current character with x.
	s	Replaces one character with text. (Insert mode)
	cw	Replaces a word with text you type. (Insert mode)
	cc	Replaces a line with text you type. (Insert mode)
	C	Replaces text from cursor to end of the line with text you type. (Insert mode)
Copy	YY	Copies a line into the buffer.
Put	p	Copies text from buffer into file following the current line.
Undo	u	Undoes the last change to the file.
	U	Undoes all changes on the current line.
Help	:help	Displays a help file.

NOTE
Commands that turn on Insert mode are noted in the table. Press <Esc> when finished inserting text to return to Normal mode.

Sample vi Editing Session

This section describes a sample vi editing session. The file to be edited contains the following contents:

```
One fith
Two fish
Red fishes
Blue fish
```

When the file opens, vi is in Normal mode. Type the following editing commands:

```
/fith<Enter>
ftrs
```

The file now contains:

```
One fish
Two fish
Red fishes
Blue fish
```

Type the following commands:

```
2j1D          (1 is lowercase L)
```

The file now contains:

```
One fish
Two fish
Red fish
Blue fish
```

Enter the following commands:

```
:1<Enter>
ddjp
```

The file now contains:

```
Two fish
Red fish
One fish
Blue fish
```

Summary

Text files are files that contain only text characters, with no formatting information. HTML files, program source code, and many Linux configuration files are text files. Although you can edit text files with a word processor, it's generally simpler to use a text editor—an application that has only the features necessary to edit text.

This chapter provides instructions for using two editors: Kate, a GUI editor; and vi, a command-line editor. Instructions are provided for basic editing, such as deleting and inserting text. Some features useful for programmers are also described.

Kate is very similar to Notepad. Editing in Kate will feel familiar to Windows users. The methods of inserting, deleting, opening files, and saving files are similar. vi, however, is a command-line editor. Its procedures for inserting, deleting, and other editing of text will be new to many users. Because it's more unfamiliar, a sample editing session is provided for vi.

One type of text file that you create and edit with a text editor is a program or script. Each line is an instruction to be executed by the computer. A useful type of script is a shell script. You can write a script that contains Linux commands, executed one by one when the script is run. Chapter 19 describes how to write shell scripts.

CHAPTER 19

Shell Scripts

Shell scripts are text files containing commands. The use of commands at the command-line interface is explained in Chapter 7, including their syntax and capabilities. The same commands, using the same syntax, can be stored in a shell script. When you run the script, the commands are executed, one by one, starting from the beginning, just as if you were typing them directly into the shell yourself, one by one. Often you can save yourself a great deal of typing by putting commands you enter frequently into shell scripts.

Shell scripts are often used to perform routine system maintenance tasks. For instance, you might write a shell script that backs up specific files to another computer on your network. Or you might want to rename all the files in your directory. Or you might want to edit all the files on your company Web site by changing your company address from an old address to a new address.

This chapter explains how to write shell scripts. This chapter is an introduction to shell scripts that doesn't begin to show the advanced power provided by shell scripts. You can learn how to create uncomplicated shell scripts for everyday tasks; if you want to do advanced shell scripting, however, you need to read a more complete treatment of the subject. Complete books are written about shell scripting.

Commands are not explained in this chapter. Chapter 7 explains the syntax of using commands. Appendix B provides a reference, with details, of the most useful commands.

A Simple Shell Script

A shell script is a text file containing a series of commands that execute in sequence when the script is run. Shell scripts allow you to run several commands at once. Create the following simple shell script in a text editor (using text editors is discussed in Chapter 18) and save it with the name dir2file:

```
#!/bin/bash
# Script Name: dir2file - A simple shell script that saves a directory listing in a file
ls -l > dirlist
echo Directory is saved
```

The first two lines are not commands, so they don't run. The lines begin with a pound sign (#), also called a hash mark, which means they don't execute. The first line tells Linux what program to use to run this script. In this case, the line (often called the shebang) calls the Bash shell. The first line of a Perl script would call Perl, rather than the shell. In this case, you could run the program without the shebang line, but the script is clearer with the line.

The second line is a comment. That is, a note to yourself. The shell ignores comments.

The last two lines are the commands that the shell script executes. The lines are exactly the same commands that you would enter at the command line. Chapter 7 explains how to use the command-line interface. Appendix B is a reference of commands. In this script, the ls command and the echo command are used. The ls command saves a long listing of the directory in a file named dirlist. When the ls command finishes, the echo command displays "Directory is saved" on the screen.

The script must have execute permissions in order to run. (Permissions are discussed in Chapter 9.) The following commands check and change the file permission, giving execute permission to the file owner:

```
ls -l dir2file
-rw-r--r-- 1 janet       janet     79  2005-01-09 15:57 dir2file
chmod u+x dir2file
ls -l dir2file
-rwxr--r-- 1 janet       janet     79  2005-01-09 15:59 dir2file
```

Now you can run the program as follows and see the output.

```
./dir2file
Directory is saved
```

If you list your directory now, you see file dirlist in your directory. If you display the file dirlist to the screen (cat dirlist), you see that it contains the output of ls -l.

The Basics of Variables and Arrays

Variables are containers that have names and hold information, either numbers or text. Variable names can consist of letters, numbers, and underscores (_). The name can begin with a letter or an underscore, but not a number. To create a variable, store information in it. The following are valid commands that store information:

```
var1=3
_var2=Hello
full_name="John Smith"
```

No space is allowed before or after the =. Notice the first two commands do not use quotes around the information. The third command requires quotes because it includes a space. Without quotes, the shell would store John and see Smith as a new command.

When you use a variable value, you precede the variable name with a $, such as:

```
echo $_var2
Hello
```

You can set one variable equal to another as follows:

```
new_name=$full_name
echo $new_name
John Smith
```

The simple script from the previous section is modified below to use a variable:

```
#!/bin/bash
# Script Name: dir2file - A simple shell script that saves a directory listing in a file
status="Directory is saved"
ls -l > dirlist
echo $status
```

When you run this script, the output is identical to the output in the previous section.

You can store groups of values under a single variable name, useful when values are related. Complex variables that store groups of values are called arrays. For instance, you might set up the following array:

```
full_name[1]=John
full_name[2]=Smith
```

When you use the value of an array, enclose the name in curly brackets, as follows:

```
echo ${full_name[2]}
```

Reading Data into Variables

You can store data into a variable from one of the following sources:

- Assigning a value in the script using the equal sign (=). This method is discussed in the previous section.

- Storing the output of a command using back ticks (`).

- Passing the information on the command line when starting the script.

- Prompting the user to enter data with the read command.

This section describes how to read data into variables using these methods.

The previous section discussed assigning simple values using the equal sign. You can also store arithmetic calculations in a variable using the let command, as follows:

```
let sum=3+4
let total=total+1
let sum=$n1+$n2-3
```

You can add (+), subtract (-), multiply (*), or divide (/). You can use modulus (%), which returns the remainder of a division (8%5 = 3).

You can store the output of a command using back ticks, as follows:

```
today=`date`
```

The shell executes the date command, storing the output in today, as shown below:

```
echo $today
Sun Jan    9 15:37:45 PST 2005
```

You can pass variable values on the command line when you start the script, as follows:

```
./dir2file 21 33 44
```

The values are stored in built-in shell script variables that are numbered, starting with $0. The above command results in the following variables:

```
echo $0
dir2file
echo $1
21
echo $2
33
echo $3
44
```

Notice that the first information item read from the command line is the name of the script, which is stored in $0.

The simple script from the previous section is modified below to use information input at the command line:

```
#!/bin/bash
# Script Name: dir2file - A simple shell script that saves a directory listing in a file
ls -l > dirlist
echo $1
```

To pass in the value for the variable $1, run the script as follows:

```
./dir2file "Directory is saved"
Directory is saved
```

The same script is modified below to request information from the user:

```
#!/bin/bash
# Script Name: dir2file - A simple shell script that saves a directory listing in a file
echo -n "Enter text: "
read status
ls -l > dirlist
echo $status
```

When the script reaches the third line (echo -n), it echoes the text. When it reaches the next line (read), it waits for input from the keyboard. When the user presses <Enter>, the remaining two lines are executed. The session looks as follows:

```
./dir2file
Enter text: Directory is saved
Directory is saved
```

The bold text is typed by the person using the script. The nonbold text is displayed by the script.

Shell scripts also provide built-in variables that you can use. One useful variable is HOME that contains the path to the home directory of the account that is running the script. Another variable is PWD, which contains the path to the current directory. To see a description of all the built-in variables, look at the man page for builtin (man builtins). You can use built-in variables the same way you use your own created variables:

```
echo $HOME
```

Special Characters and Quotes

Shell scripts can take advantage of the special meanings given to certain characters. Useful special characters are:

- *****   Represents any string of characters in a filename. Used alone, * results in a list of all filenames in the current directory, except filenames that begin with a dot.

- **?**   Represents a single character in a filename. Using file? would result in a list of filenames containing file1, file3, and file9, but not file10, file20, etc.

- **[...]**   A substitution list that contains a set of characters to be matched. For instance, if you used file[xyz], the resulting list would include filex and filey, but not filea or fileq.

- **[!...]**   A substitution list that contains a set of characters to avoid. For instance, the list generated using file[xyz] would include fileb and filew, but not filex or filez.

- **$**   Signals the beginning of a variable name.

You can turn off the meaning of special characters by enclosing them in quotes. Double quotes and single quotes have different effects. Double quotes turn off some special characters, but allow the substitution of variables values. Single quotes turn off all special characters, allowing no variable substitution, as shown by the following commands:

```
city="San Diego"
echo $city "$city" '$city'
San Diego San Diego $city
```

As you can see, the single quotes turn off the $ and echo the literal characters between the quotes. You can tell the shell to treat a special character as a literal by preceding it with a back slash, as follows:

```
echo \$city
$city
```

Flow Control

Command execution in a script flows from the first line to the last. However, it's possible to change the order of statement execution. The shell provides two types of commands that change the order of statement execution:

- **Conditional statements:** The commands in a conditional statement execute only when a condition is found to be true. Some commands do not execute when the script runs because the condition under which they execute never occurs. By executing statements only when certain conditions are met, the script provides more flexibility to respond to varying conditions. For instance, the script can delete junk files if today is Friday, but not if today is Monday.

  The shell provides two conditional statements:

  - **if statement:** Tests one or more conditions. Executes commands when a condition is true. You can define sets of alternate commands to execute when none of the conditions are true.

  - **case statement:** Sets up alternative sections in the case statement, each section containing a set of commands. A pattern is set up for each section. The case statement tests a string. The case statement then executes the commands in the section where the string matches the section pattern.

- **Loops:** The commands in a loop repeat. The commands can repeat as many times as needed. For instance, the script can process each file in a directory using the same commands. The commands repeat once for each file. Or, a loop can be set to repeat a number of times, such as 10 times.

  The shell provides three useful looping statements:

  - **for loop:** The commands in a for loop are set to repeat as long as a condition is true. Often used to set up a loop that repeats a specified number of times.

  - **while loop:** The commands in a while loop continue to repeat as long as a specified condition is true.

  - **until loop:** The commands in an until loop continue to repeat until a specified condition is true.

Testing Conditions

The shell provides a test command for testing conditions. The test commands test expressions to see whether the expression is true, as follows:

```
test $age -eq 21
[ $age -eq 21 ]
```

The two statements are equivalent. This chapter uses the second format. A space is required before and after each square bracket. The test returns true if $age equals 21.

Table 19-1 lists the options you can use to test values.

TABLE 19-1 Options for Use When Testing Expressions

Option	Tests for	Example
=	equal text strings	[$name = "John"]
!=	non equal text strings	[$name1 != $name2]
-eq	equal integers	[$age -eq $adult]
-gt	integer1 is greater than integer2	[$age -gt 20]
-ge	integer1 is greater than or equal to integer2	[$age -ge 21]
-lt	integer1 is less than integer2	[$age -lt 18]
-le	integer1 is less than or equal to integer2	[$age le 17]
-ne	non equal integers	[$age1 ne $age2]
-n	string longer than 0	[-n $name]
-z	string with 0 characters	[-z $name]

The test command can also be used to test file characteristics. Table 19-2 lists the most useful options for testing files.

TABLE 19-2 Options for Use When Testing Files

Option	Tests for	Example
-nt	file1 newer than file2	[test1 -nt test2]
-ot	file1 older than file2	[test1 -ot test2]
-d	file exists and is a directory	[-d $dirname]
-f	file exists and is a regular file	[-f $filename]
-r	file exists and is readable	[-r $filename]
-s	file exists and has a size greater than 0	[-s test2]
-w	file exists and is writeable	[-w $filename]
-x	file exists and is executable	[-x $filename]

You can test for the negative of any expression by putting an exclamation mark at the beginning of the test, as follows:

```
[ ! $name = "Sam" ]
```

This condition is true if $name does not equal Sam. It can equal anything else.

A condition can consist of more than one expression. The options for testing multiple expressions are:

```
-o   (or)
-a   (and)
```

The -o tests whether either one of the two expressions it connects is true. The -a tests whether both of the expressions it connects are true. For instance:

```
[ $age -le 50 -a $age -gt 30 ]
```

For this condition to test true, both expressions must be true. This condition tests for age 31–50. You can test several conditions, as follows:

```
[ $ age -lt 50 -a $name = "John" -a $weight -eq 200 ]
```

If Statements

If statements test conditions and execute commands when the condition is true. The if statement has the following general format:

```
if [ condition ]
   then
       commands
elif [ condition ]
   then
       commands
else
       commands
fi
```

The if statements begins with if and ends with fi (if spelled backward). All three parts are not required. Only the if section is required. The elif (elseif) and the else sections are optional. Also, notice that the if section and the elif section start with then, but the else section does not. You can use more than one elif section, but only one if and else section is allowed. An if statement can be as simple as:

```
if [ $x -eq 1 ]
   then
     echo Hello
fi
```

A more complex statement is:

```
if [ $day = "Saturday" -o $day = "Sunday" ]
   then
       echo Sleep in
elif [ $day = "Monday" ]
   then
       echo Call in sick
else
       echo Go to work
fi
```

You can nest if statements inside of if statements, as follows:

```
if [ $city = "Miami" ]
   then
   if [ $name = "John" ]
       then
          echo Hello John in Miami
   else
          echo Hello friend in Miami
   fi
fi
```

Case Statements

Case statements allow you to test a string using a series of patterns, executing only the commands for the matching pattern. The general format of the case statement is:

```
case string in
    pattern_1)
        commands
        ;;
    pattern_2)
        commands
        ;;
  pattern_3)
        commands
        ;;
...
esac
```

The patterns you can use are:

- *   Matches any string of characters.

- ? Matches any single character.

- [...]   Matches any character or a range of characters in the brackets. A range is specified with a hyphen (e.g. A-Z or 1-4).

- | Matches the pattern on either side of the | (e.g., John|Sam).

An example case statement is:

```
#!/bin/bash
name=John
case $name in
    john|John)
        echo Welcome $name
        ;;
    sam|Sam)
        echo Hello $name
        ;;
    *)
        echo You're not invited
        ;;
esac
```

The * is used for the last case, to handle all the conditions not listed specifically in previous sections of the case statement. Any string that doesn't contain John or Sam's name matches the last case.

For Loops

A for loop repeats commands once for each item in a list of arguments. The general format of a for loop is:

```
for index in list
do
     commands
done
```

The index is a variable name. It takes on a value from the list with each iteration of the loop. The list is a list of arguments through which for loops. A simple for loop is:

```
for name in John Sam Paul
do
     echo $name
done
```

Items in the list can be separated by a space or by the end of a line.

You can provide the for loop with a list of arguments by executing a command. For instance, the following script processes the output of the date command.

```
#!/bin/bash
# Script name: splitdate - outputs parts of the date in a column
for part in `date`
do
     echo $part
done
```

When you run the script, you see:

```
./splitdate
Mon
Jan
10
15:02:34
PST
2005
```

Another way to create a list of arguments is to store them in a file and read the file, as follows:

```
for item in `cat file1`
do
     echo $item
done
```

If you leave out the in parameter, the script looks for the list in the numbered variables, assuming you entered a list on the command line. Thus, you can use the following syntax to enter your list at the command line:

```
for name
do
      echo $name
done
```

Then run the script with:

```
./listnames John Sam Paul
John
Sam
Paul
```

The for loop is useful for processing each file in a directory. The following for loop echoes each file in the current directory:

```
for file in *
do
      if [ ! -s $file ]
        then
              echo Removing $file
              rm $file
      fi
done
```

The code tests whether the file is empty. If it's empty, the filename displays and the file is deleted.

The * represents all files in the current directory. You can specify a different directory with the line below:

```
for file in /home/janet/*
```

While Loops and Until Loops

The commands in a while loop continue to execute as long as the condition is true. The general format of a while loop is:

```
while [ condition ]
do
      commands
done
```

The while loop first tests the condition. If it's true, the commands are executed. When the script reaches done, it returns to the while line and tests the condition again. If the condition's still true, it executes the commands again. If the condition is not true, it proceeds to the command following the while loop.

The simple shell script below executes the while loop four times:

```
#!/bin/bash
# Script name: numbers - outputs a list of numbers
n=0
while [ $n -lt 3 ]
do
      echo $n
      let n=n+1
done
echo After loop
```

The program execution is shown below:

```
./numbers
0
1
2
After loop
```

The until loop is very similar, except it **stops** looping when the condition is true. To get the above output, you would use the following until loop, changing -lt to -eq:

```
n=0
until [ $n -eq 3 ]
do
      echo $n
      let n=n+1
done
echo After loop
```

Infinite Loops

Loops can be infinite loops. That is, loops that continue repeating forever. Infinite loops are seldom written deliberately. They usually result from a scripting error. No one is immune.

The following program results in an infinite loop:

```
#!/bin/bash
while [ $n -lt 10 ]
do
    n=0
    echo $n
    let n=$n+1
done
```

The output from this program is:

```
0
0
0
0
...
```

continuing forever because $n is set to 0 at the beginning of each loop. Therefore, $n will never become equal to 10. So, the loop will never stop.

Another common scripting mistake is to leave out the statement that increments the value being tested. For instance, if you left out the let command in the above script, you would create an infinite loop.

You can stop an infinite loop with <Ctrl-c>. Perhaps more than one <Ctrl-c>. It should break out of the script. Also, a <Ctrl-z> works. It stops the script. Sometimes the output will continue to display for a time, but it will stop shortly.

Scheduling Scripts to Run Automatically

Linux allows you to schedule a command to run at a specified time. You can use this ability to schedule scripts to run automatically. You schedule jobs using the `crontab` command.

The first time you schedule a job, you create a file with the commands you want to schedule. Each command goes on a separate line. The `crontab` format requires six items on the line, each separated by a space. The items are, in the order of occurrence:

- **Min:** Minute to run. Values can be 0–59.

- **Hour:** Hour to run. Values can be 0–23.

- **Day of month:** Day of the month to run. Values can be 1–31.

- **Month:** Month to run. Values can be 1–12.

- **Day of week:** Day of week to run. Values can be 0–6, with 0 being Sunday.

- **Command:** Command to run.

Each item must be present. If an item is not relevant for your scheduling, enter *. Below are two `crontab` entries that run a shell script:

```
59 0 * * * /home/janet/backup
0 2 * * 5 /home/janet/cleanup
```

The first line runs the script backup at midnight every night. The second line runs cleanup at 2 a.m. every Friday.

Create a file named crontab that contains entries for the jobs you want to run automatically. To schedule your jobs, type:

```
crontab crontab
```

This will schedule your jobs. If the command fails, you may need to change to the root account. As root, you can schedule the job for another user, as follows:

```
crontab -u janet crontab
```

You can see what is scheduled for you by typing:

```
crontab -l
```

You can change your scheduled jobs by typing:

```
crontab -e
```

A Sample Script

The following is a sample script. It backs up selected files from a directory:

```
#!/bin/bash
# Script name: project1_backup
# Description: Backs up project files into a subdirectory
for file in proj1*
do
    fback=project1/$file.bak
    if [ -f $fback ]
      then
        if [ $fback -nt $file ]
          then
              cp $file $fback
              echo `date` $file backed up >> backup.log
        fi
    else
        cp $file $fback
        echo `date` $file backed up >> backup.log
    fi
done
```

The script iterates through a list of filenames that begin with proj1. It checks whether the current file is newer than the existing backup file. If so, it copies the current file into the backup directory, giving it a .bak extension. Also, any current file that has not yet been backed up is copied into the backup directory.

Summary

Shell scripts are text files containing commands, the same commands you can use at the command-line interface discussed in Chapter 7. When you run the script, the commands are executed, one by one, starting from the beginning to the end. Shell scripts are useful to automate repetitive tasks.

This chapter describes the syntax for writing shell scripts, including how to:

- Create a shell script
- Use variables and arrays
- Use special characters
- Control the flow of the script using conditional statements and loops.
- Schedule shell scripts to run at specified times

Chapter 7 describes how to write commands. Appendix B provides a reference to the most useful commands.

Regular Expressions

Regular expressions are used to match strings to patterns, rather than only to literal character strings. The regular expression (sometimes referred to as regex) is a pattern you want to match, such as a pattern that matches all names that begin with B or all phone numbers. Regular expressions are used by many Linux commands and applications that find/select specific text for processing. You can use regular expressions with grep, vi, sed, awk, Perl, PHP, OpenOffice, and many other applications.

Regular expressions are combinations of the following:

- **Literal characters:** Normal characters that have no special meaning. A B is just a B, the second letter of the alphabet. It has no other meaning.

- **Special characters:** Characters that have special meaning when used in a regular expression. Special characters are not just a letter of the alphabet or a punctuation mark.

  You may have experience with special characters. For instance, an asterisk (*) is used by Windows, as well as by Linux, to mean any string of characters in a filename. You would use *.txt to find all the text files in a directory or prog* to find all the files that began with prog, regardless of the remainder of the file name.

To create regular expressions, you need to understand what special characters mean and when to use one. This appendix describes the most useful special characters, with examples of their use.

Match a Single Character (.) (?)

You can match any single character with a dot (.). A dot means there must be a character in the string.

You can make a single character optional by placing a question mark (?) after it.

Regular Expression	Match	Not a Match
.t	at, xt	ax, xx
m.x	mix	mx, miix
mi?x	mix, mx	miix
m.?x	mix, max, mx	miix, maax

Specify the Location (^) ($)

You can specify that a string only matches when it occurs at the beginning of a line with circumflex (^). You can specify that a string only matches when it occurs at the end of a line with $.

Regular Expression	Match	Not a Match
^Sir	Sir, Sir John	Dear Sir,
John$	John, Sir John	John Smith
^Sir$	Sir	Dear Sir, Sir John
^.$	a (any line with only one character)	aa (any line with more or less than one character)
^?$	a (any line with zero or one character)	aa (any line with more than one character)
^$	(any blank line)	(any nonblank line)

Group Characters (())

You can group characters together, so that they are treated as one character, with parentheses.

Regular Expression	Match	Not a Match
a(bc)?x	abcx, ax, 1ax	abx, acx
^a.(bc)5	axbc5, aqbc56	axb5, aqc5, 1axb

Match One of a Set of Literal Characters ([ ])

You can put a set of literal characters inside square brackets. The pattern matches if any one of the set of characters is found. You can indicate a range of characters within the brackets by using a hyphen (-).

NOTE

If you want to include a hyphen as a literal character, include it at the beginning or the end of the set.

Regular Expression	Match	Not a Match
a[bcd]ef	abef, acef, adef	aef, abcef
a[b-d]ef	abef, acef, adef	aef, abcef
a[,.-]b	a,b, a.b, a-b	ab, axb, a,-b
file[1-2][0-9]?	file1, file15, file20	file, file3, file40

Exclude a Set of Literal Characters ([^])

You can put a set of literal characters inside square brackets, proceeded by a circumflex (^). The pattern matches only if none of the set of characters is found.

Regular Expression	Match	Not a Match
a[^bcd]ef	axef, akef	abef, acef, adef, axkef
a[^b-d]ef	axef, akef	abef, acef, adef, axkef
file[^1-2][0-9]?	file3, file45	file, file1, file10

Match a String of Characters (+) (*) ({n})

You can match a string of one or more characters by adding a plus (+) after the character.

You can match a string of zero or more characters by adding an asterisk (*) after the character.

You can match a string of a specified number of characters by adding curly brackets enclosing a number ({n}) after the character.

You can specify a range of repetitions with two numbers enclosed in curly brackets.

Regular Expression	Match	Not a Match
ab+c	abc, abbbc, abbbbc	ac, axc
ab*c	ac, abc, abbbc	axc
ab{3}c	abbbc	abc, abbc, abbbbbc
ab(2,3}c	abbc, abbbc	ac, abc, abbbbbc
a[bc]+d	abd, acccd, abccbd	ad, axd
a(bc)*d	ad, abcd, abcbcbcd	abd, acd, axd
^.+$	a, aaa (any line with one or more characters in it)	(a blank line)

Match One of Alternate Literal Strings ((|))

You can put a set of literal strings, each separated by a pipe bar (|), between parentheses. The string matches if it contains any one of the alternate literal strings.

Regular Expression	Match	Not a Match
a(bc|de|fg)x	abcx, adex, afgx	ax, abx, abcdex
I (love|hate) carrots	I love carrots	I like carrots

Many special characters and literal characters can be mixed together to form a regular expression. Really long, complex regular expressions can be built to match any conceivable string.

A special character is sometimes part of a literal string. If you want to include special characters in a regular expression to be treated as literal characters, you insert a backslash (\ ) in front of the special character. For example, look at the following two regular expressions:

^.$
^\.$

The first pattern matches a line that has one character on it, any character. The second expression matches a line that has one dot on it. The \ in front of the dot makes it into a literal dot, rather than a special character that represents any one character. Using a \ in front of a special character is called escaping the character.

If you need to use a \ as a literal character, you would include \\ in the regular expression.

Using Regular Expressions

How you use regular expression depends on the specific application you're using. In most languages, such as Perl or PHP, you use a function in the language that compares the regular expression to a string, returning a value meaning the string matched or didn't match. In many applications with a GUI, such as OpenOffice, you type the regular expression into a field. Each application has its own method for regular expression input.

In many cases, you use characters to indicate the beginning and end of the regular expression. The characters that specify the beginning and end are called delimiters. In some applications, you can specify what delimiter you want to use. Forward slashes (/) and quotation marks are often used as delimiters.

Examples

This section provides some practical examples of regular expressions. Double quotes are used as the delimiter for these examples.

The following regular expression matches any word of normal text:

```
"[A-Za-z][a-z-]* "
```

The regular expression contains a space at the end, after the *, to indicate the end of the word.

Two regular expressions that match phone numbers are:

```
"^\([0-9]{3}\) [0-9]{3}-[0-9]{4}$"
```

Matches phone numbers of the format (nnn) nnn-nnnn. Notice the parentheses are escaped. A more flexible regular expression might be:

```
"^[0-9)( -]{7,20}$"
```

Matches a string that can contain numbers, parentheses, spaces, and dots. The string must be at least 7 characters long but not more than 20 characters long.

To match a zip code, including zip+4, use:

```
"^[0-9]{5}(\-[0-9]{4})?$"
```

Matches a string of five numbers in the first section ([0-9]{5}). The rest of the regular expression is enclosed in parentheses, making it a single unit that matches the +4 part. A ? after the closing parenthesis makes the entire +4 section optional.

The following regular expression matches a common email address.

```
"^.+@.+\.(com|net)$"
```

The regular expression includes a literal @ sign. A \ escapes the dot, making it a literal dot. Only .com and .net email addresses are accepted by this regular expression.

APPENDIX B

Command Reference

The descriptions in this appendix list what the command does, show its format, show examples, and include a table of the most useful options for each command.

This appendix lists the most useful commands. It is not an exhaustive list. There are many other commands. If you can't find a command in this appendix that does what you need done, don't quit here. Look further. Search on your system, using the man command described in this appendix. If you still don't find what you need, google for it. An amazing variety of software is available for downloading without cost.

Also, for each command, the most useful options are listed. Many commands have more options. To see all the options for a command, use the man command.

basename (display filename only)

Removes the path from a complete filename. Can also remove the extension name.

```
Format:     basename path/filename
Examples:   basename /home/janet/file1.txt
            basename /home/janet/file1.txt .txt
```

First example displays file1.txt. The second example displays file1.

bunzip2 (decompress bz2 files)

Decompresses one or more files that were compressed using bzip2. Removes the extension .bz2 from the decompressed file.

```
Format:     bunzip2 filenames
Examples:   bunzip2 file1.txt.bz2 file2.txt.bz2 ...
```

After decompression, the file is renamed to file1.txt, file2.txt, etc.

bzcat (display bz2 files)

Displays one or more files that were compressed using bzip2.

```
Format:    bzcat filenames
Examples:  bzcat file1.txt.bz2 file2.txt.bz2 ...
```

The file is decompressed and displayed on the screen. Decompressed data is not saved. After the command executes, the compressed file file1.txt.bz2 remains the same.

bzip2 (compress files)

Compresses one or more files. Adds the extension .bz2 to the compressed file. Compresses better than gzip.

```
Format:    bzip2 filenames
Examples:  bzip2 file1.txt file2.txt ...
```

After compression, the file is renamed to file1.txt.bz2, file2.txt.bz2, etc.

bzip2recover (recover bzip2 files)

Attempts to recover a damaged bzip2 file.

```
Format:    bzip2recover filenames
Examples:  bzip2recover file1.txt file2.txt ...
```

cal (displays a calendar)

Displays a one-month calendar of the current month.

```
Format:    cal
Examples:  cal
```

Opt	What It Does	Example
-j	Display Julian dates	cal -j (dates are 1-365)
-m	Display calendar with Monday as first day of week	cal -m
-y	Display calendar of year	cal -y

cat (display files)

Displays one or more files. Can also be used to concatenate files.

```
Format:    cat filenames
Examples:  cat file1 file2
           cat
           cat file1 file2 > file3
           cat > file_out
```

Example 2: If you type cat without a filename, cat waits for you to type text using the keyboard. When you type some text and press <Enter>, the text you typed is displayed.

Example 3: You can use cat to combine several files into one file. Files are stored one by one, according to the order that they are named in the cat command.

Example 4: You can create a file containing text you enter. After you enter the command, cat will wait for you to enter text and will store the text you enter in file_out. When you have finished typing the text, press <Ctrl-d>.

cdage (change password expiration)

Changes password expiration data for an account.

```
Format:    cdage userid
Examples:  cdage
           cdage janet
```

If you enter the command without any options, it prompts you for the information it needs.

Opt	What It Does	Example
-d	List date of last password change	chage -d
-E expiredate	Set date account expires	chage -E
-l	Display current values	chage -l
-mn	Minimum n days between password changes	chage -m 2
-M n	Maximum n days between password changes	chage -M 10

chgrp (change group)

Changes the group owner of a file.

```
Format:    chgrp newgroup filename
Examples:  chgrp janet file27.txt
```

The file file27.txt now has the group owner janet. Only the owner of the file or the super user can change the group. If you attempt to change the group to a group that doesn't exist, an error message displays.

Opt	What It Does	Example
-c	Display info about file changes	chgrp -c janet file2 changed group of 'file2' to janet
-R	Make changes in all subdirectories	ls -R janet file3 changes file3 in any subdirectories, as well

chmod (change permissions)

Changes the permissions of one or more files. Can specify permissions using codes or numbers.

Codes: u (owner), g (group), o (other), a (all); + (add to current permissions), - (subtract from current permissions), = (replace current permissions); r (read), w (write), x (execute).

Numbers: 1= execute, 2 = write, 4 = read

```
Format:    chmod modep filenames
Examples:  chmod a+x file7
           chmod 754 file8 file9
```

Example 1: Gives owner, group, and everyone execute permission on file7. See Chapter 9.

Example 2: Gives read, write, and execute permission to user; gives read and execute permission to group; gives read permission to everyone. The mode is determined by adding the permission numbers for each category separately; e.g., 1(execute)+2(write)+4(read)=7.

Only the owner of the file or the super user can change the group.

Opt	What It Does	Example
-c	Display info about file changes	`chgrp -c janet file2` `changed group of 'file2' to janet`

-R	Make changes in all subdirectories	`ls -R janet file3`
		`changes file3 in any subdirectories,`
		`as well`

chown (change owner)

Changes the owner of a file.

```
Format:    chown newowner filename
Examples:  chown janet file29.txt
```

The file file29.txt now has the owner janet. Only the owner of the file or the super user can change the owner.

Opt	What It Does	Example
-c	Display info about file changes	`chown -c janet file2` `changed group of 'file2' to janet`

-R	Make changes in all subdirectories	`chown -R janet file3`
		`changes file3 in any subdirectories,`
		`as well`

clear (clear the screen)

Clears the screen. Removes any text that is on the screen, resulting in a blank screen.

```
Format:    clear
Examples:  clear
```

cmp (compare files)

Compares two files to see whether they are the same. This command is used to compare binary files. To compare text files, use the `diff` command.

```
Format:    cmp file1 file2
Examples:  cmp prog1 prog2
```

The output depends on the options used.

Opt	What It Does	Example
-c	Display differing bytes as characters	cmp -c file1 file2
-l	Display location of differing bytes	cmp -l file1 file3
-s	Display nothing; return exit codes: 0=identical; 1=different; 2=inaccessible	cmp -s file77 prog3

colrm (remove columns from a text file)

Removes specified columns from a text file. A column is a single character wide.

```
Format:    colrm startcolnum stopcolnum
Examples:  colrm 1 3 <report1 > report2
```

Removes columns 1, 2, and 3 from report1 and stores the altered file contents in report2, as shown below:

```
cat report1
abcde
12345
Hello

cat report2
de
45
lo
```

comm (compare two sorted text files)

Compares two sorted text files. Displays the results in three columns: 1) lines that are only in file1, 2) lines that are only in file2, and 3) lines that are in both files.

```
Format:    comm file1 file2
Examples:  comm report1 report2
```

The differences are displayed, as shown below.

```
cat report1
Apples
Peaches
Pears
cat report2
Apples
Cherries
Pears
comm report1 report2
```

```
                              Apples
Peaches
              Cherries
                              Pears
```

The output shows Apples and Pears in both files. It shows Peaches only in the first file and Cherries only in the second file.

cp (copy files)

Copies a file into a new file or into a new directory with the same name. If the new file already exists, copy overwrites the existing file with the new file.

```
Format:     cp filename filename
Examples:   cp prog1 prog2
            cp prog1 /home/janet
```

The second example copies prog1 into /home/janet/prog1. After a cp command, two files exist: the original file plus the new file it was copied into.

Opt	What It Does	Example
-i	Prompt before overwriting a file	cp -i report1 report2
-v	Display name of file being copied	cp -v rep1 dir1

crontab (schedule commands)

Schedules one or more commands to execute at a specified time and day. See Chapter 19 for information on using crontab.

date (displays date and time)

Displays date and time. You can specify a format for the date.

```
Format:     date
Examples:   date
```

Displays date in system default format, such as Thu Jan 13 16:34 PST 2005.

Opt	What It Does	Example
+format	Specify format for date, using codes. See man page for codes.	date +"%m %d" 01 15

df (display disk space)

Displays the amount of disk space. Shows the amount used and available for each partition.

```
Format:    df
Examples:  df
```

diff (compare two text files)

Compares the contents of two text files. Displays the lines that are different.

```
Format:    diff fileordirname1 fileordirname2
Examples:  diff prog1 prog2
           diff prog1 /home/janet/dir1
           diff /home/janet /home/janet/dir1
```

Compares prog1 to prog2. In the second example, compares prog1 to /home/janet/dir1/prog1 if it exists. In the third example, compares all files that exist in both directories.

Displays the lines that differ between the two files. < indicates lines from the first file; > indicates lines from the second file. For example:

cat fileA
```
John Smith
Alice Brown
John Huang
```

cat fileB
```
Bob Smith
Alice in Wonderland
John Huang
```

diff fileA fileB
```
<John Smith
<Alice Brown
---
>Bob Smith
>Alice in Wonderland
```

Opt	What It Does	Example
-b	Treat groups of blanks as one	diff -b file1 file2
-B	Ignore blank lines	diff -B prog1 prog2
-c	Display 3 lines surrounding each changed line	diff -c file1 /home/janet
-C n	Display n lines surrounding each changed line	diff -C 5 file1 file1.bak

Opt	What It Does	Example
-i	Ignore case	diff -I report1 report2
-r	Also compare subdirectories	diff -r /home/janet/home/bob
-w	Ignore all white space	diff -w file1 file2
-y	Two-column output	diff -y file2 file5

diff3 (compare 3 text files, merges files)

Compares the contents of 3 text files. Displays the lines that are different.

```
Format:    diff3 file1 file2 file3
Examples:  diff3 prog1 prog2 prog3
```

Compares prog1, prog2, and prog3. Displays the lines that differ between the files. The lines that are different in prog1 are listed after 1:, the lines that are different in prog2 are listed after 2:, and the lines that are different in prog3 are listed after 3:. For example:

cat fileA
```
John Smith
Alice Brown
John Huang
```

cat fileB
```
Bob Smith
Alice in Wonderland
John Huang
```

cat fileC
```
Bob Smith
Alice Brown
John Huang
```

diff fileA fileB fileC
```
1:
    John Smith
    Alice Brown
2:
    Bob Smith
    Alice in Wonderland
3:
    Bob Smith
    Alice Brown
```

Opt	What It Does	Example
-m	Merge changes. See man page	diff3 -m file1 file2 file3

dir (list filenames)

The dir command is the same as the ls command, with the same options.

du (display disk usage)

Displays the amount of disk space used by a directory and each subdirectory.

Format: du *directory_name*
Examples: du
            du /home/janet

If the directory named is omitted, the current directory is used. The size is displayed as the number of KB blocks.

Opt	What It Does	Example
-a	List all files, not just subdirectories	du -a
-b	Display size in bytes	du -b
-c	Display grand total	du -c
-m	Display size in megabytes	du -m
-s	Display only the grand total	du -s

echo (display text)

Displays the text or variables specified.

Format: echo *textstring*
Examples: echo Hello World
            echo $HOME

The first example displays Hello World on the screen. The second example displays the contents of the variable HOME. $ indicates that HOME is a variable. HOME contains the path to your home directory, so the second example displays the path to your home directory on the screen.

You can use some special characters with the echo command to format the output, shown in the first table below. The second table shows the most useful options for echo.

Char	What It Does	Example
\a	Alert (rings bell)	echo \aerror
\b	Backspace	echo \bHello
\c	Suppress new line	echo $text_line\c
\f	Form feed	echo Hello World\f
\n	Start a new line	echo Hello \nWorld
\r	Carriage return	echo Hello World\r
\t	Insert a tab	echo Hello \tWorld
\v	Insert a vertical tab	echo \vHello World
\\	Literal	echo This is a backslash \\

Opt	What It Does	Example
-n	Don't start a new line after text	echo -n Hello echo " World Hello World

env (display and set environmental variables)

Displays a list of environmental variables. You can specify an environmental variable in the command to set the variable.

```
Format:    env variablename=value
Examples:  env
           env HISTSIZE=100
```

The env command alone displays a list of environmental variables and their values. The second example sets HISTSIZE to 100.

Opt	What It Does	Example
-u	unset an environmental variable	env -u HISTSIZE

file (display file type)

Displays the file type of a file.

```
Format:    file filename
Examples:  file file1.txt
```

find (find files)

Searches specified directories for files or groups of files.

```
Format:      find directories conditions
Examples:    find /home/janet -name "file*.txt" -print
             find . -type d -print
```

The first example searches the directory /home/janet, and all its subdirectories, for any files that begin with file and end with .txt. The filenames are displayed. The second example searches the current directory, and its subdirectories, for directories and displays their names.

Rather than options, find uses conditions that are listed after the argument (the path to search). Some conditions are:

Condition	What It Does	Example
-amin +n|-n|n	Find files with last access date more than, less than, or n minutes ago	find . -amin +30
-anewer filen	Find files accessed more recently than filen	find . -anewer report6
-atime +n|-n|n	Find files with last access date more than, less than, or n days ago	find . -atime -5
-cmin +n|-n|n	Find files with last changed date more than, less than, or n minutes ago	find . -ctime +5
-cnewer filen	Find files changed more recently than filen	find . -cnewer report8
-ctime +n|-n|n	Find files with last changed date more than, less than, or n days ago	find . -ctime +5
-group group	Find files owned by this group	find . -group janet
-iname pattern	Find files that match pattern. Ignore case.	find . -iname FileA
-maxdepth n	Search only n levels of subdirectories	find . -maxdepth 2
-mindepth n	Search only deeper than n levels	find . -mindepth 2
-mmin +n|-n|n	Find files with last modified date more than, less than, or n minutes ago	find . -mtime 5
-mtime +n|-n|n	Find files with last modified date more than, less than, or n days ago	find . -mtime 5
-name pattern	Find files that match pattern. use quotes when special characters are used.	find . -name lostfile
-newer filen	Find files modified more recently than filen	find . -newer report8
-nogroup	Find files with nonexistent group name	find . -nogroup
-nouser	Find files with nonexistent username	find . -nouser

Condition	What It Does	Example
-perm mode	Find files with matching permissions	find . -perm 777
-print	Display names of found files	find . -name file1 -print
-size n or nc	Find files n blocks or nc characters long	find . -size 500c
-type c	Find files of specified type: b=block special; c=character special; d=directory; p=named pipe; l=symbolic link; s=socket; f=plain file	find . -type f
-user user	Find files owned by user	find . -user janet

finger (display user information)

Displays information about users, including whether they are currently logged in. Displays information stored in .plan and .project file in the user's home directory. Can display info about a user on another computer.

Format: finger *userlist*
Examples: finger
           finger janet
           finger sam@myschool.edu

The first example displays information for all users currently logged in, showing how long they have been logged in. The second example shows information about the user janet, including the last login and contents of the .plan and .project file. The third example displays information about a user on a different computer.

fold (break lines at a specified column)

Breaks the lines in a file so that they don't continue past a certain column. The default width is 80.

Format: fold *filelist*
Examples: fold file1 file3

Breaks any lines longer than 80 columns at 80, moving the remaining columns to a new line.

Opt	What It Does	Example
-b	Use bytes to decide where to break lines	fold -b report3
-s	Break at spaces, not in middle of word	fold -s reportX
-w n	Set width to n, rather than 80	fold -w 70 reportY

ftp (transfer files)

Starts a utility program that transfers files between computers. ftp provides many commands, such as connect, disconnect, get, put, and many others, that initiate actions between the computer running ftp and a remote computer. For instance, the command "put file2.txt" moves the file named file2.txt from the current computer to a remote computer. To see all the possible commands, use the help command in ftp. See man ftp for more information.

gawk (process text)

Processes text. Using pattern matching to manipulate text. Complicated program with powerful features. Processes each line of text based on commands you provide. For instructions on using gawk, type: `info gawk`.

grep (find text in files)

Searches one or more files for text that matches regular expressions. The grep command is described in Chapter 7.

```
Format:    grep pattern filelist
Examples:  grep "^Table [0-9]:" *
```

Displays each line that matches the regex. The filename and line number is listed.

Opt	What It Does	Example
-A n	Display n lines after the match	grep -A 3 Table *
-B	Display n lines before the match	grep -B 3 Table *
-c	Display only count of matched lines, not the text	grep -c Table *
-C	Display two lines before and after the matching line	grep -C include *
-i	Ignore case	grep -I Table report*
-r	Search files in subdirectories also	grep -r Table *
-v	Display lines that do not match	grep -v Error *
-w	Match whole words only	grep -w Table *.txt
-x	Match whole lines only	grep -x "This is a line" *

groupadd (add a group)

Creates a new group.

```
Format:     groupadd groupname
Examples:   groupadd janet2
```

groupdel (delete a group)

Removes a group.

```
Format:     groupdel groupname
Examples:   groupdel janet2
```

groups (show groups)

Shows the groups that each user belongs to.

```
Format:     groups groupname
Examples:   groups janet
```

gunzip (uncompress gzip file)

Uncompresses gzip files.

```
Format:     gunzip filename
Examples:   gunzip bigfile.gz
```

The result is an uncompressed file named bigfile. See man gzip for options.

gzip (compress files)

Compresses files.

```
Format:     gzip filename
Examples:   gzip bigfile
```

The result is a compressed file named bigfile.gz. See man gzip for options.

info (display online documentation)

Displays documentation for a topic. Opens documentation on the screen. User can move through the documentation with commands. If no info file is available for the topic, info opens the man page.

```
Format:    info topic
Examples:  info gawk
```

Opens file in info, with the first page displayed. Display the next page by pressing the <spacebar>. Quit by pressing q. Press h to see online help.

less (display file one page at a time)

Displays a file to the screen. It displays one screen, and then waits. The less command is a newer version of the more command. less has both options and commands. Commands are typed while less is running, displaying the file. Commands are similar to vi commands. Pressing a key when less has displayed a screen full of text and is waiting for input tells less what to display next.

```
Format:    less filename
Examples:  less file1.txt
```

The less command has many more commands and options than the more command.

Opt	What It Does	Examples
?	Display help file	less -?
-m	Display a long prompt	less -m
-ppattern	Start display where first pattern is found	less +pa*

Command	What It Does
<space>	Display next screen
n<Enter>	Display the next n lines; default is one line
/pattern	Search for pattern
=	Print current line number
b	Skip backward one screen of text
f	Skip forward two screens of text
n	Repeat last search
q	Stop displaying files
v	Open file in vi editor

lpq (check print queue)

Displays status of jobs in the print queue.

```
Format:      lpq jobid
Examples:    lpq
             lpq jobid
```

Opt	What It Does	Example
-Pprinter	Display jobs status for specified print queue	lpq -Plaser

lpr (print)

Sends a file to the print queue.

```
Format:      lpr filelist
Examples:    lpr test.txt
```

Opt	What It Does	Example
-Pprinter	Print job to specified printer	lpq -Plaser

lprm (remove a job from the print queue)

Removes a job from the print queue.

```
Format:      lprm jobid
Examples:    lprm jobid
```

Opt	What It Does	Example
-Pprinter	Remove print job from specified print queue	lpq -Plaser

ls (list filenames)

Outputs the names of the files in a directory.

```
Format:      ls directory_name
Examples:    ls
             ls /home/janet
```

directory_name is optional. If it's not included, the current directory is assumed.

Opt	What It Does	Example
-1	List 1 file per line	ls -1
-a	List all files, including hidden system files	ls -a . .. backup file1 file2
-d	List only directories	ls -d
-l	Long listing	ls -l -rw-r--r-- 1 janet janet 579 2005-1-10 00:22 file1 -rw-r--r-- 1 janet janet 579 2005-1-10 00:22 file2
-r	List in reverse order	ls -r -rw-r--r-- 1 janet janet 579 2005-1-10 00:22 file2 -rw-r--r-- 1 janet janet 579 2005-1-10 00:22 file1
-R	List subdirectories	ls -R
-s	List with file size in bytes	ls -s 5 file1 3 file2
-S	Sort by size	ls -S
-X	Sort by extension	ls -X

man (display manual page)

Displays the manual pages on the screen. Displays one screen at a time. Press <space> to go to the next page. Press <q> to end the display.

Format: man *command*
Examples: man ls

command is the manual page that will display.

Opt	What It Does	Examples
-k string	List names of commands that include string in their description	man -k copy strcpy (3) - copies a string cp (1) - copies files and directories

merge (merge 3 files)

Merges the changes in two files into another file.

Format: merge *file1 file2 file3*
Examples: merge report1 report2 report3

First merges the changes in file2 into file 1. Then merges the changes in file3 into file 1; file2 and file3 remain unchanged.

Opt	What It Does	Examples
-p	Display changes, rather than overwrite file1	merge -p

mkdir (create a new directory)

Creates a new directory.

Format: mkdir *path*
Examples: mkdir /home/janet/dir22

Opt	What It Does	Examples
-p	Create parent directories if they don't exist	mkdir -p /home/janet/newdirs/dir23 (creates newdirs if it doesn't exist. creates dir23 in newdirs)
-m mode	Change permissions of new directory to mode	mkdir -m 777 dir24

more (display files to screen)

Displays one or more files to the screen. It displays one screen, and then waits. The more command has both options and commands. Commands are typed while more is running, displaying the file. Commands are similar to vi commands. Pressing a key when more has displayed a screen full of text and is waiting for input tells more what to display next.

Format: more *listoffilenames*
Examples: more file1 file2

Opt	What It Does	Examples
+n	Start displaying file at line n	more +10
+/pattern	Display file starting 2 lines before pattern is found	more +/a*

Command	What It Does
`<space>`	Display next screen
`n<Enter>`	Display the next n lines; default is one line
`/pattern`	Search for pattern
`=`	Print current line number
`b`	Skip backward one screen of text
`f`	Skip forward two screens of text
`n`	Repeat last search
`q`	Stop displaying files
`v`	Open file in vi editor

mv (move or rename a file)

Moves the contents of a file to another file or directory.

```
Format:    mv path/file path/file
Examples:  mv file1 /home/janet
           mv file1 file2
```

The first example moves the contents of file1 to the directory /home/janet, saving it with the same name (/home/janet/file1). The second example moves the contents of file1 to file2, in effect renaming the file. After both these examples, the file file1 no longer exists.

Opt	What It Does	Examples
`-f`	If the target file exists, overwrite it	`mv -f sourcefile /home/janet`
`-v`	Display name of file moved	`mv -v file1 file2` `file1 -> file2`

passwd (change password)

Creates or changes a password for a user account.

```
Format:    passwd user
Examples:  passwd
           passwd janet
```

Only the user account or the super user can change the user password.

pwd (show current directory)

Displays the path to the current directory.

```
Format:    pwd
Examples:  pwd
```

quota (show disk usage)

Displays disk space used and available for a specific user or group.

```
Format:    quota user
Examples:  quota
           quota janet
```

When no user or group is specified, the current user is assumed.

rename (rename series of files)

Renames files by changing part of the filename. Useful for changing several similar filenames at one time.

```
Format:    rename currentname newname files
Examples:  rename rep oldrep rep*
           rename doc projdoc *doc*
```

Changes the first string to the second string in all files that match the pattern. The first example changes files named rep1.doc, rep2.doc, rep3.doc, and so on to new names oldrep1.doc, oldrep2.doc, oldrep3.doc, and so forth. The second example renames all files with doc anywhere in their names to projdoc; for instance, newdoc1 becomes newprojdoc1, newdoc2 becomes newprojdoc2, and so on.

rm (delete files)

Deletes (removes) one or more files.

```
Format:    rm filelist
Examples:  rm file1 file2
```

To remove files, you must have write permissions to the directory where the file is located, but not on the file itself.

Opt	What It Does	Examples
-d	Remove directories, even if not empty (only available to a privileged user)	rm -d /home/janet/dir2
-f	Remove write-protected files without querying	rm -f file26.txt
-I	Prompt before deleting	rm -I test*.txt
-r	For a directory, remove all the files in the directory and subdirectories	rm -r /home/janet/dir3
-v	Display name before deleting	rm -r report*

rmdir (remove directories)

Deletes directories, but not contents.

```
Format:    rmdir directoryelist
Examples:  rmdir /home/janet/dir2
```

Directories must be empty before they can be deleted.

sed (edits text files)

Edits files. Can search for and replace in several files at once. Much faster and easier than editing the files manually. To see the sed documentation, type info sed.

sleep (pause)

Waits a specified amount of time before executing the next command. Often used in shell scripts.

```
Format:    sleep n units
Examples:  sleep 10
           sleep 2 m
```

When no units are included, seconds are assumed. The first example waits 10 seconds. The units that can be used are: s = seconds, m = minutes, h = hours, or d = days.

sort (sort contents of a file)

Sorts files by lines and displays sorted file contents. The sort command is described in Chapter 7.

tar (copy files into or restore files from an archive file)

Tar is a utility used to create an archive file, called a tarball. Files can be added to the archive file or removed from the archive file using tar. The action of tar depends on the options used.

Format: tar *options tarfile filelist*
Examples: tar -cf newarch.tar *
            tar -xf oldarch

The first example creates a new archive file called newarch and stores all the files in the current directory in the new archive. It's customary to name the file with a .tar extension. The second example extracts all the files in the archive oldarch. After extraction, the files are in the current directory and the archive is still there also.

Tar has two types of options. One option from the function options is required, determining the action tar performs. The second table lists normal options, totally optional.

Required options	What It Does	Examples
-A	Add another archive to the end of the current archive	tar -Af oldarch newarch.tar
-c	Create a new archive	tar -cf newarch.tar *
-d	Compare archived files with source files and report differences	tar -df tararch.tar
-delete	Remove file from archive file	tar -df tararch.tar file26.txt
-r	Append files to end of archive file	tar -rf tararch.tar rep*
-t	Display names of files in archive	tar -tf tararch.tar
-u	Add files if not already in archive or if they have been modified	tar -uf tararch.tar rep*
-x	Extract files from the archive	tar -xf projarch.tar

Opt	What It Does	Examples
-f file	Use specified archive file.	tar -xf projarch.tar
-j	Compress files with bzip2 before storing in archive file	tar -cjf arc.tar *
-k	Do not overwrite existing files with extracted files	tar -xkf projarc.tar
-m	Do not keep modification time with extracted files. Set modification time to the time the file was extracted.	tar -xmf proj.tar
-p	Keep the permission of the extracted files	tar -xpf proj.tar
-z	Compress files with Gzip before storing in archive file	tar -czf newproj.tar proj1*

touch (update access and modification date)

Sets the access and modification dates for a file to the current date and time. If the file doesn't exist, touch creates an empty file, setting the dates.

Format: touch *filelist*
Examples: touch report

Opt	What It Does	Examples
-a	Update only the access date	touch -a file1.txt
-c	Don't create a file	touch -c file3
-m	Update only the modification date	touch -m file4
-r filename	Change date to match filename	touch -r file2 report3

uniq (remove duplicate lines)

Stores one copy of each line from one file into a new file. The file must be sorted.

Format: uniq *filename1 filename2*
Examples: uniq addresses newaddresses

The new file contains only one copy of each line. Duplicate lines are not stored in the new file.

unset (remove an environmental variable)

Removes an environmental variable.

Format: unset *varname*
Examples: unset var2

Totally removes the variable named var2. If you want the variable to remain, but to be empty, set the variable to NULL.

useradd (add accounts)

Creates new user account. Also used to change account information.

Format: useradd *user*
Examples: useradd janet2

Opt	What It Does	Examples
-g group	Set group owner to group	useradd -g janet2 janet2
-G groups	Add user to additional groups	useradd -G sales janet2
-D	Display defaults	useradd -D janet
-M	Do not create a home directory	useradd -M specacct

userdel (remove account)

Deletes user account from system.

Format: userdel *user*
Examples: userdel janet2

Opt	What It Does	Examples
-r	Delete home directory, with its files	useradd -g janet2 janet2

w (display system information)

Displays system usage and user information. Shows whether a user is logged in and what the account is doing.

Format: w *user*
Examples: w janet2

If user is not included, w shows all the users who are logged in and what they are doing.

wc (count characters, words, and lines)

Displays the number of characters, words, and lines in a file.

Format: wc *filelist*
Examples: wc file1 file2

Opt	What It Does	Examples
-c	Show byte count only	wc -c report.txt
-l	Show lines only	wc -l report.txt
-L	Show length of longest line	wc -L report3
-m	Show character count only	wc -m letter
-w	Show word count only	wc -w myfile

who (display users who are logged in)

Displays list of users who are currently logged in, how long they have been logged in, and where they are logged in from.

Format: who
Examples: who

whoami (display current user)

Displays account name of current user

Format: whoami
Examples: whoami

▐▌ Index ▐▌▌

S

SANE (Scanner Access Now Easy), 188
saving
    files with vi, 272
    spreadsheets, 183
scaling. *See* sizing
Scanner Access Now Easy (SANE), 188
scanning documents, 188-190
scheduling scripts to run automatically, 292
screen shots, 193
screens, locking, 94
screensavers, setting, 89
scripts
    scheduling to run automatically, 292
    shell scripts. *See* shell scripts
sed (edits text files), 140, 322
selecting packages
    to install in Fedora, 44-45
    for installation procedures (Mandrake), 49
    SuSE, 57-58
sending email in Mozilla, 252
server names, 250
shapes, 169
shell scripts, 145, 277-278
    flow control, 283
    quotes, 282
    sample script, 293
    special characters, 282
    testing conditions, 284-285
shells, Bash, 97
shortcuts
    creating for long commands, 101
    path, 126
    relative paths, 126
signature, 250
signing up
    for AIM, 259
    for Gaim, 261
    for MSN Messenger, 260
sizing
    images in GIMP, 200
    panels, 91
    windows, 81
Slakeware, 15
sleep (pause), 322
software
    application software, managing, 147
    installing, 147-149
    open source software, 2
    proprietary software, 2
software licenses, 4
sort (sort contents of a file), 322
sort command, 108

sound cards, configuring, 230
source code, 147, 150
    installing packages, 152
spam, 255
special characters, 282, 295
specifying location, 296
spell checking, word processing, 164-166
spreadsheets, 175
    Calc, 175
    creating, 176
    editing content, 181-182
    formatting, 178-181
    formulas and functions, 182-183
    printing, 183-184
    saving, 183
StarOffice, 171
starting installation procedures
    Fedora, 34-35
    Mandrake, 47
    SuSE, 54
statements
    case statements, 283, 287
    conditional statements, 283
    if statements, 283, 286
stderr, 102
stdin, 102
stdout, 102
strings of characters, matching, 297
styles, 158
    copying from templates, 161
    creating, 179
    OpenOffice Writer, 159
Stylist, 156, 176
subscribing to newsgroups, 264
super user, 114
support for software, 3
SuSE, 9, 14
    configuring, 61
        sound cards, 230
    features of, 14
    installation procedures, 33
        configuration settings, 55-56
        selecting packages, 57-58
        starting, 54
    installing, 59-60, 62
        Linux, 27
        printers, 208
    logging in, 76
syntax, command-line syntax, 100-101
syntax highlighting, Kate, 270
system prompts, 97
system trays, 79
systems, planning, 24

T

tabbed browsing, Mozilla, 223
tar (copy files into or restore files from an archive file), 323
targetnames, 139
taskbars, 79
templates, 158, 160-161
terminal windows, configuring, 110
testing conditions, shell scripts, 284-285
text, 188
text editors, 140, 267
    Kate. *See* Kate
    vi. *See* vi
text files, 125
    editing, 267
        in Kate, 269
    viewing and editing, 140
Thunderbird, 247
time zones, Fedora, 42
tool tips, 80
toolbars
    Calc, 177
    fly-out toolbars, 157
    Mozilla, 221
    word processing programs, 157
Torvald, Linux, 6
touch (update access and modification date), 324
tracking changes in word processor documents, 172-174
.txt, 171
types of accounts, 114

U-V

uniq (remove duplicate lines), 324
unset (remove an environmental variable), 324
until loops, 283, 290
user accounts, 114
useradd (add accounts), 325
userdel (remove account), 325
variables, 279
    reading data into, 280-281
vi, 140, 267
    editing
        commands, 274
        files, 272
    moving files around, 273
    opening files, 271
    sample editing session, 275
    saving files, 272
video players, 235
    MPlayer, 235, 238-239
    RealPlayer, 235-237

viewing
    graphics files, 187-188
    text files, 140
virtual desktops, configuring, 92-93

W

w (display system information), 325
wc (count characters, words, and lines), 325
Web, installing Linux, 21
Web browsers, 219
    Mozilla. *See* Mozilla
Web sites, installing software, 149
while loops, 283, 290
who (display users who are logged in), 326
whoami (display current user), 326
windows, 81
    terminal windows, configuring, 110
Windows
    installing Linux, 21
    running Linux, 25
Windows 2000, disk partition, 26
wireless, 215
wizards, Mandrakefirsttime, 76
word completion, 164
word processing, 155
    autocorrection, 163-164
    columns, 166-167
    creating documents, 156
    document file formats, 171-172
    editing document contents, 162-163
    frames, 167
    galleries, 170-171
    graphics in documents, 168-170
    menus and toolbars, 157
    OpenOffice Writer. *See* OpenOffice Writer
    spell checking, 164-166
    styles, 159
    tables, 166-167
    templates, 160-161
    tracking changes, 172-174
word processing document files, 155
word wrap, Kate, 270
WordPerfect, 155

X-Y-Z

X Multimedia System, 229
Xandros, 15
Xmms (X Multimedia System), 232-233
Yahoo! Messenger, 258

Register
Your Book

at www.awprofessional.com/register

You may be eligible to receive:

- Advance notice of forthcoming editions of the book
- Related book recommendations
- Chapter excerpts and supplements of forthcoming titles
- Information about special contests and promotions throughout the year
- Notices and reminders about author appearances, tradeshows, and online chats with special guests

Contact us

If you are interested in writing a book or reviewing manuscripts prior to publication, please write to us at:

Editorial Department
Addison-Wesley Professional
75 Arlington Street, Suite 300
Boston, MA 02116 USA
Email: AWPro@aw.com

Visit us on the Web: http://www.awprofessional.com

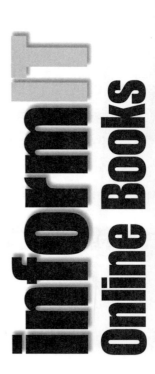